Two Gardeners

"To read their letters is to be admitted into the company of two people worth knowing, to enter a more civilized time, before e-mail. For this lovely book—beautifully designed, intelligently edited, and furnished with helpful notes—Emily Herring Wilson deserves a big bouquet."

—LINDA H. DAVIS
author of *Onward and Upward: A Biography of Katharine S. White*

"Katharine White and Elizabeth Lawrence's correspondence in the first year of their friendship was formal but burning with a passion for gardening and the joy of sharing sources and tips. . . . 'Help! Help!' White writes to Lawrence in 1969. 'I'm trying to find how often the old-fashioned Night-blooming cereus opens its white flowers at midnight in order to capture an event of my quite young childhood.' What are friends for?"

—SUSAN SALTER REYNOLDS
Los Angeles Times

"The letters are a touching testament to a friendship sparked by a shared devotion to literature and gardening and enduring, in mutual encouragement and support, through struggles with the lassitude and frailties of aging and ill health. Their many devotees will welcome these glimpses into the day-to-day lives of these much admired women."

—PAMELA HARPER
author of *Time Tested Plants*

"Gardeners and writers tend to be private people. . . . Katharine White and Elizabeth Lawrence did not need to meet each other. Their friendship grew, and their vulnerabilities were revealed to each other behind the veil of a letter. This unpretentious, human correspondence makes us remember that there is no adequate substitute for written expression between two people."

—SHEILA COBB
Winston-Salem Journal

"*Two Gardeners* is a remarkable collection of letters between two women of erudition and literary taste. Reading them is like walking around a fine garden with an amiable companion."

—BOBBY J. WARD
author of *A Contemplation upon Flowers*

"[T]he letters are full of laughter, knowledge, irrational prejudice and unexpected details. Both women belong in the company of the great early gardening writers and are admired by those who have come afterward. In this delightful collection, it is easy to see why."

—*The Economist*

"Capturing the true essence of how to be a gardener and what it means to be a friend, their letters, here lovingly collected and eloquently introduced by editor Emily Herring Wilson, offer an intimate portrait of two accomplished women whose contribution to garden literature transcends their professionally published work."

—*Booklist*

"It is a great pleasure in these troubled times to discover *Two Gardeners*, a look, through letters, at a durable long-distance gardening friendship between two wise and talented American writers. *Two Gardeners* is a splendid book to savor on a spring afternoon sitting in a comfortable lawn chair in the garden."

—ANDREW J. ANGYAL
The Greensboro (N.C.) News & Record

"This spirited and revealing correspondence illumines our understanding of American gardening and garden writing in the second half of the twentieth century. This book is a classic, no less than Mrs. White's magnificent *Onward and Upward in the Garden* and Miss Lawrence's *Gardening for Love* and *A Southern Garden*."

—ALLEN LACY
author of *A Year in Our Gardens*

Two Gardeners

KATHARINE S. WHITE AND ELIZABETH LAWRENCE

A Friendship in Letters

EDITED BY
EMILY HERRING WILSON

Beacon Press
Boston

Beacon Press

25 Beacon Street

Boston, Massachusetts 02108-2892

www.beacon.org

Beacon Press books

are published under the auspices of

the Unitarian Universalist Association of Congregations.

Printed in the United States of America

07 06 05 04 03   8 7 6 5 4 3 2 1

Grateful acknowledgment is made to the estate of E. B. White for permission to reprint the letters of Katharine S. White. The letters of Elizabeth Lawrence are reprinted here with the permission of Warren Way and Elizabeth Rogers.

Photograph credits may be found on page 274.

This book is printed on acid-free paper that meets the uncoated paper ANSI/NISO specifications for permanence as revised in 1992.

Text design by Preston Thomas

Composition by Wilsted & Taylor Publishing Services

Library of Congress Cataloging-in-Publication Data

White, Katharine Sergeant Angell.

Two gardeners : Katharine S. White and Elizabeth Lawrence
—a friendship in letters / edited by Emily Herring Wilson.

p.   cm.

ISBN 0-8070-8558-8 (cloth)

ISBN 0-8070-8559-6 (pbk.)

1. Gardening—Maine—North Brooklin. 2. Gardening—North Carolina—Charlotte. 3. White, Katharine Sergeant Angell—Correspondence. 4. Lawrence, Elizabeth, 1904–1985—Correspondence. 5. Women gardeners—Maine—North Brooklin—Correspondence. 6. Women gardeners—North Carolina—Charlotte—Correspondence. I. Lawrence, Elizabeth, 1904–1985. II. Wilson, Emily Herring. III. Title.

SB455 .W52 2002

635.9′092′273—dc21   2002000405

CONTENTS

Introduction

Gardeners are often good letter writers, and whether they write to describe what's blooming today or to remember a flower from childhood, their letters are efforts to preserve memory. After they have put away tools in the shed, they write letters as a way to go on working in the garden. Because it is impossible to achieve the kind of perfection they dream of, they try to come to terms with their dreams by talking back and forth about their successes and failures. Sometimes they like to have visitors who can walk with them along the paths and admire their handiwork, but at other times, they feel more confident if they can keep visitors at a distance. No matter how lovely the garden looks, as soon as the gardener hears that someone is coming, she feels compelled to warn, "Don't expect much; we haven't had rain." The perfect flower today can wilt under the eye of tomorrow's visitor. Even a visit to Monet's garden may find us standing in a line in the rain only to notice an unweeded bed. It is far easier to maintain the illusion of a garden in a letter.

Which brings us to the idea of the garden as an illusion, for it is the constant hope of the gardener that enriching this bed and planting that shrub will result in an aesthetic experience that lives up to the dream. So, what is the gardener's dream but a dream of the ideal order in which beauty can be expressed and loss absorbed? Often the struggle between what is hoped for and what is accomplished meets with unexpected disappointments: weeds and varmints are insistent, a flower bed looks poorly. But as the gardener moves along with worried brow, suddenly the smell of a particular flower provides transport to a garden from one's childhood (which may have been no more than one scraggly rosebush on a school playground). Memory is awakened, the world made whole, if only for a moment. But in that moment some sort of healing takes place, or so gardeners have believed for centuries.

This interplay, and perhaps it is a kind of play, between what is lived and what is remembered, between what is desired and what is accomplished, shapes the writing of letters and the making of gardens. I would observe further that this shaping is an act of evocation and is, of course, an art rather than a science.

Gardeners are as different as their favorite plants and seasons, but they share a passion for growing things. Some spend many of their gardening hours reading nursery catalogues and making plans for next year's borders, bringing the energy inside the house to bear upon fruit and flower in the outside garden. Katharine S. White was of this variety. Elizabeth Lawrence called herself a "dirt gardener," who worked outside digging and planting, bringing blossoms and leaves into the house to study. How these two different gardeners in distant places became friends is the subject of this book.

Some years ago when I began reading the letters of Katharine White and Elizabeth Lawrence in preparation for a biography of Elizabeth, I felt as if I had discovered a private garden, though not exactly a secret garden. Certainly, in leaving their letters in library archives, they had not locked the gate and thrown away

the key, and, in fact, no buried secrets, if there are any, will be un-
covered here. These two intelligent and private women—one a
New Englander, the other a southerner; one a well-known editor
of *The New Yorker,* the other a respected garden writer—present
snapshots of themselves, their gardens, and their different worlds
in letters written over almost twenty years. Amid reports of
what's growing in the garden and what they are writing, they
share glimpses of themselves that give substance to Elizabeth's
confession (to a much earlier correspondent), "Privacy is like
time. It is within."

The letters begin in the late spring of 1958, soon after Katharine and her husband E. B. White had given up their New York
apartment and moved permanently to their saltwater farm in
Maine, and they end in the summer of 1977, when Katharine
died at the age of eighty-four. In the course of the letters, the
two women discuss gardening, their writing about gardening,
and books. They also create a small cast of characters from the
past and present—family members, friends, other gardeners,
and writers. What we are shown in the letters is never complete,
for their lives were full, and their letters were often interrupted.
When they did sit down to write one another, however, they
revealed far more about themselves than people meeting them
face to face may have recognized. To acquaintances, Katharine White sometimes seemed "formidable," and Elizabeth Lawrence, "shy." Readers of their letters will have many opportunities to see beyond these limited characterizations and to develop
a fuller understanding of the two women as intelligent, opinion-
ated, sensitive, and generous friends who bolstered one another's
confidence in good times and bad.

In reading their letters, we enter a private garden rather than
a public one. For here among the persistent weeds, the briers, the
deadwood, and the tangle of branches, green shoots await un-
earthing (I use some of the language from that favorite children's

book *The Secret Garden*). As editor I have done some pruning, a bit of staking, but in the end, I hope the letters have not been changed as much as made ready for visitors. Maine winters—and mice—took their toll on Katharine's garden borders, but she went on ordering more bulbs and plants. Elizabeth liked for visitors to admire her well-designed garden, but often she had time only for sweeping the gravel walks before welcoming friends. Although both women were traditionalists (Katharine's first garden essay included a lively and humorous argument with hybridizers who made zinnias look like chrysanthemums; Elizabeth had to know the *Latin* names of plants), they liked informality—whether in borders that were allowed to spill over, flower arrangements, or letters.

Katharine White was born September 17, 1892, in Winchester, Massachusetts, the last of three daughters. Their mother, Elizabeth Shepley Sergeant, died when Katharine was three years old, and her father turned to his unmarried sister Caroline to help bring up the girls. Katharine's beloved "Aunt Crully" and her mother's sister, Annie Shepley ("Aunt Poo"), figured large in Katharine's memories of a happy childhood. Two years after his wife's death, Charles Sergeant moved his family into a handsome Georgian house on Hawthorn Road in Brookline, Massachusetts, a place Katharine wrote about in her garden essays. The three sisters—Elizabeth ("Elsie"), Rosamond, and Katharine—rode the streetcar into Boston to attend Miss Winsor's School. Katharine, especially, enjoyed visits to her father's family home on Bridge Street in Northampton, Massachusetts, where his sisters presided over a household that reminded Katharine of the mythical town "in possession of the Amazons" in Mrs. Gaskell's *Cranford*. It was a book Katharine had read and reread as a young girl, a gift from her father on her twelfth birthday. The sisters kept house and set an excellent table; the front parlor was often lively with women's club meetings and other social gatherings. Katharine was brought up on good conversation and good company, and later on, her own parties in the Whites' Turtle Bay apartment in New York would be happily remembered by her guests.

In 1915, the year after Katharine had graduated from Bryn Mawr College, she married a Harvard man, Ernest Angell, and apparently never considered any obstacles to having both a family and a career, in spite of the belief of the Bryn Mawr president, Martha Carey Thomas, that it would be unwise for ambitious women to consider both. After several office jobs, two children (Nancy Angell Stableford and Roger Angell), and a marriage that ended in divorce, Katharine found herself employed in the office of a new publication, *The New Yorker.* Early on, Katharine recommended that the editor, Harold Ross, hire E. B. White (known as "Andy"), who became what many readers regard as the best essayist in America. Katharine and Ross were putting together a group of talented people, and when she and Andy married (in 1929), her life at home had many of the same lively interests as her life at the office. Although, over the years, she and Andy moved back and forth between the house in Maine and the apartment in New York, in 1957 Andy persuaded her to live permanently on the Maine farm ("gumming up things," as he later reflected; Katharine was a city girl). In Maine, they worked in offices across the hall from one another and sometimes had staff to help with their correspondence and typing. Katharine devoted her mornings to reading manuscripts sent up from *The New Yorker* and then tried to settle down to work on a garden essay.

E. B. White loved farming in Maine and working in the barnyard (as his readers know). Katharine's domain was the house and the flower borders. She was in charge of the household staff, which prepared meals for the two of them, and often for children and grandchildren. Vegetables from the garden were great favorites. Katharine also grew houseplants (sometimes as many as fifty or sixty), and in winter months she spent hours reading through nursery catalogues to make out her orders for seeds, bulbs, and plants. Between them, the Whites had a busy, full life, one which did not seem to slow down much from the pace of their city lives.

Once in Maine, Katharine hoped to have more time to garden and to do other things she had not had time for in New York. She also set to work on her first "garden piece" (Elizabeth called it a "story"): a review of garden catalogues, which appeared in a March 1958 *New Yorker* under "Books." (After the first essay, her garden essays appeared under the title "Onward and Upward in the Garden," a phrase from the Unitarian creed.) Writing was for Katharine, as Andy observed, "an agonizing ordeal," and she had no sooner submitted her first essay than she began worrying that she would never write the next. What most stood in her way was trying to satisfy her own standards of excellence. And yet the author of the delightful and original first piece—called "A Romp in the Catalogues"—found an immediate audience of enthusiastic readers. Many of them wrote to Katharine White to thank her for her essay—and she answered every letter. The correspondent that she came to value most lived in North Carolina. Her name was Elizabeth Lawrence.

Elizabeth's first letter to Katharine White was a fan letter. Beginning with words of appreciation for Katharine's review, she quickly settled into her dominant tone: familial and helpful. She noted that they had a friend in common—Joseph Mitchell, a writer at *The New Yorker* and a native of North Carolina—and then launched into suggestions of other catalogues Katharine might read. She also added what would become a characteristic just-one-more-thing postscript.

Apparently, Elizabeth did not hesitate to send her badly typed letter filled with spelling errors, dashes, and half-finished parenthetical phrases to one of the best literary editors in America. She did, however, know her facts about plants, and that distinction was not wasted on Katharine, who always relied on the celebrated Fact Checking department of *The New Yorker*. The knowledge that showed through the smudges of Elizabeth's letter was enough to convince Katharine that she had fallen into company with yet another talented writer, perhaps one as individualistic (her word) as the writers of the nursery catalogues she so much enjoyed. From the very beginning, Katharine White and Elizabeth Lawrence struck up a friendship in letters that helped them as writers—and later encouraged them through difficult times in their lives.

Who, then, was Elizabeth Lawrence? Younger than Katharine by almost twelve years, she was born on May 27, 1904, at her father's home in Marietta, Georgia. Samuel Lawrence was an engineer, fun-loving, and Elizabeth "Bessie" Lawrence was a popular social hostess who loved order. The first of two daughters, Elizabeth lived in a small village in northeastern North Carolina until the family moved to Raleigh so that the girls could be sent to St. Mary's, a preparatory school founded by the Episcopal Church. (Elizabeth never talked about religious faith, but the calendar of the Church was as important in her letters as the Latin names of plants.) Elizabeth never liked to leave home but surprised herself by applying to and being accepted by Barnard College (the alma mater of her St. Mary's English teacher). After graduation from Barnard in 1926, however, Elizabeth paid no attention to the directives of Barnard's Dean Virginia Gildersleeve that Barnard women take their places in the world: Instead she couldn't wait to get home. Springtime in the Raleigh garden was the most beautiful she had ever seen.

Family and home always held Elizabeth close: The pattern of her childhood was not as much to be remembered as relived. She seems never to have had thoughts of separating herself from home, not for marriage or for anything else. She and her mother loved to garden and to compare closely kept records of bloom dates. Realizing that she could never earn a living by writing poetry (the poems she wrote were imitative of Edna St. Vincent Millay) and giving "talks" on the arts, which she loved, she enrolled as the first woman student in a North Carolina State program in landscape design. When she graduated in 1933, she designed several gardens, often working for a Raleigh woman who had set up a landscape practice, but Elizabeth was not suited for business: Her designs were done mostly for friends. Happily, she was taken under the tutelage of two unmarried Raleigh sisters who helped support their household by writing for publication. (Like Katharine's Northampton aunts, they had graduated from Smith College, made a home for their brother, and were gracious hostesses.) With these sisters as her mentors (one of them, Ann Preston Bridgers, appears in the letters that follow), Elizabeth began writing garden articles for *House & Garden* and other magazines, using her own large garden as her laboratory. By 1942, her garden was famous in Raleigh, and by the time she was thirty-eight, she had written her first book, *A Southern Garden.* After her father's death and her sister's marriage, Elizabeth found the large old house in Raleigh and the garden too much to manage, and in 1948 she and her mother sold the Raleigh property and moved to Charlotte to live next door to her sister Ann and Ann's family. There was a great deal of back-and-forth between the two houses, and increasingly as their mother became more of a care, Elizabeth depended on Ann to help. Family ties counted for a great deal in both the Lawrence and the White households, as the following letters make clear.

By 1958, Elizabeth began to come into her own as a noted garden writer. The year before Elizabeth wrote her fan letter to Katharine White, she had published *The Little Bulbs* and had started writing a garden column in a Charlotte, North Carolina, newspaper. Slowly, quietly, and with growing confidence in her own ability, she was becoming one of the most authoritative writ-ers and lecturers in the southern gardening world. She had made her choice: to stay at home and look after the old people. And in-creasingly, she had many responsibilities, especially after her mother became an invalid and required constant care. Looking after her mother, however, was like looking after the garden—it required both love and work. Katharine, too, knew about caring for older relatives—her own aunt Crully spent the last years of her life with the Whites in Maine. Sensitive to the needs of older people, Katharine and Elizabeth shared in their letters some of their own concerns about aging.

But what linked these two gardeners perhaps more than any-thing else was the fact that each was an inveterate letter writer. Katharine was able to make the adjustment to living in Maine in part because of her continued contact with many of the writers she edited and with friends she had made at *The New Yorker*. Eliza-beth maintained an enormous correspondence with garden-ers all over the country. Both were readers of Jane Austen and showed the same kind of anticipation as the inhabitants of Longborne in *Pride and Prejudice:* "The arrival of letters was the first grand object of every morning's impatience."

Elizabeth's correspondents ranged widely—from unlettered farm women advertising their seeds and cuttings in state agri-cultural market bulletins, to scientists studying plants, to nurs-erymen and growers. She was starstruck, however, by her cor-respondence with the wife of E. B. White (like many fans, she was smitten with the author of *Charlotte's Web*). Katharine, for her part, *appreciated* Elizabeth and told her so in almost every letter. Furthermore, she recommended Elizabeth's books, finding no fault at all (which was unusual for Katharine) with the "civilized literature by a writer with a pure and lively style and a deep sense of beauty." After each time one of her books was discussed in

Katharine White's column, Elizabeth heard from her friends—"Imagine praise from Mrs. White!" And if her stock rose among her friends, her editors were also impressed.

From the beginning, Katharine recognized that her new correspondent was an exceptional gardener and garden writer. As a result, she showered Elizabeth with questions, asking for the names of other catalogues, garden books, and plants. Elizabeth, in turn, asked Katharine for bloom dates in her Maine garden. These requests for information set the pattern for their correspondence. Over time, the letters would become a reliable source of information and encouragement to both women. Later, Katharine would say that she learned more about horticulture from Elizabeth Lawrence than from anyone else.

By the end of their correspondence in July 1977, when Katharine died, the friendship between the two women had survived long silences and many hardships. And though neither lived to complete the book she wanted to write (Katharine had hoped to turn her *New Yorker* garden columns into a book; Elizabeth hoped to use for a book her correspondence with women who advertised in southern agricultural market bulletins), both women had made their marks in garden literature. When E. B. White edited and introduced Katharine's fourteen garden pieces and saw them through to publication in 1979 as *Onward and Upward in the Garden,* the book was highly praised. Anatole Broyard, reviewing the book in the *New York Times,* wrote that it "is quite a bit more than a book about flowers. It is itself a bouquet, the final blooming of an extraordinary sensibility."

Elizabeth also was not fully recognized for her accomplishments until after her death in 1985. Garden writer Allen Lacy undertook the difficult task of making a book out of Elizabeth's wide-ranging and unfinished manuscript based on the market bulletins and published it in 1987 under the title she had chosen,

Gardening for Love. In 1990, two additional books came out: *Through the Garden Gate,* a selection of her newspaper columns, edited by Bill Neal; and *A Rock Garden in the South,* edited by Nancy Goodwin with Allen Lacy. Then, in 1997, more than a decade after Elizabeth's death, *A Garden of One's Own,* edited by Barbara Scott and Bobby J. Ward, included a selection of her articles published in garden magazines and journals. Together with her three earlier books, these new publications brought Elizabeth Lawrence renewed attention. Now, sixty years after the publication of her first book, *A Southern Garden,* she is considered one of our most distinguished garden writers, admired on both sides of the Atlantic. Elizabeth Lawrence belongs in the company of many of the earlier writers she most admired—E. A. Bowles, Louise Beebe Wilder, and Alice Morse Earle, to name a few. And she is admired by those who have come afterward—Penelope Hobhouse, Allen Lacy, Pamela Harper.

The one hundred sixty-six letters included in this book have been divided into three sections. The first section, "A Romp in the Catalogues": 1958–1961, begins with Elizabeth's first letter to Katharine. She writes to admire Katharine's review of garden catalogues in *The New Yorker* and immediately plunges into suggesting names of other catalogues. Katharine quickly answers, plans to read Elizabeth's garden books, and begins asking questions. Elizabeth becomes Katharine's teacher, and the two write each other frequently in the early years of their friendship.

Letters in the second section—the years 1962 through 1968—reflect the difficulties and also the small triumphs in both women's lives. Katharine's health worsened so dramatically that for three years during this period she was unable to write. Elizabeth, too, was exhausted from the care of her mother, who died in 1964; but she made efforts to see more friends and to travel abroad with her friend Hannah. For long periods during these years, the letters cease, then they start again, still conveying the kind of encouragement that both writers needed.

The letters of the third section, "Letters One by One": 1969–1977, document the last years of Katharine's life. These years were made difficult by her bad health and by old age; but Katharine remained intellectually alive, insistent upon helping Andy get his work done and encouraging Elizabeth to write the "market bulletin" book that Elizabeth had been working on for many years. Elizabeth became Katharine's eyes to see what was blooming in the garden. Katharine, preparing her gardening books and papers to be sent to the archives at Bryn Mawr College, began discussions with Elizabeth about what to do with their letters. And so they made plans to leave copies of both sides of the correspondence for the use of future historians and biographers.

The book closes with "Signs of Durability." In this section, I have brought together letters exchanged between E. B. White and Elizabeth Lawrence after Katharine's death. They corresponded mainly about the publication of Katharine's garden columns. When Elizabeth reviewed *Onward and Upward in the Garden* for the *Charlotte Observer* and sent Andy a copy, he wrote to express his thanks and noted that hers and other good reviews were "signs of durability" for Katharine's book. The title of Elizabeth's newspaper review had been taken from Andy's introduction to *Onward and Upward in the Garden:* "She held the world of flowers in a warm embrace."

Editor's Note

I have tried to meddle as little as possible in editing these letters for publication, though recognizing that letters not written for publication—even by a distinguished editor and a published writer—contain ordinary mistakes, repetitions, and incompletions. With the exception of fewer than a dozen letters (illegible, irrelevant, repetitive, or unclear), I have included all of the correspondence from the archives prepared by Katharine White and Elizabeth Lawrence. It was easy to read Katharine's letters—they were usually typed by a secretary, and when she added handwritten postscripts, she wrote (in the words of John Updike) in "a hand of singular clarity and erectness."* Elizabeth's letters were quite another matter—when she typed them herself, she seems never to have changed the ribbon, and her handwriting looks like the tracks of excited ants. I think I have puzzled out most of the words.

The editorial changes I have made are these: I have corrected misspellings (Elizabeth was a poor speller in English, though

*"Books: Goody Sergeant; the Powerful Katrinka; K.S.W.," by John Updike (*The New Yorker* 8/10/87).

flawless in Latin) and inaccurate dates, supplied words carelessly omitted, and changed punctuation when the meaning was not clear. I have omitted most addresses of people, nurseries, and book dealers used in the text; they would have taken up many lines and are now mostly out of date. I have eliminated use of the ampersand, which appears inconsistently in the women's hand-written notes; I have italicized all titles and Latin names of plants; and I have let stand the women's other stylistic preferences, including use of numbers and occasional ellipses. All of Elizabeth's letters were written in Charlotte, North Carolina, and she gave them no inside address; Katharine usually indicated whether she was in Maine, New York, or Florida, and I have followed her practice only as needed for clarity. Any insertions I made for clarity are indicated by ellipses in brackets.

Because Elizabeth Lawrence did not date most of her letters, I have had to make reasonable guesses (indicated by brackets) and thus to establish the sequence of letters as best I could. I retain her use of the Anglican Church calendar—she writes her first letter on Whit Sunday, for example. I have standardized salutations and closings when they are absent, while retaining each writer's preferences when they are expressed. (Elizabeth's "Aff, Elizabeth Lawrence" was always her favorite closing.) Secretaries often typed Katharine's letters, but she added handwritten insertions and postscripts. Both women added sentences in the margins and lengthy postscripts. I have entered the marginal notes in the text as indicated. I have standardized the designation of both writers' use of postscripts with one simple "P.S.," after which several paragraphs usually follow.

The letters of Katharine White contain many allusions to health problems, especially her own, but also her sister Elsie's and her husband Andy's. Family, friends, and readers of E. B. White's letters, essays, and commentaries in *The New Yorker* know that the Whites talked a great deal about health. In order to give narrative shape and flow to the letters, I had to pare down lengthy and repetitive health reports while retaining enough to reflect Katharine's character and her courage. Such editorial deletions are indicated by bracketed ellipses. In fact, a long series of surgeries and illnesses plagued Katharine for most of the years covered by these letters. Knowing that, we can appreciate even more the relief that Elizabeth's letters and Katharine's own gardening activities provided for her.

I have provided in footnotes the kind of additional information that might be of interest to readers who want to know more about a particular allusion. For frequently used citations, I have adopted the following abbreviations:

KSW   Katharine S. White

EBW   E. B. "Andy" White

EL   Elizabeth Lawrence

KSWBMC Katharine Sergeant White papers, Bryn Mawr
        College Library

ELNSUL Elizabeth Lawrence papers, Cammie G.
        Henry Research Center, Northwestern State
        University of Louisiana

NY   *The New Yorker* magazine

CO   *Charlotte Observer* newspaper

Articles by Katharine White first published in *The New Yorker* and those by Elizabeth Lawrence first published in the *Charlotte Observer* are cited by dates in the footnotes. Readers desiring easier access to the originals will find them in book form in White's *Onward and Upward in the Garden* and Lawrence's *Through the Garden Gate.*

Finally, I have divided the letters into three sections and have written short introductions in order to establish biographical and contextual meaning.

Except for italicizing plant names, I have not changed either writer's use of the gardening nomenclature, nor have I called on the advice of experts to update name changes, a tricky business at best. These are personal letters, not horticultural reports, and the voices of the gardeners speak to us in their own time and way. Since both women wrote for important publications and knew the rules, I felt no compulsion to interfere with the freedom they enjoyed in writing to one another, and I let stand their inconsistencies in such matters as use of capital and lowercase letters and quotation marks.

Emily Herring Wilson
Winston-Salem, North Carolina
August 2001

Part One

"A ROMP IN THE CATALOGUES"
1958–1961

For gardeners, this is the season of lists and callow hopefulness; hundreds of thousands of bewitched readers are poring over their catalogues, making lists for their seed and plant orders, and dreaming their dreams.

"A ROMP IN THE CATALOGUES," *The New Yorker,* K.S.W.

Katharine White's review of garden catalogues, published in The New Yorker *on March 1, 1958, apparently was the first review of its kind, and it was an immediate success. Some readers wrote to ask the name of the writer, identified only as K.S.W. (Someone with a near-perfect memory might have realized that "K.S.W." was "K.S.A.," who had written light verse about the "Seductive Spring Seed Catalogue" in a March 1926* New Yorker, *when she was Katharine S. Angell and a new staff member.) One reader who did know the identity of the writer was Elizabeth Lawrence, a lifelong reader of* The New Yorker. *Her fan letter to Katharine a month or so after the appearance of the review is the first letter in the following section.*

After a dozen letters between "Mrs. White" and "Miss Lawrence," Katharine and Elizabeth settled into a first-name basis. Elizabeth kept up a steady flow of information on nurseries and garden books and thus called forth Kath-

arine's repeated expressions of appreciation and more questions. Elizabeth clearly enjoyed researching any topics that were introduced, and she was glad to have Katharine's records of bloom dates in Maine. For more than three decades Elizabeth had been making notes on index cards about what was going on in her garden—and in the gardens of others. The unexpected availability of such a fine compatriot as Elizabeth must have confirmed the rightness of Katharine's decision to follow her first review with a series of pieces, to be presented each time under the title "Onward and Upward in the Garden." She hoped to publish them twice a year, and in 1959 and 1960 she succeeded. In March 1960 she received a letter from the publisher Alfred Knopf, proposing that she write a book, an idea that she told him she would "ponder."

The letters going back and forth between Charlotte, North Carolina, and North Brooklin, Maine (and New York City and Sarasota, Florida, when the Whites traveled) were hardy perennials. Feelings began to jostle alongside facts as the two women exchanged anecdotes and kept up one another's spirits. By early spring 1961, Katharine—who had insisted that she was an editor, not a writer—had published some 100 pages of her garden pieces in The New Yorker. She began to enjoy including some of her own memories in her discussions of flowers, recalling happy summers as a child when she and her sister picked water lilies on Lake Chocorua in New Hampshire.

Elizabeth, for her part, was also publishing her gardening column every Sunday in the Charlotte Observer. Although she worked on two or three book manuscripts at a time, the newspaper column gave her the greatest pleasure, always producing a flurry of letters. "I wish you lived next door," Elizabeth wrote to Katharine, "I would fill your garden up."

Whit Sunday

Dear Mrs. White,

I am very grateful to Joseph Mitchell's sister, Mrs. Lamm, for calling my attention to your story about the catalogues.* Our *New Yorker* is a family affair, and it sometimes gets under somebody's bed before anyone else sees it, and I sometimes miss the very thing I would have liked best.

I not only enjoyed the article, I profited by the advice, and I am particularly glad to know about "Roses of Yesterday and Today." I don't know how I managed to garden for nearly fifty years without hearing of Will Tillotson, but I did. It is a principle with me never to pay for catalogues, but I gladly sent the Honorable Secretary fifty cents. Just for Lady Caroline Howard. But do you know Roy Hennessey, Scappoose, Oregon?†

You shouldn't miss Cecil Houdyshel's little brochures . . . twice a year (LaVerne, California). I think he is in his nineties now, so you had better hurry. He always begins, "Dear Flora Friends." One issue has a picture of him with his great-grandchild. One of his letters offered a litter of cocker puppies for sale. In his spring '57 issue he says he plans to live to be a hundred, but will settle for 97, and as he had two grandparents who lived to be that old, and uncles and aunts who lived longer he thinks he has a good chance. I have all of them (the catalogues) the last twenty-two years (one was missing but I sent a dime and got it) and consider them one of my treasures. One of the interesting things in that

---

*"A Romp in the Catalogues" had been recommended to EL by her gardening friend, Linda Mitchell Lamm of Wilson, N.C. Lamm's brother, Joseph Mitchell, was a writer at *The New Yorker*.

†KSW had especially admired "Roses of Yesterday and Today," a catalogue written by Will Tillotson, the "Honorable Secretary," of Watsonville, Calif. Tillotson advertised the Lady Caroline Howard rose. EL recommended Roy Hennessey, author of "Roy Hennessey's Prize-Winning Roses," and KSW wrote about him in her next essay, "Floricordially Yours" (*NY* 3/14/59).

kind of a catalogue is to see how the gardener's taste changes from year to year: Iris, then day lilies, then African violets, then orchids . . . but always amaryllids, and always some bulb that you can't get anywhere else.

But my favorite of all is Park's Flower Book, Geo. W. Park Seed Co., Greenwood, South Carolina. The new ones on slick paper, with the same color photographs that are in all catalogues, can't compare with the old ones, but the first page still carries, in a little box (it used to have a quaint little floral design around the edge, but now just a black line), a prayer by John Henry Jowett about God's love, and beauty; and at the bottom emphasized by an arrow (it used to be a hand with a fancy cuff, and a pointing finger), "My friends, are these your sentiments? If not, why not? —Park." It still has a picture in the left-hand corner of Geo. W. Park, Founder, 1852–1935, the date of the founding 1868, a quotation from Emerson, and an adorable cut of a boy in a sailor suit and hat rolling a wheelbarrow bursting with flowers while a little girl holds a parasol over him (it is like an illustration for Mrs. Ewing*) and beneath, "Yes, sister, I buy only of Park, his seeds always grow and yield the finest flowers." Mr. Park, one of the catalogues said, is a descendant of John Knox, and he looks like it. His two sons, usually pictured, have the same grim mouth, but they have their mother's eyes. A picture of Mrs. Park, the Balance Wheel, is in the 1947 catalogue, in which Geo. B. Park, now president, pays tribute to "a heroine from real life—My Mother, a God Fearing woman" (but she doesn't look as fearful as the men of the family). ". . . During the War, Brother William (W. J. Park, Grower) and I were in service and she carried on alone of the Park family . . . sometimes she worked sixteen hours a day to get your orders to you on time." She really did get them there. They usually come by return mail. Until the war, all seeds were ten cents a package,

---

*Julianna (Gatty) Ewing, 1841–1885, editor of *Aunt Judy's Magazine* and author of the popular story "The Brownies and Other Tales," which gave the name to the junior Girl Scouts.

eleven for a dollar. Mr. Park said most people wanted only a few of a kind, and there was no use wasting them, so he just put them in smaller packages. A Jumbo was a quarter . . . still is, but the small ones are now fifteen cents . . . 15 for two dollars, forty for five . . . you can save by ordering for your friends, if you don't need that many.

I asked Mrs. Lamm if you were Mrs. E. B. White, and she said you were. So please tell Mr. E. B. that he has three generations of devoted readers in this family. My mother's favorites were the one about leaving the mirror in the apartment vestibule, and the one about homemade bread.* My niece adores *Charlotte's Web.*†

Sincerely,
Elizabeth Lawrence

P.S. I knew there was something else: Have you the charming Barnhaven catalogues? (Gresham, Oregon). You should, even if you don't want rare primroses. And do you know Harry E. Saier? Dimondale, Michigan. I subscribe to his *Garden Magazine* too. Used to be free, now a dollar a year . . . comes four times a year, if it comes.

JUNE 4, 1958

Dear Miss Lawrence,

It was delightful to get your letter, so full of interesting and helpful suggestions about garden catalogues. I had already caught up, too late, with that of the Geo. W. Park Seed Co. and I admire it, but of course I have only seen their latest. Your descriptions of the earlier Park Seed Books make my mouth water and I

---

*The favorites were "Removal" and "Fro-Joy," which had first appeared in *Harper's Magazine* and were reprinted in EBW's *One Man's Meat* (Harper, 1938).
†EL's niece and namesake was Elizabeth Way (Rogers), one of two children of her sister Ann and Ann's husband, Warren, who lived next door to Elizabeth and her mother in Charlotte, N.C.

wish I had some of them. I shall send right off for Cecil Houdy-shel's brochures and for some of the other catalogues you mention. I already have one copy of the Barnhaven catalogue, which is charming, but I can't raise primroses; they make my hands break out. I go on accumulating catalogues of every sort, though, in the hope that someday I may get time and enough good ideas to write another catalogue review, but it is quite likely that I never shall. Your suggestions will spur me on, if anything could, but I am an editor, not a writer. Of course, as a gardener, I am a rank amateur, and very disorganized because I have so little time and strength for it.

I gave your messages to my husband, who was most grateful for them. Joe Mitchell is one of our favorite friends and writers, and I was happy to hear that he recommended my review to his sister and she to you. I consider any recommendation from Joe a great honor.

Sincerely yours,
Katharine S. White

P.S. I have heard only just now of your garden book, and I plan to send to the North Carolina Press for it.*

JULY 2, 1958

Dear Miss Lawrence,

I am in New York for the moment, so it was on my desk here at *The New Yorker* that I found today your book, *The Little Bulbs*,† and a note from Mary Ellen Flood‡ saying that you had sent it to me

---

A Southern Garden (1942; reprinted 1967, 1984, 1991).
†*The Little Bulbs: A Tale of Two Gardens* (Criterion Books, 1957; reprinted Duke University Press, 1986).
‡Daughter of Ellen Flood, EL's New York friend since college days, and a secretary at *The New Yorker* 1956–1959. When EL sent her copies of KSW's letters, Mary Ellen wrote back, "She is very much the way she sounds in the long letter."

with your best wishes. I am extremely happy to have it, and proud to own a copy with your name inscribed on the flyleaf, and already I have dipped into it with delight. I shall carry it back with me to Maine next week and study it and consult it constantly for years, I know. I particularly love the *little* bulbs but the varieties I have thus far established in our garden are the obvious ones I'm afraid: the two colors of scylla,* snowdrops, snowflakes, crocuses, white and blue grape hyacinths, and among the small tulips only *Clusiana* and *Kaufmanniana*. Your book will help me to expand, I hope, if I am bright enough to hit on bulbs that will withstand our severe winters. I am anxious to try some hardy cyclamen, even though I haven't a lifetime left to do it in. Last fall for the first time I planted a mixture of small bulbs between the plants of the myrtle ground cover under some low juniper bushes on each side of the front door—a western exposure—and to my pleasure they all came up and bloomed. When we left there on June 13 some of the white grape hyacinths were still in bloom, so you can see how late we are. But in the bed [on] the south side of the house and in the long south bed beyond the lawn we get scylla and snowdrops in early March, so it is partly a matter of exposure. We shall be back in Maine next week, but I'm afraid that even the myrtle's blue flowers will have passed by then and that the pansies will be the only color in the beds to the west. It was hard to have to leave, just as the beds were getting to be lovely with peonies, lupines, bearded iris, and the first roses.

Last fall was the first time I really started out with ambitious plans—and at last the *time*—to garden the year around in a more orderly and consistent fashion, although I have been gardening and had lots of flowers in this same garden since 1932.† But this was the year when I really had dreams of glory and of success.

---

*Both EL and KSW were inconsistent in their spelling of "scylla."
†KSW must have confused the year. The Whites bought their farm in North Brooklin in 1933.

Therefore it was perfectly horrid to be hit early this spring for the first time with a doctor's command to "keep off my feet," so I have mostly had to stand around and watch while someone else did the work, if and when he had time to between farm chores. I now have much more garden than we can manage well, so I'll simply have to get back again to doing most of it myself. As a matter of fact, I am better, but I'm afraid that this year won't be the one when my dreams of glory come true. They did, though, in last winter's houseplants, and I shall use your chapter on "Little Bulbs in Pots" next winter.* Last year I had great luck with freesias, white, yellow, and lavender, but I have decided that I so much prefer the white ones that I shall plant only them next fall.

In May I sent off to the University of North Carolina Press for a copy of *A Southern Garden,* but it is out of print, as you must know, so Joe Mitchell has lent me his copy and I have had the pleasure of reading it while here in New York. It's a delightful book. I feel that I'm going to like *The Little Bulbs* just as much or even better, for already after a chapter or two Mr. Krippendorf has become a favorite character.† I don't know that I really envy him his hundreds of acres of forest but at least I do want to get our patch of woods between our pasture and our shore back to the state that it was in before first sheep and then cows were allowed to roam in it. Now at last we have fenced off this bit of woods and I hope when I am well again to restore the dogtooth violets, the lady's slippers, the wood lilies, and the white wood violets that were there when we first bought our fifty acres, before we acquired the farm creatures who have rooted them up. Most of the pasture wild flowers have survived—bluets, wild azalea, wild flag—but not the ones in the woods.

---

*In *The Little Bulbs.*
†Carl Krippendorf, one of EL's correspondents, whose woodland estate outside Cincinnati, Ohio, EL describes in *The Little Bulbs* and in *Lob's Wood* (Cincinnati Nature Center, 1971).

My only excuse for rambling on so is that you write that you like to hear from different regions, but you must already have a Maine Coast garden correspondent who is a better gardener than I am. The real point of this letter is to thank you for the book. It was generous of you to send it to me and I am very grateful.

Sincerely yours,
Katharine S. White

[JULY 11, 1958]

Dear Mrs. White,

Thank you for your very valuable letter, and the dates of white grape hyacinths, snowdrops, and scylla—I am always glad to find a lover of the classics, have you any Charybdis?

I hasten to assure you that I have no Maine Coast correspondent, and am always most grateful for any specific information, especially about anything that blooms in November, December, or January. If anything does. I asked one of the rock gardeners from Massachusetts to send me notes for that time, and she wrote that her garden was covered with snow. But I had a letter from Dr. [Helen C.] Scorgie, who lives in Harvard (Mass.) and she says that Nylon blooms there in ice and snow. I think I gave you Alexander Heimlich's name for his little bulb catalogue, didn't I? Woburn, Mass.

I must warn you that the chapter on little bulbs in pots is synthetic. I don't like to fool with pots. I got most of the information out of Mr. Houdyshel's brochures, so you may prefer it first hand. I think you can get back numbers—some, at least—for ten cents. I have them for spring and fall since 1936. Fall would probably be what you would want.

I envy you the woods. I love our North Carolina ones, but I

had never seen real woods until I went to Sargentville* one summer—all of those darling little mosses and plants, looking as neat as the pictures in Grimm.

I am sure you know that no one can be more sympathetic than I about not being able to dig.

Sincerely,
Elizabeth Lawrence

JANUARY 6, 1959

Dear Miss Lawrence,

I planted some new botanical tulips between Scylla and Charybdis in late October, and for once managed to label them all. I shall try to report my success or failure with the various kinds next spring and also how many of last year's survived. I am still uncertain how well the lady tulips endure from year to year in this climate.

I have no interesting news of winter bloomings for you and no exact dates for the last flowers of the autumn because I had to go to New York the first week of November. When I left, roses and chrysanthemums were still in bloom, as we had a very mild fall. Like a fool, I picked my chrysanthemums and gave them away, for when I got back the middle of the month, chrysanthemums in other gardens were still untouched by the frost, which is very unusual here at that date. I picked a dark red Charles Mallerin rose in Thanksgiving week, and by picking buds of Eclipse, of Golden Wings, and of White Wings—the last two are single roses as I'm sure you know—we had roses indoors up to the last of that month.

Then came our hard freezes (but I carelessly haven't the exact

*The next town over from North Brooklin, Maine, where the Whites lived.

date of the first) and December has been the coldest here since 1917. For four weeks now we have had a blanket of snow and only three scattered days of light thaw—not enough to remove the snow.

My gardening has therefore been indoors, and you are not interested in that. I shall only report on the little, or comparatively little, indoor bulbs I've grown. I had great success with Wayside's new small, all-yellow daffodil, "February Gold," both in earth and in pebbles. Twenty blossoms to twelve bulbs. (It probably isn't a new daffodil at all.) The ones in earth, planted the middle of November, blossomed Christmas week. Three pots of freesias, two of white and one of yellow, planted the end of October, and put outdoors during the day and brought in at night when below 32 degrees, have come along well and the whites are full of buds (no flower stalks yet on the yellows), but today to my horror I found green plant lice all over one pot of the white—I am in despair and only hope I can save them. We also have had the usual bowls of paperwhite and Soleil d'Or narcissus, but these are not really small bulbs, nor are my three huge amaryllis, which I am coaxing along. I have too many houseplants for the time I have to spend on them—begonias, cactuses, clivia, geraniums, strelitzia, cyclamen. The cool Maine houses just suit cyclamen.

Now I am trying to gather my wits for a try at another catalogue review but I may be too busy ever to get it written, or if I do, I may well find I have said my say last year. Anyway I have written and had returns from Mr. Houdyshell. (If he should die, would you tell me?) Also from Roy Hennessey, and various of your other good suggestions.

I gave *The Little Bulbs* to my friend Grace Root, who is a really good gardener. She had not seen it and was enchanted. She would make a good correspondent for you as a reporter on her northerly Clinton, N.Y., garden, where she naturalizes primroses. She raises among many other things the beautiful iris her husband hybridized and peonies from Sylvia Saunders.*

I am afraid that I shall not have a single outdoor winter flower to report. I am a sham as a gardener—no time to be scientific. However, I started a garden journal on January 1st.† If it produces anything—anything exact that is—in the least interesting, I shall report it to you.

Please don't bother to answer this letter, unless of course you hear any bad news of Mr. Houdyshell. I am always nervous when I write about old people.

Sincerely yours,
Katharine S. White

P.S. January 9—I am now in New York, though I started this letter in Maine, and I have no catalogues here. I may have spelled Mr. Houdyshell's name wrong.

[JANUARY 1959]

Dear Mrs. White,

I do thank you for your letter, and I *am* interested in houseplants—not for myself—but I collect notes on everything that grows! I feel I should cover everything, as I do a column for the *Charlotte Observer.*‡

I shall write to your friend Mrs. Root at once.

I guess Mr. Houdyshel is still there as I got his spring catalogue yesterday with his personal letter, and he has been on a trip! But I am sure you have it too.

*Sylvia Saunders, of A. P. Saunders, Clinton, N.Y., specialists in peony hybrids.
†KSW's "Garden and Houseplant Journal" (January 1, 1959–May 1960), KSWBMC.
‡EL's garden column, "Through the Garden Gate," appeared in the Sunday *Charlotte* (N.C.) *Observer* 1957 through 1971. Some of the columns were published in a book by that title (UNC Press, 1990).

Most all of my garden friends are at least eighty. Mr. Krippendorf never writes anymore. For a while he called me every week or so. Now he seldom does that, so when I get frightened I call him. Also Caroline Dormon*—who won't tell her age, but her friends say she is at least 80—has just had pleurisy, and has a bad heart. She is doing drawings for my book.

I was crushed when I did not find you at my darling Mary Ellen's beautiful wedding.† She said she would not ask you to come so far, but I had just hoped you would be in New York at the time.

Mr. Houdyshel makes things more difficult by his trademark of the clasped hands and the shell—naturally you would add an extra "l" [to the last syllable of his name]. I could feel your thinking that Mr. Ross‡ was looking over your shoulder.

Please forgive the scratching, and the return mail—it is now or never, and [I have a] manuscript§ in the typewriter.

Aff,

Elizabeth Lawrence

P.S. I hope you don't find me—as my grandmother used to say— too d— friendly. I feel affectionate towards you when I read your letters. But, then, I thought you might be as astonished as I was when a Mrs. Theus Colhoun (I had never heard of) wrote to ask me to come to Louisiana, and signed herself "with love." I suppose she thought she was bound to love a fellow gardener.

Have you the new *Plant Buyers Guide?* If not, don't buy it—it is not worth $15. Half the nurseries listed are either out of business, or no longer list the plant he says they list, but I got a few new names: The Tailored Tree Nursery, Edward H. Scanlon,

---

*Author of *Flowers Native to the Deep South* (Claitor's Book Store, 1958) and illustrator for EL's book, *Gardens in Winter* (Harper, 1961). She lived at Briarwood, near Saline, La.

†Mary Ellen Flood married James Mitchell Reese, October 25, 1958, in New York City.

‡Harold Ross, founding editor of *The New Yorker* (1925–1951) and KSW's boss and good friend.

§Perhaps *Gardens in Winter.*

Olmsted Falls, Ohio. He will send you matches, free, and a catalogue with a cartoon, "A city without trees ain't fit for a dog," and
a picture of Mr. Scanlon planting a maple in Moscow, a *wonderful*
picture, should be in all newspapers, the Russians looking so ten-
derly at the little tree. A *good* catalogue. Also the Brimfield Gardens Nursery, "The Home of Rare Trees," Wethersfield, Conn. I
don't know whether it is *really* the *home* of rare trees. I haven't
bought any yet as the prices are on a scale with the rarity—but he
does list trees and shrubs not to be had elsewhere in this country.
I don't know whether you would be interested in Combsie's Iris
Garden, Whittier, California.

I also love the local ones, with a special clientele. House
O'Moes Gardens, Abbeville, Louisiana, who invite you to see the
gardens of their friends; "We are especially fond of Mrs. Dave
Clarke's collection" (Baton Rouge).

I was charmed to hear of the roses at Thanksgiving—just
what I wanted. Here everyone at church wore a pink camellia—
Debutante.

JANUARY 17 [1959]

Dear Miss Lawrence,

My husband is sick in bed and I have a houseguest, so this can
be only a note to say that I forwarded your note to Mrs. Edward
W. Root, to her New York address. Her husband, who died about
two years ago, was the son of Elihu Root (the great Elihu, not his
son Elihu Jr.) and was professor of art at Hamilton College and a
collector of modern paintings. I forgot that since his death Grace
has a *pied à terre* in NYC and vacillates between Clinton and the
city. Perhaps she won't be such a good respondent after all. But
she lives for gardens and often is in Clinton—stays there late in
the fall, returns early. I know she will feel honored to be asked.

Mr. Houdyshel's new book did come; I have about fifteen of

them now and read them in a trance all one day this week, but I am now beginning to despair of writing my *New Yorker* piece this year. Too much is descending on me all at once, including two *little* grandchildren,* next week. I am much obliged for the new catalogue names and for your delightful letters. I have had the same fear about you—that I get to be too damned friendly. If I do, forgive me, for I love your letters. We were not asked to Mary Ellen's wedding. If I had known you were to be there and if I had had an invitation, I would not have missed the occasion. Mary Ellen looks beautifully happy.

As ever,
Katharine S.W.

MARCH 30, 1959

Dear Miss Lawrence,

I am writing you from Florida where we are having a month's vacation from the bitter Maine winter of this year, and as usual I am turning to you for help. [. . .]

I want to acknowledge the great help that your tips to me on nurseries and catalogues were in writing my this year's garden piece for *The New Yorker*.† It would have had no Cecil Houdyshel but for you, and several of the other names came from you. I wrote Mrs. Houdyshel and she gave me the information about his age and his present interest in camellias, and she said he would be glad to have these facts used.

The help I beg for is this: what do you know about Will Tillotson's *Roses* as of now? I wrote about the firm in both my pieces and the roses I ordered thrived. Also before I first wrote about this catalogue in 1958, I asked two friends (one the wife of a famous private rose grower and one a good rose grower in a smaller way)

---

*Steven and Martha White, children of KSW's and EBW's son Joel and his wife, Allene.
†"Before the Frost" (*NY* 9/26/59).

what they knew about Tillotson roses. All the reports were good and the nursery was described by one of them as a thing of beauty. Now comes a letter from two San Francisco women saying that on the strength of my 1958 piece, they had been to Watsonville last summer to see the Tillotson roses and had found no roses at all—only an office. They claim that the Tillotson roses are grown by a wholesaler in San Jose, are sent to Watsonville, retagged, and shipped to customers. Why they didn't write me when it happened, I don't know. They claim misrepresentation in the catalogue and if what they say is true, I fear they are right. I am trying to gather facts from outside before writing directly to Mrs. Stemler* or sending someone to investigate. I feel like an utter fool, of course, and feel I have cheated *New Yorker* readers. Naturally, too, I feel that I am probably too unknowing to write on garden subjects any more, although up to now I had thought my amateur status perhaps an advantage. Oh dear, what pitfalls! [. . .]

I hope you can read this awful scrawl. I have no typewriter here.

Another point I seem to have been ignorant about in my last article is *Dictamnus.* A reader has written me that the gas plant makes many people who handle it break out in a bad rash. And on top of all this Alfred Knopf, the publisher, writes me he has never paid cash to *any* seedhouse or nursery.† I think the size of his orders and his name must carry more weight than mine do!

You can see why I am discouraged by my unnerving sashays into the world of gardening. The Tillotson thing is the only one that really bothers me, for if they are distributors only, they should say so in their book and I should say so in my pieces, if I ever mention them again. [. . .] I would be grateful if you would not speak of my present doubts until I really have time to investigate thoroughly, and if you have facts, I would welcome them.

*Dorothy C. Stemler, who ran Will Tillotson's rose business after his death.
†KSW had advised readers that most companies did not offer charge accounts.

Despite all my self-doubts, I just may, if I have time, write a short autumn or late summer piece on houseplants and bulbs, and on some books on gardening. The latter got crowded out of the latest piece. I had even written out a paragraph on your two books but I was not satisfied and I had overrun my space. If you have any suggestions on houseplants and bulb catalogues and on books you value, I'd be grateful. But why should I ask you to do this when you yourself are writing on gardens? I wish I ever saw your column. If I did, I would be less ignorant. You are one of the two writers in this field I know is learned, is not sentimental, and who is a writer. The other is the gardening Drinker sister* and she can't write as well as you.

Gratefully yours,
Katharine White

[APRIL 4, 1959]
Don't give it another thought department

Dear Mrs. White,

I never heard of the Tillotsons until I read your first article, and so I can't answer firsthand. I suggest that you write to Drew Sherrard.† [. . .] At San Jose, I suggest you write to Leonard Coates. I don't know anything about him except that he is a reputable nurseryman, that I have heard of for years, and he is probably ninety, too, but I have a postcard from him this morning saying he no longer ships, sad to relate. Then I would write to Mr. B. Y. Morrison.‡ He is under eighty and answers by return mail. He knows all of the intrigues of the horticultural world, but you should tell him all. I would have written these letters myself ex-

---

*Ernesta Drinker Ballard, *Garden in Your House* (Harper, 1958).
†Author of *Roadside Flowers of the Pacific Northwest* (Metropolitan Press, 1932), columnist for the *Portland Oregonian,* and a pioneer in bringing native plants into Oregon gardens.
‡Morrison had been director of the National Arboretum in Washington, D.C., before moving to Pass Christian, Miss., to open his own nursery, specializing in azaleas.

cept that you said not to mention it. In the meantime I shall ask around, but I am sure no one in these parts knows any more than I do.

In any case you are silly to worry. There is no reason for you to feel guilty. You were writing about catalogues, not nurseries. It is certainly a charming catalogue, and worth fifty cents.

[. . .]

I love the Merry Gardens.* They have a wonderful ivy list, and the little plants that come in plastic pots are enchanting. [. . .] The Rosses look so young and trusting in their pictures. The way I found them is, a visitor to the garden gave me an adorable ivy called fleur de lis that came from there. I don't know how she ever got as far as Charlotte, much less to Maine. They also have some hard-to-get tender vines that I have been looking for for ages. I just got from them yesterday a *Muehlenbeckia*, a passion vine, and the most enchanting little evergreen grape. Even if they don't prove hardy here, I can enjoy them this summer. And I should think window gardeners would like the way they divide the list into plants for sun and shade. It drives me crazy. I like an alphabetical list. [. . .]

The reason I haven't written you about *The New Yorker* article is that I have been rereading Willa Cather and herb books for a lecture, and hadn't got around to the last numbers.

As to garden books, the old ones are the best, and mostly out of print. Do you know Caroline Dormon's *Flowers Native to the Deep South?* She published it herself and couldn't afford review copies, so it is very little known. She said Macmillan said they couldn't do it for less than twelve dollars a copy, and her friends hadn't that much money, so she mortgaged her place† (paid off now) and did it herself.

---

*Merry Gardens, Camden, Maine. Ervin and Mary Ellen Ross ran the nursery.
†Briarwood, Dormon's 100-acre woodland estate in northern Louisiana, now open to the public as the Caroline Dormon Nature Preserve.

You can't worry about people with *allergies*. I never heard of *Dictamnus* giving anybody a rash, and it has been a favorite family plant for many generations. [...] Mrs. Loudon* says, "The leaves have a pleasant smell like lemon peel when rubbed," and I am sure she wouldn't have led her readers on to rub it and get a rash. Mrs. Wilder† in *The Fragrant Path* (my favorite of her books) speaks of it as a plant to have close by and touch; and so do all of the books that I have on hand, and think of at the moment. I enclose a review I did of Miss Dormon's book. A friend made some copies for me to send around to various garden editors in hopes of getting them to mention it.

I find most plantsmen send their wares without cash, even when they have never heard of you, but I certainly would never ask them to. I am always in debt to Mr. Saier because he sends things at odd times, and I wake up in the night and remember that I have owed him a quarter for three years. The reason I don't send a check is that they often don't list the price of rare things, and then you don't know whether they still have what they list. Some give the prices, and say that they will send the plants when they have the money in hand. You really can't blame them.

Aff and sympathetically,
Elizabeth Lawrence

[APRIL 1959]
Department of Correction and Amplification

Dear Mrs. White,
    I was so incensed over the unjust slur your reader cast on the gas plant that I spent most of the night looking into it, and having spent so much time decided to write it up. I am sending you a car-

*Jane Webb Loudon, *The Lady's Companion to the Flower Garden* (William Smith, 1842).
†Louise Beebe Wilder.

bon,* so you can let me know if you have any objections to what I have said about you or the article. I'm sorry it is so fuzzy, and hope it won't put your eyes out. I won't get it in the *Observer* before the last Sunday in April, and can scratch you out if you don't want to be quoted. I never know. I am so in sympathy with people who can't bear to have their names in newspapers—I am one of them. "I will thank you to leave my name out of the paper," my great-grandfather used to say, and I was brought up on it. On the other hand, a friend was furious because I put forth some of her theories without mentioning her name. [. . .] Then a darling old lady said I could write about her garden if I wouldn't mention her. The charm of it was that the rock larkspur came from a cousin's farm in Virginia, and the Trillium grew by the spring at her grandfather's place in Cabarrus County [North Carolina]. But in this case I felt I shouldn't use your name without asking.

Floricordially yours,
Elizabeth Lawrence

APRIL 8, 1959

Dear Miss Lawrence,

I am relieved that you can defend the gas plant and I don't mind your mentioning my piece as a takeoff for your very interesting and learned piece on *Dictamnus,* but I must have worded my letter to you intemperately and I'm afraid I must ask you to reword your lead. I am now back at the office and able to reread the letter from my reader. She did not "take me to task." Instead, out of the kindness of her heart, she wrote me a warning as follows: "I feel I should warn you about *Dictamnus.* Did you know that some people are allergic to the secretion that comes from the plant? We didn't until my poor Mother suddenly developed the worst rash

---

*EL had written that an "indignant" reader "took Katharine White to task" for not warning gardeners about the poisonous effects of the gas plant.

I've ever seen on her arms and legs. We have a very alert M.D. here who diagnosed it. [. . .] What a mess. So beware."

Now this letter to *me* is not going to be published, and of course I can't give you permission to quote from it so perhaps you can word your lead either without mentioning my piece at all or else by saying that I was a floral friend and had told you that after writing about the gas plant in *The New Yorker*, a friendly reader had sent me a warning that some people were allergic to the flower, and that I now was worried about it. Then you could go on to say I need not worry and to defend the gas plant.*

I can't tell you how to do it but I think you'll see why I feel it would be unfair to my correspondent if you used the present lead to your piece. She was not indignant; she was merely reporting and warning. I guess I wrote you in a moment of despair. The ladies who did not find Tillotson roses growing at Watsonville were the ones who really took me to task and I transferred the indignant tone of their letters to my correspondent on the gas plant.

You don't mention Tillotson. I now feel better about that, too, since getting a detailed letter from Mrs. Edwin Bechtel about what she knows about the firm. She also says it is not unusual for nurseries that issue catalogues to have plants and cuttings they own grown in other nurseries. I do think, though, that hereafter I *must* know whether the plants I describe are grown at the addresses I have to give, and it seems to me that if they are not, it would be only fair if the catalogues did the same thing. Have you ever had an experience of this? My ignorance, you see, leads me into many pitfalls.

Sincerely yours,
Katharine S. White

*EL did revise her lead according to KSW's suggestions (*CO* 5/10/59) and acknowledged that KSW's article in "Onward and Upward" had brought to light three cases of people who had been poisoned by handling *Dictamnus*. She went on to say, "I have never heard of this before (and I hope it won't keep Mrs. White from planting it)."

P.S. Your second letter has just come and I shall have to answer it later. A *second* reader has written me that *Dictamnus* is as bad as poison ivy for her.

[APRIL 1959]

[Dear Mrs. White,]

I keep thinking about gardening books: I can tell you four that are *not* my favorites: *Garden Clubs and Spades* by Laurence McKinney (which I none-the-less treasure for the Helen Hokinson* drawings). [. . .]

Surgery with a Spade by A. Z. Godunov, which begins, "Have you ever heard the whispering among the tall trees?" A sample of plant conversation is "Move over you fellows. I need more room. That's why they call me Spreading Juniper."

Garden Rubbish, of which Dean Nuisance and Broccoli Bill are the main characters.

And *A Sense of Humus*. I forgot who wrote that. It is always being quoted to me. And I nearly forgot a fifth: *Adam's Profession*, by Julian Mead. [. . .] I am like that critic, who said about Molnar's play that if he had to hear a goat sing he would rather read about it in the newspapers. If I have to hear flowers talk, I would rather read *Through the Looking-Glass*, which *is* my favorite garden book. "It says 'Boughwough!' " cried a Daisy. "That's why its branches are called boughs!"

Did Mr. Mitchell tell you about *Wild Flowers in Britain*, by Geoffrey Grigson? He (Mr. M. I mean) sent me an enchanting and lengthy review of it, and when I have twenty-five dollars (or some such) that I can spend for pleasure (when I *think* of having to pay seventeen dollars for the miserable *Plant Buyers Guide*, the poorest and most inaccurate attempt I have come across in years) I am going to have it for my own. Hannah Withers† gave me *A*

---

*Helen Hokinson was famous for her *New Yorker* cartoons satirizing society matrons.
†EL's friend and near-neighbor in Charlotte.

Treasury of English Wild Life, which has an essay by G.G.; and Mr. Krippendorf gave me the charming little Penguin [edition of] his *Flowers of the Meadow.* These two are beautiful in the way that only English books are. Another Penguin is *Tulipomania.** If these Penguins are still in print, people ought to know about them: three shillings (or more).

[Aff, Elizabeth Lawrence]

MAY 11, 1959

Dear Miss Lawrence,

Can you ever forgive me for having been so rude as not to write you long before now to acknowledge all the helpful things you have done for me and for your good letters and postcards? What happened was that almost immediately on my return to Maine on April 11—just a month ago—I began to get sick, and I have had a fairly miserable month, just when I really needed to be active and vigorous and working hard outdoors. It was some sort of infection of the kidneys or bladder—the most repellent of all organs and my weak spot, apparently—which left me weak as a kitten. After a morning of work on my *New Yorker* daily stint, I just took to bed. Finally the doctor gave me achromycin for a week and now I am a lot better, though still not able to do the physical work I need to, especially as Henry Allen, our wonderful young farmer-handyman and all-around helper on these fifty acres, is also ailing.

Well, enough of troubles here, which I really think are now improving. [. . .] The Tillotson thing is pretty well settled and all is well. I did not have to write the people you so kindly suggested, because I got from my friend Louise Seaman Bechtel a lot of information. [. . .] In another piece I shall try to put in a general

*By Wilfrid Blunt (1950).

warning on this point, possibly even say (when I know it) whether
visits to a nursery named would be rewarding or not, from the
point of view of picking out one's own plants and seeing the gardens in bloom. [. . .] The whole business of modern rose growing is a fascinating theme, and methods have drastically changed
now that plants are refrigerated and shipped in plastic bags. Louise Bechtel says the contracting for rose growing is very common.
Many of Jackson & Perkins roses are grown in California under
contract.

The *Dictamnus* story is interesting and I am much indebted to
you for sending me Prof. Totten's letter.* Before it came I wrote
Wayside of whom I had ordered one plant of *D. Fraxinella caucasi-
cus* to ask if the men who handled it for them had ever been poisoned and they replied no, except if one scratched himself with a
seed pod, and that not everyone was affected even by that. I have
now had a letter from a reader saying he hoped I would get *D. albus,* as it was so much more beautiful than the pink *Fraxinella*—
the white, he said, grew four feet high and two feet wide. Well,
one is enough for me, and the pink it will have to be. I have no
room for monsters either in spite of the fact that we now know we
have lost dozens and dozens of perennials.

This has been one of the crushing blows after our bitter winter
and our frigid and six-weeks-late spring. All but two chrysanthemums are gone, four clematis vines, about two dozen established
delphiniums, two new climbing roses, two new shrub roses, and
every hybrid tea we did not dig up and bury. (We bury most of
the fine ones.) The oddest losses to me are lupines—all wiped out
completely, and they've been there for years; all the ajuga is gone

---

*Henry Totten, professor of botany at the University of North Carolina (Chapel Hill) and
coauthor with William Coker of *Trees of the Southeastern States,* quoted W. C. Muenscher in
Poisonous Plants of the United States as including *Dictamnus albus.* EL wrote on the copy of Totten's letter, "Don't bother to return this, as I have ordered the book, which I should have
had long ago—but poisonous plants are such a bore, but I think I should write something
about them."

and it is just like a weed, it grows and spreads so, also all the fox-gloves, many Canterbury bells, two huge *Echinops, Thalictrum,* all the *Platycodon*s, and much much more. Well, the long borders were much too crowded and now I'm trying to start fresh. [. . .] I do not think simple very low temperatures would do all this and I think that what must have happened while we were in the South was a thaw and hard freeze after it. [. . .] Up till we went away we had a safe snow cover all winter and no serious thaw.

I want to ask you as an expert on bulbs whether you think a freeze and thaw or simple cold or some other thing is the cause of so many of the daffodils being very short-stemmed this year, and of the odd phenomenon that happened to my Red Emperor *Fosteriana*s. They came up as the daintiest of miniatures and are very pretty right now. (I rather prefer them to the Emperors when big.) The *Kaufmanniana*s are out now, too, and are normal, and *saxatilis* survived, but I have lost many small bulbs (*leucojum* for one) and many that are up, like the grape hyacinths, are stunted. All the crocuses that were in the grass are either gone or not blossoming; those in beds are normal. Now my largest number of spring bulbs are in a bed on the south side of the house—the first bed to thaw in spring. Since it is the most conspicuous of the flower beds I usually have taken up the bulbs and dried and stored them through the summer and planted annuals there. Last summer I got tired of doing this and left the bulbs in the bed and planted annuals between them. Would this fact have hurt them, do you think? Would the soil have been called on to do too much, even though fertilized, and made the Emperors turn up as dwarfs? The new bulbs of all kinds that I put in last fall are for the most part better than the old ones, though not in every case. Those Emperors were new in 1958 and 1957—two different batches of them. Do they merely tend to play out?

Only the commonest of my lilies have shown up so far (I don't mean day lilies; they are okay). Our troubles are compounded by this being the dryest spring on record; we are in the midst of drought just when I must transplant.

I am very grateful to you for your information on books. I long to get Caroline Dormon's [*Flowers Native to the Deep South*]. [. . .] I shall try to see whether that book store in Baton Rouge still has a copy. [. . .] I am with you in detesting most garden books and their sentimentality or their jokes. I must tell you something funny about *A Sense of Humus.* Years back, when Andy (my husband) was writing "One Man's Meat" for *Harper's* magazine, he made that bad pun in one piece, but I think justifiably as I remember it. Anyway it did not offend me. (Perhaps he was taking a poke at the organic gardening nuts or else he was talking about our own compost piles.) When it came out, he got a furious letter from a woman who said he had stolen her title. Stolen it in advance, that was, for her book had not yet been published, but she wanted to give him fair warning that she had thought it up herself and was going to use it! [. . .]

I love Merry Gardens catalogue, too, and I shall certainly make a trip there this summer. I am told that they get very flustered with visitors, have too much to do, poor things, to sell plants except by mail. My correspondence with George Park has been lively, for I sent them an order for both seeds and plants. He wrote me the nicest letter about my piece; it sounded just like that first page of the catalogue. I fear my piece may have offended the Houdyshels, for she gave me all the information and wrote me that he would be pleased to be written about and said I could use anything in her letter, yet she has not written me since. [. . .] One nice thing has happened. Charles Wilson of Harris is going to send me a copy of the original Harris catalogue.

This letter is much too long and I must wind it up fast. Our first calf was born today and another will be along soon. We have only two cows—Herefords for beef. The first bantam chick has cracked its shell and it is suddenly hot, so spring must be here at last. The seventy-five chicks for broilers and laying hens have come out from under the brooder stove. We try to do much too much and our lives are too full. I'm sure yours must be, too, especially when you get letters of this length.

Oh, I shall add one thing that is on my mind. I have often longed to subscribe to your paper and read your column regularly. I have resisted it, though, for fear it would make me feel so uninformed that I'd never dare write again on gardens, and for fear too that I might unconsciously lift something from you. I think it is safer if I don't read it, but I do love it when you send me excerpts and copies of what you have written. Do send some more from time to time. I owe you more thanks than I can ever say for all your help. And I find myself quoting "Elizabeth." Do I dare call you that? Anyway, I'll sign myself,

Katharine

[MAY 1959]

Dear Katharine,

First, please believe that I never even *notice* when letters are not answered, much as I love the answers when they come. I can't bear to think that you would ever have answering on your mind. And in turn please don't fault me if I don't answer. If I don't by return mail, I probably never will. I have had to give up writing to my close friends. And answer only business letters; and garden ones, for as you know that is the only way to get any real information.

My mother had a stroke three years ago, and is now in bed, with two nurses. Even the practical ones (colored, thank the Lord) do only eight hours duty, so I am the third. Even when the day nurse is here, I am really on duty. I have to keep up my lecturing, consultation and garden column, as illness is such a drain financially, and I am frantic over not being able to get the book I am working over* (I mean to say on but over is right!) done. I suddenly realized that I am fifty-five, and have spent all this time collecting material to write about and when will I write about it.

I do feel for you about the devastation, and don't think it has anything to do with Maine. We had a late spring freeze several years ago, and the borderline things have never recovered. It took my garden three years to look like anything.

I can't answer your questions because I don't know the answers. Far from being an expert, I am the most casual gardener. I don't even own a spray. When things get sick I destroy them. I haven't divided daffodils for years. I just put out things and let them take their chances. When I write about the way things should be done, I quote an expert. I am a writer. In my garden everything grows on top of everything else, and I let them fight it out. Some take root and grow forever. Most disappear. I never had any big tulips go back to species. Could you have planted a species and forgotten? I never take anything up. [. . .] I throw the tulips away, and get new ones in fall. Also hyacinths. Squills get better and better. A few years ago I had one of those bad daffodil seasons, and was completely discouraged, but this year was one of the best ever. Your turn will be next. I wish you lived next door and I would fill your garden up. My garden is so small that the trouble is to get rid of what grows too well. The *Kaufmanniana* tulips seldom last more than a season, but Mr. K. [Carl Krippendorf] dotes on them and is always sending me more. I don't think shallow rooted annuals hurt big bulbs, but I am sure they are the cause of my losing the darling tiny ones. I have never found *any* ground cover that is satisfactory for little bulbs.

Heavens! You are welcome to anything I say, and anyway aside from being welcome, I thought anything in print was anybody's. I consider anything out of it the same. Never heard of

Gardens in Winter.

anything else until I went to New York to college and was rep-rimanded for using a story told to me. It was only in a college theme. Never heard of not giving away receipts until we gave away one that had been given to us. I'd be glad to send you a batch of clippings of my column if you would like to see them, and if it wouldn't be too much trouble to return them. I have only those that I clip myself. I'm afraid that there will be a lot of that you won't be interested in, as I have to cover local things like gardens to open.

[⋯]

Don't worry about the Houdyshels. I am sure that they could not be anything but flattered—though he *is* very touchy. I doubt very much that they ever read the article. Couldn't you send it to them? Mr. Houdyshel hardly ever writes letters. Just when he wants something, which I don't mean critically. He says he can't write. There would be no end. You'd be surprised how many people never heard of *The New Yorker*. And also how many have. The other day my niece (13)* and I stopped in Columbia for lunch on our way to Summerville to a wedding. When Fuzz found that I had never seen Mrs. Gibbes (79),† she was scandalized. I told her that I knew her much better after several years of correspondence about old daffodils than many people I had known all my life. Mrs. Gibbes was concerned that Fuzz might get tired of listening to us while we talked about gardens, so she had laid out *The New Yorker* and *Eloise in Paris*.

When I was at Miss Dormon's I read a most delightful book, one that I had never heard of, called *A Mirror of Flowers*.‡ I can't remember the author (a woman) but can dig it out of my files (or piles more likely!) if you want me to, though the library will prob-

*EL's niece and namesake, Elizabeth Way (Rogers), called "Fuzz" by family members. See note on p. 6.
†Mrs. Alexander Gibbes, a frequent garden correspondent who reported on bloom dates in Columbia.
‡By Dorothea Eastwood (Houghton Mifflin, 1953).

ably know. You will love *Saints and Their Flowers*, by Gladys Taylor. My bookshop was never able to get it for me, but a friend says the Church has plenty. How about herbs? Eleanor Chalfin has done two little paperbacks that are the most useful I know.* How about a general information book? I can find more definite information in Mr. Wister's *Woman's Home Companion Garden Book* than any other of the kind.† Mine was borrowed so much that I had the library get it.

I hope you are better and going onward and upward in the garden.

Aff,
Elizabeth

P.S. I thought you did call me Elizabeth. I always call you Katharine in spirit. I have great difficulty with my friends who think my signing my full name is unfriendly. It is just a family custom. Mr. K. nearly parted company with me over it. My family always ended with "Your devoted mother, Elizabeth B. Lawrence"; "your loving grandmother, Nannie F. Bradenbaugh"; "your affectionate grandfather, Robert de Treville Lawrence." Grandpapa always began, "My dear Miss Elizabeth." He never called any female by her first name, even his wife, who was "Miss Ann Eliza."

I enclose a letter from the Parks to the Raleigh postmaster, to show you that the spirit of John Knox is still with them, and they really do do what they say they do.‡ I had carelessly (as often in the past ten years since we came here to live) put Raleigh, and they took all of this trouble to get the seeds to me. I am right proud

---

*Eleanor Pierrpont Chalfin, *Herbs Described* (Mutual Press, 1955) and *The Useful Herbs* (Chalfin, 1957).
†John C. Wister, editor (Doubleday, 1947).
‡When the George W. Park Seed Co.'s shipment to EL in Raleigh was returned marked "unknown," a staff member appealed to the Raleigh postmaster to help find her new address. The postmaster wrote back, "This lady now lives in Charlotte, N.C."

of the Raleigh post office, too. The Charlotte post office doesn't remember people who moved away ten years ago, or even those who live here now.

MAY 26 [1959]

Dear Elizabeth,

I am just in after supper from watering my transplants. We are in the midst of a severe drought—unheard of in this region for May. My tulips are at their best, and most of them at once— the Darwins and other late big tulips, and to my delight, quite a number of species and hybrid species tulips too—*Clusiana, Marjolettii, acuminata,* which just delight me as I grew them for the first time this year, and wonder of wonders, two *saxatilis* bulbs have bloomed for me. The Red Emperors have passed and I've decided that they are simply played out. They were not new last fall. We are spoiled here, for so many tulips live on for many years, but a neighbor's Emperors have suffered the same fate. The blue grape hyacinths are at their height, but the white, which I have not had until this year, are gone already. I was surprised to discover how greatly the two colors vary in earliness. To give you an idea of how the seasons work here I'll add that the pear trees and crabapple are in full bloom but the other apples are still in pink bud. The pasture is edged with the purple-pink of wild azalea.

I am writing chiefly to tell you how terribly sorry I was to hear about your mother and how sympathetic I feel for the sort of life this means for you. I know a little about the sorrows of caring for the older generation because the aunt who brought me up and was like my mother lived with us summers here for years and then spent all of the last two years of her life here before she died of a stroke, at ninety-three.* In these last years she had to have a practical nurse, but it was mostly because of her extreme age.

*Caroline Sergeant (Aunt Crully) died in 1955.

[. . .] I am especially sorry to think of you, burdened with nursing and with the expense of two nurses. [. . .] But the worst of it all for you, I know, must be seeing your mother in such a pitiful and sorrowful state. I can't imagine how you manage to accomplish all that you do. I *know* you will get that book written and you simply must do so, for it would mean so much to so many people. I promise to shut up and not burden you with any more letters or questions. I'm ashamed to think how much I have impinged on your time.

I am behind on everything, too, and I can see that I can't even think about writing a catalogue or garden piece again until August or September, if then. I have to go to New York next week to see my aging sister and catch up at the office and see doctors and get some summer clothes, and then rush back to receive my two youngest grandchildren—age four and five,* while their mother goes to the hospital to have her third child. And after that two other families of children and grandchildren† will be turning up and I shall be inundated.

I was charmed by your paragraph on your family's method of addressing each other and rather wanted to start this letter, "Dear Miss Elizabeth," but such courtliness from a Yankee, I felt, would sound too mannered and even impertinent.

Do not despair of that book. Fifty-five seems to me very young and you have years ahead. I am sixty-six and the sister I am going to see is just winding up a book on Robert Frost and she is seventy-seven! She is Elizabeth Shepley Sergeant—Elsie in the family—and possibly since you once wrote you were to lecture on Cather, you know my sister's book on Willa C.‡ They were

*Steven and Martha White. See note on p. 16.
†KSW's daughter Nancy Angell Stableford, her husband Louis Stableford, and their children—Kitty, Jonathan, and Sarah; her son Roger Angell, his wife Evelyn Baker Angell, and their children—Caroline and Alice. After Roger's first marriage ended in divorce, he married Carol Rogge, and they had a son, John Henry Angell.
‡*Willa Cather: A Memoir* (J. B. Lippincott, 1953). The Frost manuscript Sergeant was writing became *Robert Frost: The Trial by Existence* (Holt, Rinehart and Winston, 1960).

friends in their younger years, and the book is sentimental in part. No one tells the real Cather story.

Affectionately,
Katharine

P.S. This letter must *not* be answered. I loved the Parks' persistence on getting your seeds to you. It's characteristic of them.

JUNE 15, 1959

Dear Elizabeth,

Here I am back again with a question, in spite of my promises. I imagine that to the initiated it is as simple-minded as if I asked what the address of Harvard University was. The question: do you know the address of Jan de Graaff and does de Graaff bring out a catalogue? I have been studying the lily offerings for the autumn of this year and every one of them, both in specialists' catalogues and in those of the big nurseries, of course brags of lilies from the great de Graaff. [. . .]

We have been to New York and missed Mary Ellen at the office, but it's good news that she plans to return after the baby. A baby here is the reason for my trying to line up now some facts I may try to get on paper in my August vacation. Beginning next week, when the new baby comes and we take on two little children for the new baby's mother, I shall have no time, through July.

As ever, and with apologies
Katharine

P.S. It is 48 degrees here today and has been this for 48 hours. Discouraging.

[JUNE 1959]

Dear Katharine,

I was just about to write to you anyway, to thank you for telling me about your sister's book, and to assure you that I wouldn't dream of lecturing on Willa Cather. I only talk on general subjects such as religion, art, poetry and gardening. I ordered the book but it hasn't come yet. I can't think how I missed it.

I know Mr. de Graaff is wholesale only, and I am pretty sure that he is The Oregon Bulb Farms, Gresham, Oregon. They probably have a catalogue, but I have never seen it. He is a great friend of Mr. Krippendorf's, and Mr. K. sent me the lilies. But I seldom buy any myself. Caroline Dormon does, and I shall ask her. Isabelle Henderson has a story about taking Stella Haydon to Chapel Hill to hear Mr. de Graaff speak to the Garden Club.*
He told about the long search he had for some yellow lily that was essential to his breeding, and how when he had failed to find it, someone wrote that she thought she had the lily in her garden, and was sending two bulbs. He almost threw them away, it seemed so unlikely, and he had been disappointed so often, but he planted them, and it *was* the lily. After the lecture Stella went up to him and said, "And I am the person who sent them to you." If you could use it, I am sure Stella would be pleased to tell it to you correctly. She is Mrs. Haydon, Raleigh.

[. . .]

Thank you for your sympathy and encouragement. My grandfather took up writing just before his ninetieth birthday, and privately published *Meditations on Current Religious Subjects by an Octogenarian*. Grandpapa is the one who called his wife "Miss," and he could not have his name appear in print, even on a brochure that was never seen by anyone except the friends he gave it to. When he was ninety the governor of Georgia appointed him to fill out

*Isabelle Henderson and Stella Haydon, friends of EL's in Raleigh.

the term of director of the Confederate Home in Atlanta. He commuted every day from Marietta, and when the term was out ran for re-election—but his rival won.

Aff,

Elizabeth Lawrence

JULY 1, 1959

Dear Elizabeth,

The new grandchild was born four days ago—a huge boy named John Shepley White, for my maternal great-grandfather —and because of this we have his older brother and sister here, aged four and five; also, as a surprise, my oldest granddaughter, aged 16.* If this letter makes no sense, you will understand why.

Mrs. [Ellen] Flood sent on to me the copies of all three of your "Garden Gate" pieces and I'm glad she did, for I was charmed by all three of them. I return the copies now as I'm sure they must be precious to you. I took great liberty in having the chief column on Mrs. Bennett† copied for future reference, just in case I ever get around to doing that piece on garden books—or use old books as a lead, or something of the sort. I would hesitate to follow you on Mrs. Bennett, you have done her so delightfully. I know you must have written reams on Mrs. Loudon but some day I may mention my old family copy. It is *Gardening for Ladies* and *The Ladies Companion to the Flower Garden*, combined into one volume except that, annoyingly, the kitchen garden sections have been omitted. You will doubtless know whether my volume is the first American edition. The date is 1846, the publisher Wiley &

---

*Katharine "Kitty" Stableford, daughter of Nancy Angell Stableford and Louis Stableford.
†EL wrote about Ida D. Bennett, author of *The Flower Garden* (McClure, Phillips, and Co., 1903).

Putnam, and the preface makes it sound like the first published in this country. It is taken from the third London editions. What I don't know is whether Mrs. Loudon wrote other books or whether these two were her major works. Is there a *magnum opus* I have missed entirely? Don't bother to answer now—just sometime when you send me a postcard. I *mean* this. Besides I can find out at the Bangor Public Library if I need to.

Your and Ida Bennett's remarks on castor bean foliage remind me to tell you that last year Stanley Walker,* who now raises cattle in his native Texas, sent Andy some of his very special beans last spring to plant, the idea being that the best cure for cattle warts is the crude oil of the castor bean. We have a tiny herd of Herefords (five) and Stanley feels it important to instruct a beginning Easterner in Western cattle lore. We did plant them but we got them late and they did next to nothing. I was glad, for with little children about I think the castor bean is something to skip. This year we have none.

I hope Mrs. Flood will stop in here if she comes to Maine this year. I wrote her and said this. I'd love to meet her and we could talk about *you.*

I have written Mr. de Graaff on the chance of getting a wholesale catalogue if one exists. Thank you for that address and all the information.

Affectionately,
Katharine

[JULY 1959]

Dear Katharine,

Mrs. Loudon wrote *The Ladies Flower Garden of Ornamental Annuals, The Ladies Flower Garden of Ornamental Bulbous Plants, The Ladies*

---

*Stanley Walker had retired after a career as a writer for the *Herald Tribune* and later *The New Yorker.*

Flower Garden of Ornamental Perennials. I have the text of the bulbs, which I got for a dollar from a gift shop in Chapel Hill after they had torn out the hand-colored engravings to make into lamp shades and cigarette boxes. And I have a battered little copy of *The Ladies Companion to the Flower Garden,* which my mother got for a quarter from the old book store in Columbia, S.C. [. . .] I suppose you could call the *Annuals, Bulbs,* and *Perennials* her *magnum opus,* as they are so handsomely bound and illustrated. Billy Hunt* has them along with other treasures in his horticultural library in Chapel Hill, but every time I go over to work on them, I find myself listening to Billy—not but what I'm glad to do that, too. Then there is the *Ladies Magazine of Gardening,* complete in one volume. [. . .]

Your words about the use of material gave me pause, and I began to worry about writing a book with a great deal of Caroline Dormon in it. As Mr. Krippendorf was not going to use what he had written to me, I never worried about that, but Caroline (at eighty her contemporaries say . . . she doesn't tell her age) is writing and making drawings for *two* books. So I wrote to her, and she replied, "Honey, quit fretting. If there is anything I don't want you to use I'll tell you." I really had no choice about some of it, as, instead of drawing the things sent her, she did bulbs she gathered up in old gardens, and shrubs I had never seen.

Then I found in my file a record that Fuzz made of her garden when she was nine, and, thinking of you, I asked her if I could use it for a column, expecting her to say she would be delighted. Instead she said, "No!" I said, Oh dear, I'd already written it, so after reading it she said reluctantly that I could do as I liked.

I was just about to write to you to tell you how much I enjoyed

---

*William Lanier Hunt (1906–1996), gardener and garden writer, who gave land to the University of North Carolina in Chapel Hill for the Hunt Arboretum of the N.C. Botanical Garden.

your sister's memoir of Willa Cather, and her picture of herself as well as that of her subject.

Aff,
Elizabeth Lawrence

JULY 28, 1959

Dear Elizabeth,

I haven't thanked you for your letter about Mrs. Loudon because we have been, and are, in trouble. My husband is in the hospital in New York, as of today, for medical tests. I am still here, because I was too sick and virusy to go with him, and I shall follow him there on Thursday. [. . .] And in three days more I was to have settled down to a month of vacation and an attempt at an autumn piece for *The New Yorker.*

The prospects look dim, but who knows—maybe it will work out even so. If only Andy is all right.

I have sent to one second-hand book dealer in quest of some of the Mrs. Loudon books. If you know of a store that specializes in her, I'd be glad to know the name on a postcard—or one that specializes in gardening books of all sorts. But no rush.

The garden was never more beautiful. I hate to leave it. And Andy even more hated to leave his new calf and his boat.

Aff'y,
Katharine

P.S. Don't be alarmed by the hospital. These tests are precautionary following weeks of indigestion. It may be only nervous indigestion, so please don't speak of him to anyone as being sick.

[AUGUST 1959]

Dear Katharine,

I am distressed to hear of troubles, and it is well you warned me. I was going to write at once to Mary Ellen to tell her to write to Mr. White, whom she adores.

If I knew where to get any of Mrs. Loudon's books, I would have pawned the family jewels long ago. You might try Mr. Lynn Ranger, 41 Lynn Shore Drive, Lynn, Massachusetts. He has gotten me several rare books, things I've hunted for years. He says please don't address him as Miss Ranger. Everyone does. He seems to have more sources of supply than anyone I know.

Hannah Withers and I also got books from the Landsman Bookshop, Llangollen, Denbs, N. Wales, U.K. (specialist for farmers and gardeners). We write to a charming gentleman, Mr. K. H. Young, and send him a list of our wants.

With love and sympathy. I hope you are both all right.
Aff,
Elizabeth Lawrence

NEW YORK
SEPTEMBER 15, 1959

Dear Elizabeth,

As usual, I am terribly late in thanking you for your last letter, this one with its suggestions on book dealers who might track down Mrs. Loudon's trilogy. I have small hope but I may try. August was a sort of horror. I didn't finish the "Onward and Upward in the Garden" piece before the final batch of children and grandchildren arrived; the time was just too short after Andy's release from the hospital and our return to Maine to get it done before the arrival. Andy's tests, by the way, turned up no sinister things beyond the usual and eternal nervous causes of his indigestion and general bad health. These seem to be the hardest of all to conquer, and not easy now that his sister* is dying.

I finished up the piece, if you can call it finished, which I don't, just before Labor Day, in the midst of a young family shut in the house for five days by storms, and mailed it off with many misgivings. It is the poorest I've done yet, to my mind, but it will be published in the issue of September 26. I feel particularly badly because I did try to do a paragraph on your latest book [*The Little Bulbs*] and also one on my American edition of Mrs. Loudon. I have never seen your reviews of her books—only your references to the books—or else I could not have dared to write about Mrs. L. at all. [. . .]

Since we got to New York it has turned cold and I'm dead sure that we shall get home at the end of the week to find most of the annuals frostbitten and my houseplants on the terrace ruined. I left stern injunctions that they be brought indoors at the first sign of cold but that means little, especially when the cold sets in on a weekend, when Andy and I usually hold the fort. I have put in far too big a bulb order—that will be the next thing—to get them planted. I was undone by ordering from de Jager, who sells by the dozen.

Affectionately,
Katharine

[SEPTEMBER 1959]

Dear Mrs. White,

Thank you so very much for writing to me about Mr. White. I had worried all summer, and wanted to write to ask but didn't like to.

A nice person called me the other day to ask about *A Southern*

---

*Marion White Brittingham.

Garden. She said a friend had written to her, and you had written to the friend. She said, "Do you know Katharine White?" and I heard myself saying, "Oh yes! She is an old friend of mine." [. . .]

I was very much dashed to get, in the morning's mail, Mr. Ranger's supplementary list, which included "Lawrence, Elizabeth, *The Little Bulbs.* A nice little book."

I shall look forward to the book and bulb piece. I am sure you need not worry. The kind of writing you do will always come through. It's just when you are exhausted you think it doesn't.

I hope this doesn't smell like garlic. I just went out to see if the British Soldiers are in bloom, and I picked off some heads of allium that were going to seed.

Affectionately,
Elizabeth Lawrence

OCTOBER 4, 1959

Dear Elizabeth,

I have been corresponding with Mr. Ranger—bought Mrs. Wilder's *The Fragrant Path,* partly because I am thinking of taking up the subject of flowers that have lost their fragrance in my midwinter piece. In his last letter (Sept. 30), Mr. Ranger writes as follows: "Yesterday I saw Miss Lawrence's *The Little Bulbs* for the first time and stopped everything to skim it through before mailing it to a customer in Portland, Maine. I was impressed by its style and surprised by its scope as I did not know of it until Miss Lawrence mentioned it." This sounds odd to *me,* for if he only saw it first on Sept. 29, how could he then list it earlier as "a nice little book"? I have asked him to try to find me a copy of *A Southern Garden,* which I can't buy anywhere, it seems, and have read only hurriedly in a copy borrowed from Joe Mitchell. [. . .]

Mrs. Wilder is so learned and interesting on fragrance that in the end I'll probably not dare touch the theme. I am trying to list, though, the flowers I used to remember as sweet but that have lost their fragrance in the modern hybrid or fussed up forms. Roses, sweet peas, and violets seem obvious examples. Petunias, too. White nicotiana is still wonderfully perfumed in the tall varieties but the colored ones have no scent at all that I can detect, though Mrs. Wilder notes merely that they have less scent. [. . .]

If you have ever written something on this theme, and I'm sure you must have, I wish you'd tell me where to look for it, so I can get some facts from a real horticulturist and botanist who could set me on the right track. I don't suppose I need to know too much to say, as I think I might, that I wish all catalogues reported on fragrance as well as on color and form.

I do hope that your mother is no worse and that everything goes well with you.

[. . .]

Affectionately,
Katharine

P.S. If anyone asked whether I know you, I would say, "Of course. She is a great friend." But I wish your picture had been on the jacket of your book.

[. . .]

[OCTOBER 1959]
Sunday

Dear Katharine,

Mr. Krippendorf called the day after *The New Yorker* came out, to ask if I had seen your article.* Evidently, he doesn't take it anymore, since Mrs. K. has been blind, though she read it from cover

*KSW had reviewed EL's *The Little Bulbs*, about EL's garden in North Carolina and Carl Krippendorf's in Ohio. KSW described reading the book as a "literary pleasure" and EL as a "botanist and horticulturist; still better, she is a writer with a sense of humor and a sense of beauty."

to cover, always. So I sent him mine, and he will be so pleased. Really, you are a genius. He says he has no heart for planting flowers that Mrs. K. cannot see, and I know how he feels, for I feel the same way when something new blooms, and I pick it for my mother, and she doesn't look at it. She used to go out every morning and turn over every leaf to see if anything new was in bloom.

I have been getting all of your fan mail, which seems very unfair. Mr. Mitchell's sister, Mrs. Lamm, wrote to congratulate me, and say what a good article it is. She said, "Imagine praise from Mrs. White!" I particularly enjoyed the nurse and Leo; and the squirting cucumber,* which I found in Park's catalogue when I was doing an article on gourds. And you almost converted me to houseplants, but I know I would never take care of them. Fuzz comes over every fall, and pots something up, and then in a few days brings back the dead plants. This year she carried off a sweet little ebony spleenwort and a small *torenia,* and they met the fate of all the others, but she still wants plants in her room. The best thing in the garden now is *Oxalis Bowiei*—have you tried it in pots? It has never bloomed this early, and usually gets caught by frost.

I also had a letter from Mr. Ranger thanking me for providing him with such a delightful correspondent.

Please tell Mr. White how much I enjoyed his article, too.† And forgive my worse than usual typing. I have torn my fingers to pieces trying to get the double Cherokee out of the Indian hawthorn and into the pine trees.

Aff,
Elizabeth Lawrence

---

*KSW had written in *The New Yorker* (9/26/59) about a practical nurse in the house who had hated KSW's pot of begonias named "Leo" and about a cucumber plant.
†EBW, "Khrushchev and I (a Study in Similarities)" in *The New Yorker* (9/26/59).

OCTOBER 8, 1959

Dear Elizabeth,

Your letter came today and this is thanks for it, following hard on my letter that imposed a question on you. (I always feel guilty when I do that.) This one should have no answer, nor the other, either, unless it is convenient. I was relieved to hear from you about that miserable piece, which I disliked quite intensely. I feared that you had hated it, too. I didn't do justice to you. I wanted to bring in that *A Southern Garden* should be re-issued and I hope I can later, when I have the book before me.

I am sad for Mr. K, and for you. Here we are in a state of suspension and sorrow too. Andy's sister is still alive although she has been in a coma and without food for weeks now. We jump, whenever the phone rings.

A sea of bulbs has arrived from de Jager. We have to wait for colder weather to plant the outdoor ones but I am potting up the indoor bulbs. I have never *seen Oxalis bowiei* let alone grown it. The only *Oxalis* I ever had was a pot of *Crassilis,* which grew outrageously, got aphids, and was thrown out. I seldom use poison sprays indoors, and very few outdoors—just throw away in most cases. I am nursing some violets and one gloxinia.

As for Mr. Ranger: he plunged in and began suggesting poor and silly subjects for *New Yorker* pieces, and I had to slap him down. I can hardly imagine that I am a "delightful correspondent." But he *is* good at finding books.

My best flowers now are a new small bed of chrysanthemums. They are in full bloom now and heavenly colors. We had a big wind last week and I picked all the roses to save the bushes. I picked *eleven* yellow roses from one bush of *Eclipse.* [. . .]

I gave your message to Andy and he was pleased. At this very moment he is answering a lady from Warner Bros., who says he was unfair to Mr. K.*

I am awfully sorry if I repeated you on the squirting cucumber. Speaking of gourds, for the first time my small decorative gourds did not mature in time for me to wax and polish them while watching the World Series. I am a baseball fan, I hate to confess—have *played* baseball since I was a child.

[Affectionately, Katharine]

[NOVEMBER 1959]
Friday morning

Dear Katharine,

I would have written to you right away if I could have been of any help, but I don't know anything about modern flowers that have lost their fragrance. I think some hybrid roses are as sweet as old ones. At the fall flower show I was intoxicated by the scent of one flower of Sutter's Gold.

[. . .]

I think I had better change to the typewriter, or you will never read this. I do envy your beautiful clear handwriting. It is like a scientist's.

Hannah Withers says she went to a meeting of the board of the Crittenton Home† the other day, and someone said they thought the expectant mothers would be cheered by having some magazines to read. Someone else said that was a good idea, and she would take down a lot of *New Yorkers*. And someone else muttered,

---

*EBW's *New Yorker* essay, "Khrushchev and I," was vintage White—its humorous and lyric descriptions (of himself as a man like Khrushchev, recently described in a newspaper article as a family man who liked to walk in the woods with his grandchildren) giving way to irony at the end. It isn't clear why the lady from Warner Brothers objected, and EBW's letter to her has not turned up.
†The Florence Crittenton Home in Charlotte cared for unwed mothers and their children. It was one of many Crittenton homes in the United States.

"If they were bright enough to read *The New Yorker*, they wouldn't be there."

My nephew Chip (16)* is away at school. His first letter to his father, always called Dad, began, "Dear Father," and was signed, "Yours truly, Warren Way, Jr."

Later

How in the world do you accomplish all you do? I have been interrupted five times since I came to my desk an hour ago, the last by a friend who wouldn't take the plants I offered on a day I was in the garden, and would like to have them right now. I told her to come on. If she doesn't she will choose a still worse time.

Aff,
Elizabeth Lawrence

NOVEMBER 28, 1959

Dear Elizabeth,

Just about everything that could happen to us of an adverse nature has happened in the past month, most of which I've had to spend in New York because of the serious illness of my sister Elizabeth. [. . .] I got home, temporarily, three days ago, when she was better and I was sure there was to be no operation for the time being but this is only a small spell here to catch up on my duties and follow my life as a wife, mother, and grandmother. Meanwhile, what did I do yesterday but ruin my bad back which years since was fused and put together with screws. I am in pain, so this is only a note to thank you for yours, tell you that Mr. Ranger found me a copy of *A Southern Garden*—what a pleasure to *own* it! And also to report that on Thanksgiving Day, the 27th, all I could pick this year was one pansy and one viola. There would

*"Chip" was the family name for EL's sister's son, Warren Way, who lived next door.

have been some chrysanthemums, and much more if Henry, during my absence in the city, had not become panicked by the first spell of severe weather and dug up and buried the hybrid teas that grow on the terrace and also covered all the borders and beds with evergreen boughs. [. . .] Thanksgiving morning Andy and I spent hours removing the boughs. This started my back troubles and I finished it up Friday by trying to lug our heavy dachshund upstairs, where he sleeps at night. Something has happened in our absence to scare him, possibly a fall on the stairs, and he refused to go up under his own power. Never leave home, I say!

The reason for removing the boughs may not be clear. After the cold spell, we had torrential rains and flood conditions and those flower beds simply had to dry off before freezing weather or a sheet of ice would have formed over all the perennials with sure winter killing. [. . .] winter protection is to keep the ground frozen during thaws, not to keep it warm. Today it is snowing hard after four days of rain. So now I must wait for a thaw to melt the snow, cold weather to freeze the ground, and then get the boughs back on. And Henry is on his vacation.

The house, at least, is full of bloom—paperwhites, soleil d'Or, saintpaulias, cyclamen, begonias and geraniums and in the cellar various daffodils and a pot of scilla are almost ready to bring upstairs and the freesias are upstairs and the cactuses have buds. My clivia-miniata finally blossomed.

My sister's trouble is heart and gallstones. The heart is too poor to make them want to operate unless they absolutely must. She also has had anemia and edema in the lungs but these are improving. The big thing now is to devise a better way of life for her when she goes home and this means putting in a downstairs bathroom, finding a nurse to live there nights when her old maid is not there, etc. etc. As you see I must return to the city as soon as possible. (But my problems are as nothing compared to yours!) Elsie (i.e., Elizabeth) did finish up her book on Frost before she collapsed. The book really did her in, but it will be published in the spring, which seems to me an achievement at seventy-seven years, no matter how good or bad it is. I have not read it.

No answer expected!

Affectionately,
Katharine

[DECEMBER 1959]

Dear Elizabeth,

I send you for Christmas, with my love and deep gratitude, this battered volume. I do it with some hesitation, lest it trouble you and make you think we are on Christmas present terms and that you should send me something. I should be very cross if you did, for this is not my intention at all, and this is a one time thing that I just happen to send at Christmas time. I bought the volume of *Ornamental Annuals* for myself months back, but it kept coming to my mind that it was *you* who should have it and that, if you don't own it already, you might enjoy it, even though, as I know, annuals are not your interest, really. I wish it was the *Ornamental Bulbs* volume and I wish its cover was not broken. You see, it was you, really, who first introduced me to the pleasures of Mrs. Loudon and it was you more than anyone who gave me courage to go on writing the "Onward and Upward" garden pieces, and it was you whom I've been pestering for two years with questions when I, a total stranger, had no right to take your time. So this is just a token of my gratitude, like that of a student to a professor who had taught him the things he cared about most. I do thank you everyday for what you've taught me by your books and your letters. So *please* don't be mad at me. [. . .] I hope that 1960 will be an easier and less sad year for you. *I* am glad to see 1959 go.

Affectionately,
Katharine

[DECEMBER 1959]

Dear Katharine,

I never heard of anyone so darling as you. How anyone could part with a volume of Mrs. Loudon's I cannot imagine, but I promise you (as Fuzz says, "I *promise* you, Aunt") no one shall (could? will?) make as good use of it as I. It arrived at the moment when I thought I could go no further, so I dropped everything, and sat down on the floor and read, and thought, How wonderful (and remembering Mrs. Loudon's family life) was ready to jump up and start all over.

I am glad it is annuals, as bulbs I have. [. . .] But the annuals are even better, chatty detail (how *could* you part with it?) especially Viola tricolor, and mesembryanthus. I don't know how I gave the impression that I wasn't interested in annuals, probably I said modern annuals. I spent years and years hunting up Mrs. Loudon's annuals, but I must admit I haven't done much with them, here (after the first year, when I had all of that lovely bare ground to work with) for the space gets smaller and smaller. I certainly never thought I would possess a volume with the beautiful plates. The only one I had ever even seen is the little frontispiece to *The Ladies Companion to the Flower Garden* that my mother picked up for thirty-nine cents.* It is not completely backless as are most of the garden books that I have read to death. In her letter to her young friend Annie, on managing her household, Mrs. Loudon tells her to see that the maid does not dust the books too often, as pulling them in and out of the shelves will wear them out. I wonder if she rationed reading. (I bet she was like my great-grandmother who used a plated silver coffee pot for everyday, and I always had to carry the silver basket up to her room every night.)

I had a note from your dear and invaluable friend, Mrs. Root,

*The value has increased from EL's original estimate of a quarter in her July letter.

who sent a list of things in bloom at Thanksgiving, and she said she would be here in the spring. I would love to have her stay with me if she would not be depressed by our household, and would not get indigestion from my cooking. I would always rather talk than eat, and found one person who feels exactly as I do: Miss Dormon. When I stayed with her in her cabin in the woods we got up and had eggs and toast and coffee. Everything was left on the table, and we went right out into the woods where we spent the morning. When we came in, we pushed the breakfast dishes to one end of the table, and had tea and toast and jam. And when it began to get dark we had bread and butter and some chicken and vegetables that she had cooked beforehand. When we weren't out of doors, or both talking at once, she rested, and I read a delightful book that I had never come across, *Mirror of Flowers*,* but we never wasted any time washing dishes—except to rinse the coffee cups before putting in the tea. At present I am not able to run my own household along those ideal lines, as the nurses insist upon eating.

In spite of our having frosts nearly every night the camellia, Dawn, is in full bloom, and only a little tarnished, and the wintersweet pure gold. There is a little clump of Corfu snowdrops, and the Buis and Kessen Hellebores are almost open. The autumn cherry is blooming for Christmas, *Clematis cirrhosa* and *Crocus laevigatus*.

I have been wondering how your sister is, it is so much harder to take responsibility for a person who is away from you than for one who is with you. I am enclosing a card for her address in case you think she would like a note from me. And I have been worrying about you. You did not say anything about your neck.

I cannot imagine what I could possibly have done for you, except to be unable to answer your questions. It is you who have

---

*By Dorothea Eastwood.

done for me, for I would never have gathered strength to get this book organized if you had not written me that wonderful letter saying that it could be done. It is still very difficult, as I seldom have a whole hour without interruption, but once well started you can keep going. I really don't see how you can do without the *Ladies Annuals*, for it is as valuable to you as to me. Couldn't we share it?

Aff,
Elizabeth Lawrence

DECEMBER 28, 1959

[Dear Elizabeth]

Thanks for lovely letter. I wanted to report to you that on Dec. 15 I found two Hellebores in bloom—Niger, the Christmas rose. Atronubeus, the "Lenten."

[. . .]

My sister is out of the hospital but her future remains a problem. I'll write a real letter when the rush dies down here. If all goes well, we go to Florida Feb. 14, probably by train but we just might drive. If it worked out, could I call on you for an hour? I expect we'll go by train so don't worry.

Love,
K.S.W.

DECEMBER 28, 1959

Dear Elizabeth,

Good Heavens! What I did this morning is a sign of the state of mind and fatigue I'm in.* I read your letter with delight and

*KSW had returned EL's self-addressed stamped postcard (intended for Elsie's address) to report on bloom dates.

one from my son Roger Angell and one from my secretary and then carried all three of them upstairs to Andy, who has been in bed all day with a sore throat, and needed cheering. Then, this being a day when no manuscript came from the office because Friday was a holiday, I set out to try to clean up my desk and do some filing of *New Yorker* papers. (I am miserable on filing, for I've been spoiled, having worked all my life with a secretary at hand to do it.) There on my desk lay your p.c., stamped and addressed, so what did I do but forget your kind offer, and mail it off not for the purpose you sent it for. And it was so dear of you to offer to write my sister. Her address until Jan 8 or 10 is Miss Elizabeth S. Sergeant, The Cosmopolitan Club, New York. After that she goes home, Piermont, New York. [. . .]

She left the hospital the Sunday before Christmas and when I talked with her on Christmas Day, she sounded better and more cheerful than she had in months. A very dear friend was there with her for a week and she was beginning to talk about how she would soon be reading the proofs of her book on Frost, and all was hopeful and good. [. . .] Elsie, when sick, is as stubborn as a mule, and she hates to take help or advice from her younger sister and even from her doctor. [. . .]

After you finish your present book, I wish you would write a life on Mrs. Loudon and a commentary on her books and her life work. It ought to be fascinating. Has one ever been done? You seem to know all about her. I know nothing, except that I gather her husband was a well-known horticulturist and perhaps this was an avocation? What *was* her life like? I must say I never heard of such an indefatigable worker as she. I have just got hold of a bound volume of the *Ladies Magazine of Gardening* she brought out for a year or two and concluded in 1841 with the words that what with all the others' works she had in hand, she was unable to give it her attention, but she hoped it would remain useful to those who love flowers but were not gardeners or florists. That made it seem aimed at *me*. But what do you think has happened since I sent you the book on annuals? Months back I had asked Mr. Ranger to look out for me for the whole series and he suddenly turned up the volume *Ornamental Bulbous Plants* and *Ornamental Greenhouse Plants!*

I feel guilty that you have the *Annuals* with the cover gone, for these are intact. But though I've hardly had time to read them at all, I can see that the greenhouse book is not very chatty. So perhaps you will get more out of the annuals and I can leave these two others to you in my will, and until I die if either of us want to borrow and lend back and forth, we can. [. . .] Did Mrs. Loudon, like Miss Dormon, do the flower paintings herself? They do not seem to be attributed to anyone else. They are heavenly.

Now no more for a long time. If I can grind out a catalogue piece next month I must. But so far I have no good ideas—just a carton full of catalogues, few of them interesting. And I am way behind in my work on *The New Yorker Book of Stories* from the last decade. This is due to be handed in in April or May but I have to determine its length now, so a publishing contract can be drawn up. And all this must be done without working in the morning, for morning hours go to editing. I am a fool to take on so much when I moved to the country to take it easier! [. . .]

Aff'y,
Katharine

SECOND SUNDAY AFTER CHRISTMAS

Dear Katharine,

I was delighted to hear that there is a possibility of your coming our way, and hope you will stay with me if you don't mind, and don't mind staying with people. If you don't drive, do you fly? There is a wonderful Delta non-stop day-coach flight from New York. The train is miserable: awful hours, awful food, awful late.

In any case you must plan to stay long enough to see one or two of the lovely gardens in the neighborhood.* Mine you can see at a glance as it is so little. I wrote a little note to your sister, and I hope she can read it. What I had to say wouldn't type.

[. . .]

I don't really know anything about Mrs. Loudon. Both Mr. Free† and Mr. Harkness‡ were horrified by my saying that I pictured Mr. Loudon as a middle-class merchant,§ and informed me that (as I had already begun to suspect) he was no other than the author of *Arboretum et Fruticetum,* the most celebrated horticulturist of the nineteenth century. Mr. Ranger got me a copy of his *Encyclopedia of Plants,* 1,574 pages of fine print "comprising the specific character, description, culture, history, application in the arts, and every other desirable particular respecting all the plants indigenous to, cultivated in, or introduced into Britain." It was edited by Mrs. Loudon, who was his amanuensis, as he had lost his right arm. That was what I meant by her family life. As I remember, their little garden was four acres and they grew something like three thousand species and varieties, and traveled all the time. They had one little girl whom they dragged about with them, and *she* is the one I'd like to write about. There is no life of either Loudon as far as I know, and the little I have gleaned has been picked up here and there. Bill Hunt says Mrs. L. kept a corps of lady water-colorists to paint the engravings. I don't know who did the drawing. I think she had a sort of book factory.

*EL probably wanted KSW to see the garden of Elizabeth and Edwin Clarkson, now open to the public as Winghaven Garden and Bird Sanctuary in Charlotte, N.C.
†Montague Free (1885–1965), first president of the American Rock Garden Society (now the North American Rock Garden Society). Author of *All About the Perennial Garden* (Doubleday, Doran and Co., 1955).
‡Bernard Emerson Harkness (1907–1980), president of the American Rock Garden Society (now the North American Rock Garden Society) from 1968 to 1972. Author of *Seedlist Handbook.*
§In *The Little Bulbs,* p. 194. In a letter to EL (6/12/57), Free said that her remarks "were enough to make the old boy turn over several times in his grave" (ELNSUL).

The notes on hellebores are very valuable, and also timely.
[. . .]

I do hope that your sister will get on all right, and you have all of my sympathy. I know what it is to have responsibility without authority.

Aff,
Elizabeth

[FEBRUARY 1960]

Dear Katharine,

[. . .]

I hear sleet against the window pane. I just got in in time from picking the day nurse up after the early service. My mume* was almost out for the second time, also the apple blossom, quince, and all the little very early bulbs. I do hope that you will come, and that everything will not be blighted. Last week camellias were in bloom everywhere—then down to 15 degrees.

I have just got back from flying to Atlanta to see my uncle† who is dying of cancer, and came home utterly dejected. My uncle has always been the one I loved most in my family, and the only person left who remembers the past that I love. He is still mad because General Sherman burned his grandfather's house, and was telling me about a cousin (called Laura-dear) who calls her son-in-law Jackson, because his real name is Lincoln, and that word has never passed her lips.

Aff,
Elizabeth

---

*_Prunus mume,_ the Japanese apricot tree, with light pink, fragrant flowers.
†Maryon McDonald Lawrence, Marietta, Ga.

FEBRUARY 8, 1960

Dear Elizabeth,

[. . .]

Alas, we are not driving south. We leave here Sunday by train. We came to this decision because Andy has a slipped disc in his back which has been cutting up and long drives are not good. I feel terribly grieved not to see you and your garden, this time anyway.

I am dreadfully sorry about your uncle. It must be very sad for you; since we've just been through the same thing with Andy's sister,* I know how dejected you must feel.

I have just heard that my garden piece has been accepted, which is a relief because [. . .] I lead off on a subject I know nothing about—fragrance. I have too much to do, so no more for now.

With love,
Katharine

[. . .]

P.S. The most recent garden writer I want to study is Miss Jekyll.† Can you suggest a couple of her books that are the most representative, so I can see if Mr. Ranger can get them for me?

[FEBRUARY 1960]

Dear Katharine,

We are disappointed not to see you and distressed to hear of Mr. White's back, but when I woke this morning to the tune of sleet on the window pane, I was comforted to know that you are not setting forth in an automobile.

*Marion White Brittingham died of cancer in 1959.
†Gertrude Jekyll (1843–1932), renowned English gardener, garden designer, and author of more than a dozen gardening books.

[. . .]

Miss Jekyll's best book is *Home and Garden*—more about the building of Munstead Wood and her cats and country rambles than her garden. Her best garden book is *Wood and Garden*, because it is partly made up of her charming early writings for the *Guardian*. But you might find color schemes in the flower garden more useful than the cats. There is also *Gertrude Jekyll, A Memoir,* by Francis Jekyll, which doesn't tell any of the things you really want to know, and most of it can be found in her writings, but still I am glad to have it.

Please tell Mr. White that I asked Mitty* why she left two dirty looking brown balls dangling over her window, and she said, "Oh, they are spider eggs!" She and her two big football-playing sons watched the spider all summer—"and when she laid the eggs, she died." I said, "Did you read *Charlotte's Web?*" and she said, "Oh yes, that's why we were so interested."

[. . .]

I hope you will both find sun in Florida, and be better.

Aff,
Elizabeth Lawrence

SARASOTA, FLA.
MARCH 17 [1960]

Dear Elizabeth,

I owe you thanks for a letter that's so far back I'm ashamed. I have been thinking of you almost constantly—that is, whenever there has been a report of snow in the Carolinas, and it seems to me that has been constant ever since we got here. What a dreadful winter and spring! I do hope that your garden is not destroyed

---

*Mitty Wellford was one of EL's gardening friends in Charlotte, whom she often quoted in her newspaper columns.

The young Katharine in 1929

Katharine White, editor, at her desk at *The New Yorker*, where she had worked since 1925, when she was hired by the founding editor, Harold Ross.

Katharine and E. B. White's nineteenth-century house on a saltwater farm in Maine, which they purchased in 1933. Katharine's office was in the right front corner of the house, across from Andy's in the left corner.

and that your spirits are not even more devastated. Ours, I know, are pretty frazzled, even in this milder climate. We have been here for a month and three days and have had only three really *good* days. Wind, cold, violent winds, violent electrical storms, etc. The trouble with us Northerners is that we come all set to relax in the sun and swim in warm Gulf waters. When we congeal in inadequate Florida houses with louvered windows we feel frustrated. We deserve no pity, being so much better off than those in the more northerly states, but we do feel cheated. But you, I fear, have really suffered—not only yourselves but you have the sickening thing of watching spring in the garden, and maybe the garden itself, being destroyed. I shall worry about you until I hear how you have fared.

Thanks to your help, I have sent off for three volumes of Miss Jekyll, and Mr. Ranger tells me one is en route here at the moment. I hope so, for now at last I am on vacation. The first month here was all work for both of us. I had the proof queries on my endlessly long March 5th garden piece to clear up—and to my vast annoyance they came by long distance phone instead of in proof, although I turned the piece in in ample time for a proof. The result was that many small errors crept in that were not my fault. Next, I had to wind up a huge job I've been working on for six months—*The New Yorker* stories—1950–1960.* (This was in addition to a daily envelope of manuscripts to read.) The book will be out next fall but it still is not quite settled as to contents, order of stories etc. etc. It is a compromise selection, to suit the taste of five editors. I merely headed up the chore, but Bill Shawn† of course has the final word. Most of what we have together is, I think, first rate writing but the trouble is that in the last decade our fiction writers use only "I" and their favorite themes are death, childhood, or the past. It was a jigsaw puzzle to fit it

*(Simon & Schuster, 1960).
†William Shawn became editor of *The New Yorker* in 1952.

together. The South and Ireland are also in the ascendancy. I love the South but not Ireland (I confess) and I would gladly have cut out a couple of Irish stories but was voted down. My feelings do not apply to Frank O'Connor.

—And this was as far as I got on March 17. It is now April 3 and we leave here in three days. We have had a burst of ten days of glorious warm sunny weather since I started this letter. [. . .]

I will only add that I've been reading *Home and Garden* and already Miss Jekyll has cleared up a part of a mystery I've been trying to solve. At home in my childhood we had a big bed of shrub roses which my father called "Guelder Roses." Remembering their heavenly fragrance and the way they grew a half-story high, and the clusters of white single roses, with gold stamens turning to a rich brown, I wanted to try to find some old Guelder shrub roses for Maine, but there *were* no such things to be found. Now I know why; my father had the name wrong, for according to Miss Jekyll, the Guelder rose is a water-elder, not a rose. [. . .] The unsolved part of the mystery is what these white roses of ours really were.

Have you written much about Miss Jekyll? Her personality both fascinates and at times irritates me, but I can see what a great and beneficent influence she must have had on gardening in England and everywhere. She reminds me of many energetic New England women I have known, especially in the first decade of this century. I love her emphasis on simplicity in flower arranging and in planting, yet the way she went about building a house was far from simple! What a fussy woman she was.

I do hope that your mother is no worse and that life is easier for you. *How is the book coming?* Did I ever tell you that my sister was most grateful for your letter and asked me to thank you for it, hoping you would forgive her for not writing? [. . .] I stop over in New York for ten days to see her, as well as to catch up at the office. John Lardner's death was an awful blow, and FPA's a gentle sorrow.* (He had lost his mind.)

Forgive so long a letter.

Affectionately,
Katharine

[APRIL 1960]

Dear Katharine:

The reason I haven't written to tell you how much I liked your last article is that I am waiting for strength (not time, I have plenty of that at night, when I am too exhausted to even read) to go into it in detail. So I had better tell you now that I did, and that my sister Ann sends word that she read it all and loved it. She says it is the only thing about gardens she was ever able to read.

[. . .]

I do hope your vacation was not ruined by the weather. We did not get out from under the snow until St. Patrick's Day. The last bit in a north corner melted yesterday. The garden is devastated. I hope to do better later.

Oh. The main thing I wanted to say is, I think you would be interested in the chapter on fragrance in [William] Robinson's *English Flower Garden.*

Aff,
Elizabeth Lawrence

---

*John Lardner, a sports journalist like his father Ring Lardner, and Franklin Pierce Adams, newspaper columnist and editor of the popular column, "The Conning Tower," belonged to the NYC writing scene the Whites had known for decades.

NEW YORK
APRIL 8, 1960

Dear Elizabeth,

Our letters crossed. Yours came just as I was leaving Florida
for New York. I hurry to write how distressed I am by what I read
between the lines—your terrible fatigue can mean only that your
mother is worse and that you are having over-taxing days of sorrowful nursing. I wish there were some way I could be of help. I
am touched that you should take the strength to write me about
the garden piece and while I'm thankful to hear you liked it (for I
would rather have your approval than anyone's), it bothers me
that you went to the exertion, and also took time to tell me about
the iris guide book. I shall write off to Placerville. Also, I must ask
Mr. Ranger to get me Robinson's *English Flower Garden.*

I weep for your garden. We went through North Carolina after dark last night, so I could not see how far along your spring
had come. When we get home, next week, there will still be snow
on the ground. Do not bother to answer this note. It is only to take
you my love.

Affectionately,
Katharine

P.S. I was far more upset by the changes in the Park catalogue
than I wanted to say in my piece. It is *ruined,* so far as looks and
charm go. He hasn't written me this year, either, and I guess he is
mad at me. Do you suppose my describing the catalogue last year
as old-fashioned and complex made him feel he had to change it?
If so, I could knife myself, for I meant everything I wrote last year
as *praise.* I do know that a lot of people wrote me to thank me for
introducing them to the Geo. W. Park Seed Co., so I certainly
could not have hurt him commercially. Oh, dear!

[APRIL 1960]

Dear Katharine,

What a New England Conscience: I am absolutely sure that you had nothing to do with the decline in the Parks. It is the fault of the Garden Writer Association. In the early days of the garden club I used to chauffeur my mother when she went around to the nearby hamlets to talk to the small country clubs and take them plants and encouragement. Once at a meeting in a bare little hut, after we had opened with a prayer, sung "Bringing in the Sheaves" and listened to a portion of the Song of Solomon, one of the more observant members said to me suspiciously, "Is this customary?" She needn't have been suspicious of me, for I was brought up in a village just like hers,* and I loved every bit of it (to the distress of my grandmother who, when she heard me singing "Water, water, pure and bright, Clear as crystal, free as light. This our song shall ever be, loyal temperance boys and girls are we" ordered my parents to send me right off to St. Mary's).†

Mr. Park is now sending the garden writers (and probably you) postcards like the one enclosed,‡ and "releasing" little tracts about his latest introductions and inviting them to come and spend the day and see his trial gardens (I should love to go to Greenwood) and any moment I expect an invitation to cocktails. I cannot blame him. He has to make a living.

I am writing in haste to beg that, if you get a copy of *An English Flower Garden,* you see that you get a reprint of an old edition and *not* the foul sixteenth edition revised by Roy Hay "and reset with New Materials." I am furious with Hannah who has the old one, and did not save me from getting the sixteenth. [. . .] Hannah

---

*Garysburg, N.C., in the rural northeast corner of the state.
†St. Mary's, an Episcopal school for girls in Raleigh, N.C., which EL attended from 1916 to 1922.
‡Enclosure not preserved.

says if she could have only one garden book that would be it, but I am not so attached to Robinson as she is.

Did you read *The Fires of Olympus* in the April 2 *New Yorker?* [The author] Charles Bracelen Flood is Mary Ellen's brother.

My mother does get steadily worse, not physically, but more unquiet, and I am in constant terror that one of my two good nurses (or both) will give out. I have learned by experience that three years is as long as they last (and Mary* has been here nearly that long). My experience is great, as I started at thirteen with my great-grandmother.†

The garden got so far behind when the snow was on the ground for a month that I thought (especially as my good yard-man took to drink) I would never catch up. But Helen Mayer‡ telephoned last week that she and a friend were coming to spend the morning weeding. My sister took over my duties within, and made sandwiches, and Helen and Sarah§ and I worked steadily from nine until two. Then Ivey‖ got a half-grown colored boy to come and chop the gravel paths, and now things look so much better I almost believe that I can catch up again. We had a real frost last night (almost unheard of for mid-April) and *Magnolia Lennei* is covered with brown rags. I am going to chop it down, for this happens too often. I hope you found your sister better and spring in your garden.

Aff,

Elizabeth Lawrence

---

*One of the several women who helped nurse EL's mother.
†As a young girl, EL spent summers in Parkersburg, W. Va., visiting her grandmother, Ann Neal Bradenbaugh, and her great-grandmother, Elizabeth Neal, both widowed and living together. EL was thirteen in 1917.
‡Helen and Walter B. Mayer were gardening friends in Charlotte.
§Perhaps Sarah Hodges, a Charlotte friend.
‖A Charlotte, N.C., housekeeper who helped nurse EL's mother.

APRIL 15, 1960

Dear Elizabeth,

I hasten to say that I not only read Charles Flood's *Fires of Olympus* but read and voted for it in manuscript.

Thanks for the warning about the bad edition. [. . .] I have written [Mr. Ranger] it must not be the 16th edition.

Your description of the early garden club meeting somehow reminds me of the time I found myself at a public luncheon in Maine, to raise money for the salary of the local public health nurse. Or so I thought. It proved to be a county affair and at the start of it, I found myself standing with the others and singing to the tune of "Little Sir Echo" the following chorus:

> *Hancock Health Nurses, Hello, Hello,*
> *Hello, Hello, Hello, Hello,*
> *Hancock Health Nurses, Hello, Hello,*
> *Hello, Hello, HELLO!*

The school superintendent had written the words and led us in song. I will sing it sometimes, if pressed.

I know that Mary will stay on. She simply must.

Affectionately,
Katharine

P.S. We leave for Maine today and I called home and learned that mice had eaten and destroyed *nine* of my old-fashioned rose bushes, so I am extra sympathetic about the magnolia. [. . .]

MAY 10, 1960

Dear Elizabeth,

Life is too mixed up for me to give you absolutely *exact* dates and it is probably far too mixed up for you to even want to receive them. Today—maybe yesterday—out came *N. Hawera,* a first

time for me, a day before that *Tulipa biflora,* and about a week
ago various *Kaufmannianas,* among the grape hyacinth—now out
since 10 days are *Armeniacum, botryoides album,* and for the first
time this year as of four days ago *Armeniacum Cantab*—a very new
color blue for grape hyacinths (for me anyway). A week to ten
days ago *Leucojum vernum* and snowdrop *nivalis viride-apice.* The
old-fashioned snowdrops and crocuses were blooming when we
arrived from the South on Good Friday. The scillas are almost
gone. This year I had some new pale blue ones—*Tubergeniana.* I
failed to note the date but I think about April 30—very pretty. All
my big narcissus are in full bloom, including "Mrs. R. O. Backhouse," a name that kills Andy.

Today I replanted the half-dead (winter-killed) chrysanthe-
mum bed.

I am sorry not to be a better date-keeper for you.* One trouble
is that Augie the dachshund has eaten my labels of new bulbs.

[. . .]

I *hope* things are no worse for you. I have a toothache so no
more now. I have been too occupied with my family to tend to my
own teeth. Also very much occupied on a huge cutting job on an
eccentric very long book-length *New Yorker* manuscript. *Time* is
about to roast *The New Yorker* of William Shawn,† but we have to
expect it I guess. I will write a better letter when I know what is
making Andy sick.

Much love,
Katharine

P.S. The bluets are in flower in the fields. [. . .]

---

*Perhaps there was also too much to report. By mid-June, the garden was "at fever pitch,"
perennial borders "works of art," according to EBW (*Letters of E. B. White,* p. 470).
†"The Years without Ross," *Time* (5/16/60). It turned out not to be a "roast." Shawn was
said to have "talent," Ross, "genius." Current writers were not as good as the old ones,
especially KSW's husband. The *Time* reporter observed, "E. B. White's civilized despair

[MAY 1960]

FRIDAY AFTERNOON

Dear Katharine,

I can't answer all your letter, but I want to tell you that I am distressed to hear that Mr. White is sick again, and am so sympathetic about teeth, and thank you for the dates. [. . .] Also that Hannah Withers has promised to let me know when her Musk Rose is in bloom, and we will send you some flowers to check. Maybe you will be able to root them; anyway, we are going to try to root it for you. Hannah's came from a cousin (also a Mrs. White, who lived in Chicago but was from South Carolina) who found it on an old house, and got cuttings. Hannah is sure that it will be hardy. [. . .]

I have had a number of things on my mind to say, but have dropped everything to try to finish my book [*Gardens in Winter*]— except clients whom I have already promised, and my column, of course.

With love and sympathy,
Aff,
Elizabeth Lawrence

MEMORIAL DAY [1960]

Dear Elizabeth,

I am touched that you want to bother to send me clusters of the Musk Rose.

[. . .] Just press a truss* and some leaves and mail them to my office. I shan't be here to try to root a cutting, but I'm sure I could identify by scent and the dried flowers.

---

and gentle celebration of nature is now rarely to be found in 'The Talk of the Town,' while he hibernates in Maine."
*A flower cluster.

I am so happy that you are trying to finish your book. *Do not answer this!* Keep at that book! [. . .]

Aff'y,
Katharine
[. . .]

P.S. I was *supposed* to go to Bryn Mawr, my college, on June 3, taking care *en route* of Miss Marianne Moore* and my sister Elizabeth, both of whom are ailing and fragile. I hope I can make it, so I can carry their bags where there are no red caps, but now I'm not sure. The college is having its 75th Anniversary and has dreamed up the awful idea of "citing" 75 alumnae—of which the three of us are three out of the 75. It's all about business, and I never should have let myself in for it.

JULY 25, 1960

[Dear Katharine,]
[The musk rose] bloomed while Hannah was out of town. The day she returned she brought a branch with one little last flower—I pressed the flower separately and you can tell its habit from the spray—flower creamy and about the size of a nickel.

E.L.

P.S. I'll try to get it off right away.

JULY 19, 1960

Dear Elizabeth,
Do you, from your learned flower background, know of any book that covers or even touches on the subject of the names of

---

*KSW solicited Marianne Moorè's poems for *The New Yorker* and continued to correspond with her after retirement. MM encouraged KSW to collect her "Onward and Upward" pieces for a book.

flowers, particularly their familiar names? The reason for the Latin names is often easy to trace by the Latin root, and so are the descriptive familiar names but it occurred to me that someone might sometime have written down the reasons for naming a certain flower for a certain person or for giving it an odd name and that this might make a bit for one of my garden pieces. Probably I should know who Mrs. R. O. Backhouse of the unfortunate name was, or who Madame Baron Veillard was, the lady for whom my favorite clematis is named. Etc. etc. [. . .] *No* time, *no* research on your part—only a postcard. It is wicked to impose on your time.

I do hope that your book is progressing well and that you have been able to get adequate help to take care of your mother. I think about you often and worry.

We've had bad luck. I was sick for two months. [. . .] This prevented my going to Bryn Mawr. Now I'm having a vacation from editing and feel much better, but whether I can pull myself together to write a fall garden piece next month I don't know. My mind is empty as a sieve. I hope to write on shrubs and wish I knew the title of a good shrub book.

[. . .]

The usual inundation of children and grandchildren has begun. One,* the oldest, is tending pregnant mice at the Jackson Lab in nearby Bar Harbor and comes here between litters!

Forgive all this chatter.

Much love to you,
Katharine

---

*Kitty Stableford.

[JULY 24, 1960]

Dear Katharine,

[. . .]

The sort of information that you want is what I have been try-ing to acquire for twenty-five years, and I still know next-to-noth-ing. I once wrote Clarence Elliott* about *Ornithogalum balansae,* and asked him for whom it was named. He wrote back very snip-pily that he did not know, and why didn't I put my questions to American horticulturists. The reason was, they don't know either. I found out after a long search that it was named for the French botanist, Benedict Balansa. Now, with the wretched mod-ern method of small letters for specific names, I wouldn't even have known whether balansa was a place or a person. Generic names, of course, are explained in the *Cyclopedia of Horticulture,* and most plant dictionaries. Only they don't all agree. I did a lecture on plant names once, but my notes got lost, and I want to gradu-ally collect them again, and put them little by little in my column. I refuse to write about sprays and fertilizers all of the time.

Mrs. Backhouse (and why is her name unfortunate . . . it is pro-nounced like the god of wine, isn't it? the only thing I can think of is that you might call what we called the "garden house," when we lived in the country, the "back house") was an early breeder of daffodils (1857–1921). Her husband worked with her, and they introduced the early red cups. Two I still grow and love are Ha-des and Scarlet Leader. They lived at Sutton Court, Hereford, and don't seem to have been connected with William or Henry.

I looked all through the lists in my file of garden books, but couldn't find those that I had in mind. The trouble is that there are so many half-baked books all telling what you know already, and nothing that tells what you want. My filing system was com-

---

*Author of *Rock Garden Plants* (E. Arnold and Co., 1935) and coauthor with C. A. Johns of *Flowers of the Field* (George Routledge and Sons, 1916).

pletely broken down, both card index and catalogue. My desk is piled with unfiled cards. And I shall have to go to town to get more filing cases before I can get things cleared up. I sometimes feel as if I never shall.

[. . .]

I am sure I had other things to say, but can't remember what.

Affectionately,
Elizabeth Lawrence

P.S. Mr. McAdoo* thinks he will get the book out in January—I don't know whether they are the kind who dilly-dally. Right now I am struggling to keep him from re-writing it, but he will probably win. I am not a fighter. Nurses all right at present.

P.P.S. Did you ever hear of a poet called Vernède? The quotation I have is in English,† but may be a translation. I have two libraries working on it, they can't find any such person—but he is quoted in a garden magazine.

SEPTEMBER 4, 1960

Dear Elizabeth,

I seem to have had to walk out on all my friends this summer and I have walked out on you the worst of all. It is perfectly terrible and I hope you can forgive me after the many kindnesses, still unacknowledged, for which I am indebted to you. [. . .] I had to write a garden piece for *The New Yorker*—before my daughter and her three children arrived a week ago. Two families of young departed by car this morning after one breakfast at seven and another at eight at this house, so the melancholy end of summer has come for us. We ourselves leave in three days for two weeks in New York. [. . .]

---

*EL's editor at Harper for *Gardens in Winter.*
†EL had spent years trying to identify the source of a favorite line, "It is July in my garden and steel-blue are the globe thistles," which she had quoted in her column (*CO* 7/17/60).

The thing I feel the worst about is never having answered your question about the poet named Vernède. I never heard of him or her but I shall ask *The New Yorker*'s checking department if it can turn up any information in any of its reference books. [. . .]

Well, maybe I feel even worse about not thanking you right away for the sample of the musk rose, and your kind friend who bothered about it, too. [. . .] I really think you probably found it, but what about its wintering in Maine? [. . .] The cluster of flowers looks very much as I remember them, in size, and your description of creamy white about the size of a nickel exactly fits. [. . .] The scent I remember as heavenly but I did not know enough about scents and roses then to know whether it was a musk scent. Very likely. But there is one big trouble. Our rose grew in Brookline, Massachusetts, and *Hortus II** says that the musk is not hardy in the North. [. . .]

[. . .] I am not happy about this piece in spite of the fact that Shawn says he likes it as much as the others. To me it is dull and hurried and superficial, and it gives absolutely no dope on shrubs, I'm afraid, for the person who knows something about them. I know nothing. But then I know nothing about anything in the gardening line in any solid sense. The only section of the piece I like at all is about Miss Jekyll but I may have guessed her all wrong. You will know. You should see our garden and lawn now—desiccated by drought, all flowers in the borders except the very latest gone. We do not dare water much as the spring is not overflowing. It usually does. It has never been known to give out, but this has been the longest drought in history and we have had to use lots of water in the house.

If you read the piece you will see how much in it I owe to you— Miss Dormon's book, the books by and on Gertrude Jekyll, the Backhouse thing which I may or may not cut in proof. I only

---

*_Hortus Second_, reference book on botanical nomenclature by Liberty Hyde Bailey.

wanted to use it because of Jackson & Perkins' absurd change of the name.*

[. . .]

My filing system, such as it ever was which was nothing, has completely gone to bits, and letters, files, catalogues, and sundry notes make my study a horrid mess. I despair of ever catching up for now I must start in editing again. I can hardly wait for your book and trust it will be out in time for me to read it before I write my spring piece in Dec. and January. *Who is the publisher and what is the title?* I'd like to place an order early in hopes of getting a copy promptly. I find I'm not even sure what the book is about, but I hope it has something to do with the notes you have been collecting about dates of bloom, etc. I do hope you write up your notes on plant names. One thing I find I do not know about you and wish I did is whether you still practice landscape gardening or now spend all your time on writing your column and your books.

I have a question. Could you use some ordinary tulip and daffodil bulbs in October if I find I have some extra when my de Jager order and Heemskerk order come?

[. . .]

Affectionately,
Katharine

[SEPTEMBER 1960]

Dear Katharine,

[. . .] I don't see how you do so much. You and Mr. Krippendorf (Mr. K. formerly—now, no longer, alas . . . he is going to pieces just like my mother, only not bedridden yet. I am always so thankful that what you wrote about him came out while he could

---

*In the final proof KSW did not cut out what she had written about the pink-cupped daffodil, Mrs. R. O. Backhouse, in which she argued that Jackson & Perkins's calling it "Mrs. R. O. Pinkhouse" in its catalogue was "a confusing and dispiriting change."

still appreciate it. It gave him so much pleasure. And that was the last time he was able to really talk to me on the telephone—the time when he called to ask if I had seen your article.) always make me feel ashamed of myself.

[. . .]

Please, please, don't ever again worry about thanking or answering. Especially for the dead roses, and don't *think* of thanking Hannah. Next time we shall try to get them to you with their perfume in the box. I work so hard, I never know whether I have heard from people, and I had forgotten the roses. [. . .]

I am sorry you worried about Vernède, but glad you haven't forgotten, as you may come across something. I shall also put Ellen Flood on it. She loves such jobs, and often goes all through Mme. De Sévigné* hunting a phrase for me, or finding the original of "the laurels all are cut." I didn't want to find Vernède for any particular reason, just that I thought he might have said more charming things about gardens.

Yes, I still do a little designing and consulting. I can't make up my mind to give it up. I turn down nine calls, and answer the tenth if she sounds desperate—and nice. Then I sometimes take on people who bother me long enough. One of my problems this spring and summer is that I *couldn't* refuse to do the planting for the new Nalle Clinic, as my mother's doctor,† who has done for us things far beyond the call of duty, asked me to do it. [. . .] I thought I could just design it and plant it. I had no idea of getting involved with contractors and engineers and foremen and graders. All saying things can't be done, that my yardman, Willie, and I have been doing for years without any fuss.

Heavens! Don't dream of buying the book. I have already taken the liberty of asking Mr. Harris, the publicity man (if that's what you call him) to see that you, personally, get a review copy.

*Marie, Marquise de Sévigné (1626–1696), French writer.
†Dr. Walter Brem Mayer, also a well-known Charlotte gardener.

[. . .] I am sure that Mr. McAdoo would jump at a chance to send you a galley or proof, or whatever they send and I shall ask him to, if you like, or you can. He hopes to get the book out in January, and galleys should be coming soon, if he can read the corrections on the copy-edited manuscript I just sent back to him. The publisher is Harper, and the book is *Gardens in Winter*. Caroline Dormon did the most beautiful drawings for me. [. . .] It took Caroline two years to do them, as I had to send her many of the bulbs and plants, and she had to grow them first. Others she had already.

I always love having bulbs, but I have left so many unplanted in the last two years, I dare not accept. I keep promising myself to stop writing so furiously and catch up on my garden, but I find it hard to ration writing.

I apologize for the way *I always answer by return mail*. I hope that doesn't make you feel the need to write any sooner. It is just that otherwise I won't answer at all.

Aff,
Elizabeth Lawrence

P.S. Mary Ellen's so happy about having another baby about Christmas. Ellen says she doesn't know what she will do with *two* grandchildren, as she cannot keep up with one. You will be amused by that!

[SEPTEMBER 1960]
Saturday morning

Dear Katharine,

Hannah, the wretch, came to dinner with me last night, and was fascinated by what you wrote about the rose, and said, "Well, it's bound to be hardy, because Virginia got it from a garden in Marietta, Ohio." I said crossly, "Well, why didn't you tell me that?" And she said, "You never asked me." I guess I didn't. I just took for granted that Hannah's cousin, Mrs. White, who inherited The Borough, one of the old places at Statesburg, South Carolina, and gathered together a collection of old roses to add to those in the garden, had found it thereabouts. Especially as the only other specimen I have come across came from an old North Carolina (or maybe it was a Virginia) garden. Mrs. White said she smelled the wonderful fragrance before she could see the shrub. It was clambering all over the house, and was in full bloom. She was given five canes, which she took back home (to Cleveland) to have rooted in her greenhouse. She sent one to old Mr. Bobbink,* who was then living, and he told her that it was the Musk Rose. So that is why Hannah feels sure of it.

[. . .]

Aff,
Elizabeth Lawrence

NEW YORK
SEPTEMBER 19, 1960

Dear Elizabeth,

I worried about you during Donna's visitation to New York, hoping that you were not again subjected to terrible devastation. It is so shocking and sad when this happens. We were lucky in Maine this time, I learned by phone, as the storm petered out to only sixty miles an hour winds. The hollow old Balm O'Gilead trees in front of the house are still standing. They bring us the raccoons and the birds, and we almost lost them in two earlier hurricanes.

I am delighted that Harper is sending me a review copy of your book and very much hope they can get a copy to me early, in

*Bobbink and Adkins was a famous rose nursery in Rutherford, N.J.

hopes that I can cover it in the spring "Onward and Upward" piece I'll be writing next January. Perhaps if they sent it direct to North Brooklin it would speed things up. How wonderful to have Caroline Dormon as your illustrator! I touched on her wild flower book in the piece that will be in this week's issue. I'll buy some copies of your book for *friends* and keep the review copy for myself.

Did I or did I not apologize for lifting so much about Mrs. R. O. Backhouse from your letter to me? You will see why I wanted to speak of her name, but actually it is you who wrote this paragraph.* This makes me uneasy; I sponge far too much. All through this article I am indebted to you, as you will see.

I am more and more convinced that the Sergeants' "Guelder roses" were the musk rose. If in Marietta, why not in Brookline? [...]

Joe Mitchell and I had a long and happy talk about you at a party last week. And I passed on to my sister your paragraph about her book. It will please her, I know. She looks and is better than she was in June when I last saw her. We drive back to Maine on Thursday.

No answer expected to this letter. It's nice about Mary Ellen's baby.

Affectionately,
Katharine

P.S. Just heard from our Checking Department that your poet is Robert Ernest Vernède,† 1875–1917—and he is *English*. The Library of Congress has him listed, with titles, so you could write

---

*KSW discussed the Mrs. R. O. Backhouse daffodil and silently quoted EL on the pronunciation of the name ("War in the Borders, Peace in the Shrubbery," *NY* 9/24/60).
†EL filed away information about Robert Vernède and later wrote about him (*CO* 7/31/66), acknowledging White's help.

there, but I dared not use our checkers' time to get all the titles. All they presented to me were "War Poems" and they said there were also novels and short stories.

[SEPTEMBER 1960]

Dear Katharine,

I hasten to again assure you that anything that comes from me is yours and welcome, and Mrs. Backhouse doesn't belong to me anyway. When everyone is so generous to me, I could not but be eager to pass on anything I can. Thank you so much for finding out about Vernède. I didn't know about writing to the Library of Congress, but I shall, and I'll ask our librarian to get the books for me.

[. . .]

Aff,
Elizabeth Lawrence

NOVEMBER 3, 1960

Dear Elizabeth,
[. . .]
Did I tell you that I heard from two dwellers on Hawthorn Road,* the first from #17 asking me if I could mean Hawthorn Road, *Brookline*, and had I lived at #17 as a child? I replied yes, it was Brookline but that we had lived on the corner, at #4. Next I got a lovely letter from the mistress of #4 who was told by her neighbors, asking me to call on her when I could and telling me that almost none of the shrubs still existed and the lawn had been cut up to make room for a garage, etc. Sad. But, I thought, here's

---

*KSW's readers must have seen her 9/24/60 column, "War in the Borders, Peace in the Shrubbery," in which she had written about her family's house and garden on Hawthorn Road in Brookline, Mass.

my chance about the "Guelder" roses, so I wrote right back and asked if they still grew under the east windows of the library, and could she send me some leaves if they were still on the bushes— or, if they had fallen, a cluster of flowers next June. No answer yet, either the roses are gone or the leaves had fallen, or else the dear lady, a busy surgeon's wife with three children, was too busy to have time for an unknown, eccentric old lady. I think I will hear again eventually for it was a lovely letter. She did tell me lots of things that were pleasant to know such as that her daughter, age 11, walked up the hill to High Street and down the hill to Brook-line Village to take the streetcar, just as I always did, in to town to the Winsor School. (In my day, "Miss Winsor's.") I shall try to go there sometime.

As usual my lack of knowledge is catching me up. Those "broken" tulips, for instance.* The Crops Research Division of the Department of Agriculture has a bulletin that says they must be planted apart from other tulips and from lilies because all of them offered by bulb dealers have a virus, which is the cause of their interesting markings. [. . .] Isn't it possible that the tulips could have been raised from seed free of the virus? [. . .] I need to know the answer, for if I've given *New Yorker* readers a bum steer, I must issue a warning when I next write about tulips. Do tell me if you know the answer.

Then another thing I did wrong, apparently, was to give the impression by my wording on Gertrude Jekyll that England had never had naturalized plantings until Robinson and Jekyll came along. Of course it had, and I knew it. I'm not learned enough to know where the craze for bedding out and for copying formal European gardens started but I remembered a passage in *Mansfield Park* where all the Bertrams and the Crawfords and poor

---

*KSW admired "Broken Tulips" from de Jager & Sons, flaked with bright colors or mar-bled with white (*NY* 9/24/60), which provoked letter writers to warn that the bulbs were infected with a virus.

Fanny Price went to spend the day at Mr. Rushworth's estate to consider how to remake his landscaping and gardens, and Fanny mourned because Henry Crawford recommended cutting down an avenue of old trees. This made me wonder whether it was not between 1800 and 1820 that this all started. Jane Austen commenced this novel in 1811 and it was published in 1814. Do you, with your real learning, know about this? I would love to use this reference to *Mansfield Park* (and some others in the Austen novels) in a later piece if by any chance my hunch is right that Jane was satirizing a new fad in gardens. [...]

One reader who queried me on my time implications said she thought there were naturalized gardens in Shakespeare's day. Do you know this? I know there is a garden of Shakespeare's flowers at Stratford but I have no clear impression of Elizabethan gardens except to suspect they were formal. What do you think?

The mail is going and I won't burden you with my errors, which you probably knew all along, but were too polite or too busy to point out. (Actually, I'm eternally grateful for corrections.) Oh, yes, there was one other whopping error I've discovered. Not all hollies are dioecious; some are polygamous or hermaphrodite. [...] I often wonder how I dare write on garden catalogues at all when I'm such an ignoramus. I find I am in a state about the election and I seem to think how I just can't bear it if Nixon wins. Oh, dear! Very likely you feel the exact opposite way.

Affectionately,
Katharine

[NOVEMBER 1960]

[Dear Katharine,]

I'll lend you an article I have on Repton and Jane Austen,* and I think it will answer all your questions. [. . .]

The "naturalistic movement" came at the end of the seventeenth century with the Earl of Shaftesbury, Addison and Pope. But it wasn't very natural, I gather: ruins, romance and rustic seats. Bedding out seems to have been in full swing in the eighteen fifties.

I never heard of any naturalized gardens in Shakespeare's day, but it depends on what you mean by naturalized. I imagine the English cottage gardens were the same all the way back, if that is what is called natural. It is really a question of defining terms.

I think all hollies *are* dioecious (that is all species), but some forms, *Ilex cornuta Burfordii,* for example, always have berries (or so they say). I find that many general are like this, mostly dioecious, but individuals have perfect flowers—or at least bear fruit without being pollinated, but I'm not sure that it's the same thing. I gruel over things as you do, but I learn more by making mistakes than any other way. Even with the greatest care I find errors creep in, and when I learn better I write and correct what I've said before. But I try not to let it bother me. Everyone makes mistakes, but the really despicable people are those who protect themselves by never making a definite statement. That's why it is so hard to get any real information.

[Aff, Elizabeth Lawrence]

---

*EL must have sent KSW a copy of "Jane Austen and the English Landscape School," by Elsa Rehmann, *Landscape Architecture,* 25 (April 1935): 127–135. Rehmann, a landscape architect herself, argues that Austen's novels reveal "a comprehensive knowledge" of the landscape architecture of her time and a familiarity with the work of Humphrey Repton, who wrote about the English gardens at the end of the eighteenth and the beginning of the nineteenth centuries.

[NOVEMBER 20, 1960]

Dear Elizabeth,

I owe you thanks for so many things that I am appalled. First, your letters; second, the article on Jane Austen and Repton, and now the six little bulbs. The last went into the ground today—not in the bed where I usually plant the small bulbs, for a red squirrel has discovered these treasures and until Andy shot him (not for this reason but because he so stirred up Augie, the dachshund, that Andy could not write), he was busily carrying off all my miniature treasures.* Therefore, since there are other squirrels I put Queen Anne's Jonquils in a different spot, under a Persian lilac in the south border, near the front of the bed where there are Maggi Mott violas and snowdrops. [. . .]

Do you need the *Landscape Architecture Quarterly* back right away? I can have the article copied if you do. Otherwise, if you would trust me, I would love to be able to keep it until I see whether I can write anything fresh about Jane Austen and the English scene—come January. I can't do it now, for we have to be away in New York for at least two weeks, and then Christmas will be upon us. [. . .] I admit I was crestfallen to find that Jane Austen had been so thoroughly explored, but I also think the author of that piece and even Jane's famous editor [R. W.] Chapman, didn't quite see that the novelist was satirizing a current fad, in somewhat the same way, except more mildly, that she poked fun at the gothic novel. At least that is my theory, probably false. Before I can even write anything, of course, I must read Repton and I hope I can find him in the New York Public Library next week. And I must also reread all the Austen novels, which is no chore for me. I keep doing it anyway.

[. . .]

---

*What most likely happened is that the squirrel stirred up KSW, who stirred up EBW, until he finally gave in, then retired to his bed with a sick headache. EBW's enemy was the fox, when it threatened his geese.

My pursuit of the truth about "broken" tulips has brought me two fascinating letters, one from [S. L.] Emsweller of the U.S. Ornamentals Division, who says flatly that all are virus ridden, one from Willis Wheeler of the Daffodil Society who wrote not to me but to John Wister who had sent him my letter. Mr. Wheeler says this is so of the real "broken" tulips but he adds that there are many that are colored like the broken ones but are not strictly "broken." All named cultivars appear to be free of virus and since these are the ones de Jager sells, his are safe. It is really a matter of semantics. I'm with you in not caring about pests and diseases too much. We hate poison sprays and won't use any that are really dangerous and haven't time to use the others much.

[. . .]

No more now except to wish you belatedly a happy Thanksgiving Day. [. . .]

Affectionately,
Katharine

[NOVEMBER 1960]

Dear Katharine,

I should have told you to keep the article as long as you like, even if you wait until fall to use it, and do not worry about the subject's having been covered, for that is so long ago, and I am sure no one but me remembers it, and few people must read that publication. I did because I was so interested. I don't know of any book that really covers the history of Landscape Architecture here and in England; probably Richardson Wright's *Story of the Garden* would be helpful.

Don't be disappointed if the little Queen Annes don't bloom, for the jonquils are supposed to do in the South only. But ever since I found lavender growing at Sargentsville I have wondered if more things would grow along the coast.

[. . .] I don't understand why Mr. Wheeler says all cultivars are free of virus, because *all* broken bulbs would be cultivars, so all would be free . . . if you follow. I hardly follow myself. I would be most interested if you write about it, and I should think everyone would. Do you know the dear little Penguin book, *Tulipomania* by Wilfrid Blunt? I could send you mine if you would like to see it.

[. . .]

I have been interrupted so many times that I keep forgetting the things I want to say. One is that Mary Ellen has another little boy. The other is that they say that animals don't eat bulbs of daffodils or any of the amaryllis family. The bulbs are supposed to be poison, but I read somewhere that they have little crystals in them. No, wait a minute. I am sure I *did* read that somewhere, but all I can find at the moment is that some daffodils, and some other amaryllids contain toxic alkaloids. I have been collecting material on poisonous plants, for a chapter in my next book, but I haven't made a separate file yet, so it is hard to check. What I gather is that practically everything that grows is poisonous to some person or animal at some time.

Just as we were about to sit down to our Thanksgiving dinner my nephew (17) arrived unexpectedly, having gotten a ride from the Virginia Episcopal School in Lynchburg. As we sat down, he looked around the table and said, "Well, how did you all like the results of the election? *I* was pleased, and (looking at me) I believe *one* other member of the family was." I don't think his Uncle Roger will ever recover. He had just spent the whole of the cocktail hour telling me that he is not half as worried about integration as he is about the communists in the country, who will now take us over, aided and abetted by Mr. Kennedy, who is even worse than Mr. Roosevelt. And I hadn't said a word.

Affectionately,
Elizabeth Lawrence

E. B. White's province was the barn, Katharine's the flower borders. Here in a photograph from the early 1940s Katharine helps feed the sheep.

Katharine admiring her borders. Even when she was working in the garden or giving instructions to the Whites' longtime helper, Henry Allen, she did not "dress down" to the garden.

Katharine at home among her books and papers. The windows looked out on perennial borders and, in the front, on Andy's celebrated "coon tree" that eventually came down in a storm.

Katharine enjoyed arranging flowers in favorite old containers; in this case, a big copper vase on a corner bookshelf.

[JANUARY 1961]
Epiphany

Dear Katharine,

When I opened the package I sat right down on the floor, and began to read *The New Yorker Stories*, the ones I remembered and the ones I had missed. I remembered "Kin" [by Eudora Welty] and when I finished rereading it I got up and wrote a letter to Eudora. No one but Eudora remembers things like the polar bear and the spark from the North Star. I think of myself as reading every *New Yorker* all the way through, but then someone asks me about a story, and I find I haven't read it. Just before Christmas I had reluctantly gathered up all the old copies that had got piled on my studio floor because there was no place else to put them, and sent them off to the Salvation Army. Having the new volume is like getting them back.

We have had continuous cold all winter . . . once down to eleven which stops the camellias for a while at least. But the wintersweet has never been hurt. Caroline Dormon wrote on New Year's Day, "The ground was frozen like a pavement for days, but in spite of it all there are lots of Paper-whites, the wintersweet is still full of bloom, buds of the white magnolia are swelling, and a big bud of Anemone de Caen." This morning there was ice in the birdbath, but by noon the first crocus was out.

I am sure it is hard to give up your work on *The New Yorker*,* but you are so wise. I never did see how you do all that you do. I am sure I would not be in such a miserable state if I would give up designing gardens, and do nothing but write. [. . .]

I am terribly upset about my [*Gardens in Winter*] book. Mr. McAdoo has [not?] *mentioned* a publishing date. I can't imagine what happened, after he rushed me so to get proof back. He kept

*On January 1, 1961, KSW gave up her part-time editorial work with *The New Yorker*, ending a career of more than thirty-five years.

saying that it *must* come out in January, and I agree that in spring no one will want to read about winter.

I hope you are going to Florida, and that you will be coming our way, and will come to stay. I can always put you up if you will bear with our household.

Affectionately and gratefully,
Elizabeth Lawrence

P.S. Hannah was so touched by your thinking of her.

FRIDAY, FEBRUARY 3 [1961]

Dear Elizabeth,

Thank you for your dear letter. We are here in the city and to-morrow I go to the hospital, just to check in and hold the room until Monday when the tests start. I couldn't get a room unless I entered on Saturday! I'm sure the tests will prove that nothing very bad is wrong. We resolved the scribbling* in a fraction of a garden piece. I enclose a segment of it—the part I have to write on—broken tulips—to see whether you will allow me to quote the sentences from your letter in this section.† I *do* hope you will, as I need backing on my casual attitude. You are not explained here because there's a paragraph on your book earlier, which proves that as a horticulturist or writer you are "redoubtable."

Please reply to me at *The New Yorker* as I'll need your answer for the *New Yorker* lawyer. It is technically illegal to quote from a letter without permission and our magazine lawyer makes us follow this to the letter.

Love, haste,
Katharine

*KSW sometimes sent her "scribbled" letters and manuscripts to her office to be typed by a secretary.
†KSW was asking for permission to quote EL's letter in her continuing discussion of "broken" tulips, acknowledging, "My most encouraging reply came from the redoubtable Elizabeth Lawrence."

Dear Katharine,

I have just written a formal note to you in care of *The New Yorker.* Of course, Jerry Nelson has just written me, "you have my full permission . . . and I must say, that I am very flattered." Jerry is Mr. Krippendorf's great-granddaughter, now fifteen.

I was so relieved to have your letter in the morning's mail as I had wondered what had become of you in the storm, and I wanted to write, but didn't know where to send a letter. Now that I do, I hope you will have escaped from the clutches of the testers before you get it.

I have just been out in an almost freezing rain to pick you some sodden blossoms, which will probably be a pulp when they get to you, but I thought I'd take a chance (after consulting the Post Office, where the clerk said he could promise me that they would get off the ground in Charlotte, but not that they would be airborne farther than Washington, *D.C.*—they always say D.C. in these parts as it is not considered as important as Washington, N.C.): The little hoopskirt was the last and least battered of a clump that has been in bloom without interruption since the fourth of January. It has scarcely been above freezing for some time, and they have been through two sleet storms. The Christmas rose is Harney's form, and should be much finer. The narrow green leaf is sweet box. I do wish the tiny flowers would open for you to know their fragrance. They look as if they were just waiting for a little warmth. The round leaf is galax, a very small one, and the one that is like it but more oval is *Shortia galacifolia.* The tiny-leafed twig is the true myrtle, not perfectly hardy here as you see from the brown tip, but I do love the smell. This form is not typical; it is the variety *compacta.* The cotoneaster with the shriveled berries is *C. lactea.* The berries don't take much cold, but I do love the dark leaves and grey stems—though I find few to share my enthusiasm. The twigs wired together are *Cyrilla*, from the evergreen shrub bogs, but it doesn't seem to mind the very dry garden. The leaves are supposed to hang on only until Christmas, but this year they have been lovely all winter. The ivies are fleur-de-lis and needle-point. The nandina is a seedling, which is why the leaves and berries are so small. These are the first flowers of the Mume, and the poor little brown camellia is Dawn. (The fully-out flowers of the Mume were forced.)

I am most interested in the story of the virus. [. . .] You must have had great fun digging out all of this. I have had fun hearing about it.

I must stop this, and put the flowers in the mail.

Aff,
Elizabeth Lawrence

NEW YORK
FEBRUARY II [1961]

Dear Elizabeth,

I am dictating this letter to Andy because I am flat on my back with one of three post spinal punch headaches. If I don't raise my head, the headache leaves.

You can't imagine what a surprise and pleasure your letter and your box of flowers from your own garden were. The flowers are my prize possession and I have had the greatest fun trying to identify them. A few were shattered and so I still don't know which one is the mume and I am a little vague about the nandina, neither of which I have ever seen growing. But the Christmas rose and the camellia and the autumn cherry were fresh and lovely and even the little hoopskirt daffodil was charming. The sweet box smells good even without the flowers opening. I am with you in loving the color of the cotoneaster leaves. I am touched that

with all you have to do you did this for me. I forget the witch ha-
zel—it came through beautifully.

Thank you for allowing me to quote you. I turned in the article for better or worse yesterday, minus the houseplant section
and minus most everything else as you will see.

I have to wait out this headache in the hospital although the
tests are over, and the doctors say the headache lasts a week if you
get it at all. They know now that I did not have a stroke and that
it is not hardening of the arteries. What they think it most probably is is a very small scar on the outside casing of the brain (probably from an embolism) and they believe they can control the
nerve irritation by drugs. We are to go to Florida on February 21,
if I am well enough, and my address there will be 4444 Ocean
Blvd., Siesta Key, Sarasota, Florida. We are probably having our
car driven down and if we are able to drive back in mid-April it
might be we would pass through Charlotte. [. . .]

Affectionately,
Katharine

[FEBRUARY 1961]

Dear Katharine,

It was dear of you to write to me, for when the letter came I was
sitting here worrying, and thinking that I had no way of finding
out how you are.

I enclose another leaf of Nandina and in with it is *Prunus Mume*,
which was the one I sent. The autumn cherry bloomed all fall,
but when the really cold weather came it gave up. I am going to
send you a seedling Nandina in the spring. If it is hardy for Mr.
Krippendorf, I bet it will be for you. It is certainly hardier than
lavender, which I found flourishing in a Maine Coast garden. It
wouldn't fruit, of course, but the leaves are enough. I enclose the

last flower and a seed pod and a leafy tip of *Clematis cirrhosa,* which has been blooming without ceasing since Thanksgiving, though not very impressive. I would like to look at the feathers under a microscope. The heart leaf is one of the *Asarum*s from the North Carolina mountains. It came from The Three Laurels as *A. Shuttleworthii* but I don't think the botanists really know them apart. This is not one of the prettiest patterns (I never seem to get the silver hearts, though I see them in other gardens) but I put it in for your nose. Also another twig of myrtle. Though neither seems to have as much of the essence in winter. I have noticed this about herbs too. It takes twice as much thyme this time of year.

Oh dear. I can't imagine why I said I couldn't find *Viola rosina.* It is in *every*thing—even *Wayside.** I must have looked under *V. rosina* instead of *V. odorata.* I am like that. But would you think I would go out of my way to be so stupid. Well.

Please thank Andy for writing, and tell him Mr. Morrison remembers meeting him at Harvard once. It sounds like seeing Shelley plain.† Mr. M. was in the [Cornell University] Landscape school with Andy's brother. I hope you will be able to come our way in April.

Aff,
Elizabeth Lawrence

[MARCH 1961]

Dear Katharine,

I am terribly upset that you have not been well, even more at the idea of your being at the mercy of the Harkness Pavilion.‡ I feel sure that small coats, overshoes and leggings are at the root of the trouble, and that a rest from them will clear it up entirely.

*Nursery in Hodges, S. C.
†Robert Browning's poem "Memorabilia" begins, "Ah, did you once see Shelley plain."
‡Of the Columbia-Presbyterian Medical Center in New York City.

I have never been able to understand how you write as you do under the circumstances. Far from writing easily (When I read "Onward and Upward" . . . I always think how easily *you* write) I write with the greatest difficulty and mostly in despair, and never get through even a letter without several interruptions. My mother's illness becomes more and more of a burden to me as well as to her, and it is only with the greatest effort that I have been able to keep myself together. I exist on the verge of collapse, and cannot persuade kind friends that what I need is rest, not distraction. Dr. Mayer was really angry when I refused an invitation to drive to Hilton Head [South Carolina] (where my great-grandfather was born, and where I have never been), knowing how I love the Low Country. He said, "I order you to go." I say this not in complaint, but in sympathy. I got to a point where I not only couldn't think, I couldn't type. That really scared me. And as you see I am not much better now!

You would not envy me if you were here today. The trees are glazed and the ground covered with a white sleet. I think this winter must be a record for steady cold, though the lowest temperature was eight degrees—so far. Still a few flowers bloom on. Yesterday when it was never above freezing an iris unfurled. But the wild rabbit who has taken refuge in the garden is frisking about—during the cold clear days he stayed in a huddle under the dead bracken fronds—and all of the birds are out.

Did I tell you that I wrote Eudora Welty about how pleased I was to see her story in the album and had a letter from her? She said: I, too, with two other nurses, am taking care of my mother.

Caroline Dormon will be so pleased that you liked her drawings,* and the [cover] photograph of the snowdrops, which she tracked down. She always asks if I have heard from that darling

---

*KSW had praised Dormon's pen-and-ink line drawings "as delicate and precise as the author's prose" in her review of EL's *Gardens in Winter* (*NY* 3/11/61).

Katherine White . . . she is just like me, and has never noticed the A, but she is incensed if anyone spells Dormon with an A.

Everyone will be disappointed if you can't write "Onward and Upward" this time; I wonder if you know how many people look forward to it—in the provinces I mean, and not the kind of people who write to *you,* but the kind who quote it to me, but please let reviews be the least of your worries. It is enough for you to like the book [*Gardens in Winter*]. The trouble with *The Little Bulbs* is that it got to be a specialist's book, which was just what I didn't want it to be. Nobody wants to know that much about little bulbs.

I hope you are better by this time and will be all right, and will try not to worry.

Aff,

Elizabeth Lawrence

P.S. This didn't get mailed. We are still glazed. It is 8 A.M. and the sun shining in the still-brilliant berries of the fire thorn, and the icy buds of the Mume. The Mume is very late, and not a flower is open—but the buds are almost coral. We are promised more snow and sleet tonight. I never know whether the night nurse will make it. She lives miles in the country.

MARCH 18, 1961

Dear Katharine,

All of your fans give me such pleasure by congratulating me on all your pieces. I had not seen the March 11th issue* when Dr. Mayer called—how he found it and read it between the time he got home from the clinic and the time he called, I can't see. The next day a postcard from Mr. Morrison to say how right you are about the beauty of Blue Beauty—that night a long distance call

---

*KSW had praised EL's *Gardens in Winter* as "the best" book for winter gardeners and described EL as "a classicist" and "discriminating horticulturist."

from your devoted admirer Linda Lamm,* and on and on. I loved it all, especially the old catalogues—I can hardly bear it when I think of ones my great-grandmother must have thrown away. I wish she had thrown away her Thackeray—with print too fine for anyone to read (we weren't allowed to, and to this day I have never read *Vanity Fair*) instead.

And I can't bear for Mr. Krippendorf not to hear about Lily Pons,† how he would love it. But Rosanne [Mr. Krippendorf's daughter] says he does not listen when she reads to him, and he can no longer read himself.

And I am most interested in all the research on the tulip, and of course like to read about myself.

I hope you can read this scrawl, which I am writing as I sit with my mother. Her day nurse always picks her most restless moments to go in the kitchen and get her punch. Since the time my mother crawled out of bed, I am always terrified when she is alone and not asleep. The bed has sides, but that does not stop her, and being a hospital bed it is a long way to fall.

I am trying to clean my desk (except for unfiled index cards and pamphlets—I have to go to town to get more files before I can do that—so they are in little dusty piles on my desk)—so that I can get off for New York in the morning. Perry Daniel‡ and I are driving my nephew and a friend of his back to Lynchburg, where we lunch with a cousin who also has a son at the Virginia Episcopal School. She will take the boys back to the school at the last possible minute—Perry and I are going on to spend the night in Leesburg with her mother, and then leave the car with a friend in Baltimore, and go on on the train. I will be back some time in Holy Week, I hope in time to get the garden in order for you. This

*Linda Mitchell Lamm, sister of Joseph Mitchell.
†KSW had written about the "punning name" associated with Three Springs Fisheries, a nursery in Lilypons, Md., specializing in water lilies (*NY,* 3/11/61). Lily Pons was also a famous singer.
‡A Charlotte friend.

is the most beautiful early spring I have ever known. The garden is losing that first gauzy look, and *Magnolia Lennei* is in full bloom [. . .] quinces and daffodils still lovely—dogwoods just nearing bud.

I shall have to send this to New York. If I have your Florida address, I can't find it—though *all* your letters are now in the file.

I do hope you are all right—Mr. Ranger is terribly upset about you.

Aff,

Elizabeth Lawrence

P.S. I can't tell you how I admire the ground you cover in "Onward and Upward." I don't know how you do it.

SARASOTA, FLORIDA

[MARCH 1961]

My dear Elizabeth,

I am absolutely appalled that you, who are so overworked and so constantly anxious and so tired, should have written me three such wonderful letters and that I have not even acknowledged one of them except the first through Andy. The truth is that I cared so much about them and wanted so much to thank you adequately that I kept waiting till I felt more able to write, for sitting at a desk has been next to impossible for any length of time. I have been awfully sick nearly all the time since I came south—sick chiefly, Andy and I think, from the hospital tests and the strong drugs. [. . .] So I am up and down, up and down. On top of this the medicines have given me great depression of spirit and are very hard to adjust to. [. . .] Since the doctors still frankly say they don't yet know what is wrong with me, it seems crazy to be taking dilantin—the drug they are giving me on the *guess* that I have a scar on the surface of my brain. Yet maybe it is working for

I have had fewer dizzy spells. It's the drug they give after strokes
or for epilepsy—neither of which I have or have had. They say
this is *proved*. But because of its connotations, please do not use
the word "dilantin." Well, enough of me and my horrid ailment.
We'll know more by May 1st, for we have to go back by train and
are leaving here April 13. I couldn't possibly drive. I look healthy
and am fat from so much inactivity but I really am undone and
to me it seems now that I shall probably never be able to write
another word for publication. This saddens me—I had so many
plans. [. . .]

I am woefully disappointed not to be able to stop off in Charlotte to see you. But hope lives eternal. I trust you had a pleasant
trip north and hope the change did you good. Up till yesterday
our weather here has been perfect and I walk in a stately way into
the salt water when I can. [. . .]

I am glad you sent the extra dried leaves and flowers as I had
had them all wrong. It was kind of you to take the time to gather
them. I'd love the Nandina when and if I get home. But you must
tell me how high it grows and what exposure it likes and acid or
alkali soil. All our soil is acid. This year my garden will really
have to go to the dogs. It was next to impossible for me even to
make up seed orders so I don't know what the results will be. I
shall probably have to postpone planting the water lilies till another season. As for roses and chrysanthemums, we are certain to
have had many winter deaths, but it's hard to calculate how many
to order as *we* won't know till May. Maine is still under snow.
Andy is selling the beef cattle, alas.

[. . .]

I hope your book is selling some. I did not do it justice. Two
readers so far have written me they've ordered it. Except for a
few really wonderful letters like yours my mail on this last piece
has been scantier than usual, uninteresting except for a few like
yours. Deservedly so, as I covered so little, really. I liked my one

sentence letter from Alfred Knopf, Sr., who said "I think your book is making progress."* Of course I then had to write him that the book I'd planned to devote the next ten years to seems now merely a myth. I had planned to write the omitted houseplant section of that piece while here but I can't possibly. But maybe I shall learn to write, one paragraph at a time.

This poor letter has been written in short takes. It is now April 1st. I send you good wishes, belatedly, for Easter. I owe you so many thanks that I don't know where to start. *No need to answer this letter.* Only write when you have nothing else to do (which will never happen) or have something on your mind. If you have time to read a long piece, you might enjoy Andy's "Letter from the North (Delayed)" in the March 28 issue.† It is very funny to me— also very honest. It's not easy to write about one's callow youth and it took him 18 months to write this. He alternately likes and hates the piece.

Your letter about my piece gives me courage to hope I'll ever be able to write another and I am more grateful than I can say. This year, though, I must discount letters for some are written just to be kind and encouraging. I am at least enough on the ball to know that.

Affectionately,
Katharine

[APRIL 1961]

Dear Katharine,

I was terribly upset to have your letter from Florida, for though I had worried about you, I had been reassured by the last one

---

*Knopf had encouraged KSW to turn her *New Yorker* garden essays into a book, if that's what she wanted to do. He simply wanted a book "by Katharine White."
†EBW's essay, "The Years of Wonder," described a trip he had made through the Bering Strait and into the Arctic in the summer of 1932, when he had embarked on what would

from New York. I hope by now the headache and the effects of the medicines have passed, and that you are feeling better. There is *one* thing I can reassure you about, absolutely and positively: you need not worry in the least about being able to write. Anyone who could write such a letter as your last one to me, can write anything (given time and a chance to concentrate—which, like me, you never seem to have either of).

[. . .] I sat down to write to you the day your letter came (with the address in hand) but I was interrupted, and never got back. As I follow the Southern plan of visiting friends and relatives all along the way, I have never got through bread-and-butter letters (and more have been added by two short trips since, one to S.C. for my goddaughter's twenty-first birthday; and one to Tryon [N.C.] to lecture, and then back to S.C. to visit), and I never got to the bottom of the pile of mail waiting, and of course get more and more snowed under. I don't see how you ever do all that correspondence for "Onward and Upward" (I am one of your admirers who really *knows* how much) and answer all the mail you must get each time. Even my small amount (from my column, I mean) sometimes takes a morning. And people call all day to ask what to do, and if I don't know, which I usually don't, I look it up, usually in several books before I find the answer (if ever) and read it to them. I have just been doing a piece for the *Observer* on *Garden in Your House* [by Ernesta Drinker Ballard], for which I am indebted to "Onward and Upward." [. . .] I do appreciate you, as so few people who write about gardens ever say anything.

If, when you get home, you find a hoop-petticoat daffodil in bloom in your garden, it will be what I sent you for Queen Anne's double jonquil. I don't know whether Mrs. Gibbe's or I made the mistake, but for you it was lucky, as I think the hoop-petticoat

---

become eight years of a young man's wanderings. Reprinted in *The Points of My Compass* (Harper and Row, 1962).

much more likely to survive your winters, and it is easiest to grow. I hope you love it as I do. As soon as I know you are there, I will send the nandina. It will grow in sun or shade, and in any soil, but I guess it would appreciate a protected place.

The Mitchells came to spend an evening with us when I was in New York. Joseph's sister Linda [Lamm] was here week before last with his sister Laura [Braswell], and they came to have lunch in the garden. Linda is one of your greatest admirers. All of the family are as individual, as unspoiled and as delightful as Joseph. The husbands and wives as well as his brothers and sisters.

This has been the most beautiful spring I have ever known, with none of the blistering winds we usually have, but even cool weather, and things in perfection for days, even weeks. The last daffodil, *Narcissus gracilis,* came out yesterday, and the garden is full of tulips, and the iris are just coming. Dear Katharine, I do hope you are both much better.

Aff,
Elizabeth Lawrence

MAY 16, 1961

Dear Elizabeth,

You will think me a very careless and ungrateful friend, but I hope you can forgive me because my silence has been entirely due to the inability to sit up and write. The news was good when I spent a week in the hospital in April, for my neurological tests were no worse than in February and the doctors were elated as it showed I had no quick-growing malignant tumor. We got back to Maine the last day of the month and I stood the two days' drive from New York fairly well. Then, Bango! two days later, I began having bad headaches again and from there on things have gone up and down but always progressively a little worse. Now I spend most of the time in bed, trying to get up three times a day for an hour. I am at my desk now, feeling less bad because of some new caffeine pills they are trying for my headaches but in a few minutes I shall have to retreat to bed and continue this in pencil while lying down. I have only been able to get out into the yard and look at the gardens twice while dressed, but every day I creep out in my wrapper to see the daffodils and early tulips. This is why I'm afraid I shall have to postpone until another year your offer of the Nandina. Everything is at sixes and sevens here. It would never get planted right. Poor Andy is distracted what with a sick wife who can't do a thing and a calf with pneumonia. Henry is our only hand at the moment, our usual extra man for spring not being available. He's off on an island on a more lucrative job. We are at least one month behind on planting.

On top of this, we chose this spring to put in a guest bathroom—a long postponed plan—and the house is swarming with plumbers, electricians, and carpenters. [. . .] Like all old houses this one is queer and we only have one bath on the second floor, way out at the end of the ell. This was uncomfortable for guests and Andy decided that he, by now, disliked dodging visitors and taking turns in the bathroom. When our live-in cook departed, her empty room gave a space next to the guestroom for a second bathroom. But what a mess it all makes.

I'm the worst mess of all. We have a good local doctor and he keeps in touch with the two in New York who are watching over me. [. . .]

As you can see my plans for gardening and writing must be forgotten for the moment. The spring is a month or six weeks late here. Only in the last few days has the grass turned green. The first thing I hunted for was the hoop skirt daffodil but it is missing, alas. So are the *Trevithian* and *Thalia* daffodils that were behind it, and in the same patch of ground, the scillas and grape hyacinths. Something happened just there, for all the rest of the two beds on each side of our front door are full of little bulbs. It may have been a rooting animal or it may have been that ice formed there too heavily or that the cover of boughs got dislodged. I wasn't here to see or know. I am terribly disappointed and feel, too, that I have failed your trust in me as a gardener. These beds are to the West of the house. To the South the bed of larger bulbs is now perfectly lovely, with hyacinths and narcissus and, so far, only Red Emperor and Gudoshnik and the little *Kaufmanniana* tulips. The crocuses on the lawn and the snowdrops and snowflakes have just passed.

Before I got really sick here, I was able to stand or sit outdoors and tell Henry where to plant the hybrid tea roses. We take them up and bury them, you know, and didn't lose a one this year. But it was a winter of great losses otherwise. Nearly all the chrysanthemums are dead, a good many delphiniums, and bearded iris, violas, various perennials and lilies. But thank goodness, my extravagance of last fall—five new Silvia Saunders hybrid peony roots—has survived. Four have shoots up and the fifth is coming. From now on I shall have to compress, not expand, the flowers. Andy is trying to sell the cattle. The thought of not having them in the pasture and the barn is sad but he's right, I'm afraid. He gets too tired when Henry isn't here to tend them—every cow emergency comes at night or on Sunday of course—and then there's the haying—four weeks of it with extra help needed. We shall just give it away to anyone who will cut it. But how sad to have no cows in the landscape and no manure pile for the garden and compost heap.

I was delighted today to read in the *Journal of the N.Y. Botanical Gardens* the wonderful praise of your book [*Gardens in Winter*] by Wister. I can't think of anyone whose praise would mean more —to me, anyway. I was going to clip and send it to you in case you hadn't happened to see it yet, but I have momentarily lost it. (That happens when one is in bed.) I'll leave this letter open and hunt for it tomorrow. I blush when I think of Mr. Wister, who led me to van Slogteren,* for I haven't even yet managed to tell the broken tulip story right, or so I now see. There of course have to be two different vectors to cause breaking—not just the peach aphid. Well, nothing could matter less just now to anyone but me. I shall just have to get well so as to make that correction in the book I am going to try to make out of my *New Yorker* pieces some-day. Meanwhile I reread *you.* [. . .]

Those caffeine pills have certainly taken hold; I haven't writ-ten as long a ramble as this in months. I'm sorry my burst of en-ergy had to be taken out on *you,* and in this dreadful pencil scrawl.

Affectionately,
Katharine

P.S. I hope your book is selling well; any number of people have written or told me that they've bought it and love it. And I do hope that your mother is no worse and that your life is not too hard.

MAY 24, 1961

Dear Katharine,

The reason that you have not heard from me is *not* that I have never finished writing bread-and-butter letters for my trip to New York, and never answered the nice letter Mr. Wister wrote me in February, to say nothing of the other unanswered mail on my desk, but that when I did not hear from you that you were not well, I was afraid if I wrote even a note you would try to answer it. (As you see from its battered state, this had to come out of the typewriter some days ago, and I am just now getting back to it.) Besides I knew that you would know that I was worried and would let me know about yourself as soon as you could. And I am distressed to hear that you are not all well again, but you mustn't

*Dr. E. van Slogteren of the Flower Bulb Research Laboratory, in Lisse, Holland.

feel discouraged about your book, but must take the advice that you gave to me.

[. . .]

I agree about Mr. Wister. The first time I saw him was in Winston-Salem [North Carolina], when I was just out of college. One of the rich tobacco people had flown him down with arms full of daffodils to talk to the first meeting of our State Garden Club, and I had driven my mother and the other members of the Raleigh Club over to hear him. I thought he looked just like the illustrations to Richard Harding Davis,* and I went home and began a collection of daffodils.

When he came to Charlotte some years ago we asked him to come to stay with us. He arrived in a Cadillac about the size of our house, and having greeted us very formally went out into the garden, where my nephew and a small friend were playing by the pool. One of them put his finger on the fountain and sent a jet of water right in Mr. Wister's face. He walked on as if nothing had happened, and did not even take out his pocket handkerchief to wipe his face or his immaculate suit. I learned afterward that he has nephews of his own.

On the morning he was to leave, my mother and I got up early and packed a lunch for him, and when breakfast was over we presented it to him. He thanked us, and sat down by the fire, and when lunchtime came he was still sitting there. So I said he might as well get the lunch out and eat it, which he did at length.

Heavens, don't think of the hoop-skirts. There are plenty of them, and I could not bear to have you ever worry about a plant. Besides, I did not really expect them to come through the winter. What I really want to send you is some of Mr. Krippendorf's seedling hellebores. That is, seedlings of his seedlings. Most of

*Richard Harding Davis (1864–1916), reporter called "the Beau Brummell of the Press," war correspondent, and novelist whose theatrical flair in life and in stories gave him a reputation for being the ideal American male.

them are so superior to anything in the nurseries now. I have been saving some good sized ones for you, and I am so afraid someone else will get them. So let me know when you have someone to put them out (fall would be all right, as they are very hardy), and promise me that you will not mind if they don't survive. [. . .]

I hope this will find you with the headaches gone as suddenly as they came. Please don't ever have writing on your mind.

Aff and hopefully,
Elizabeth

AUGUST 3, 1961

My dear Elizabeth,

By now you will have given me up entirely as a friend. It is shocking that I have not written you in so long and especially that I have never answered your letter offering me some of Mr. Krippendorf's hellebores. Perhaps you can forgive me, though, when you hear all the things that have been happening to me since May 24, the date of your letter. In May and June I was in bed a good deal with severe headaches. About the first of July I began to feel better and even made my first drive into the village on July 4th to watch the town's funny annual shindig and homecoming day for an hour. Two days later I was writhing in pain, which had nothing to do with my head, and by the end of the day was rushed to the nearest and poorest hospital—the one in Blue Hill—for an emergency appendix operation. [. . .] After fifteen really horrible days I was able to come home. [. . .]

My desk is in the same clutter it was when I returned the first of May and my little workroom is an incredible mess of unfiled material. [. . .] So here it is August 8, *not* Aug. 3 when I began this scrawl. I have to go to the hospital in New York, so I hardly know what to say about the hellebore seedlings, for if they are planted in the fall they should go in in early September here. [. . .] The real trouble is I can do no gardening yet (even flowers, if low, must be picked for me) and I have to breakfast in bed and sleep half the afternoon, so Henry's and my hours seldom coincide. His are 7 to 3:30. I've been living only half a life. [. . .]

But this last week I have suddenly seemed much better. Perhaps the turn for the better has come and I can fool [the doctors] yet! [. . .] Keep your fingers crossed!

I've had to give up any idea of writing a fall piece this month, though. As you can see I can't write anything without effort or in an interesting way and I haven't the stamina to put on any pressure. My only hope in the next month is to dig my way out of the mess of this study and sort and file catalogues and letters. All three of my young families are all in town, so this is a great pleasure. Only five of the eight grandchildren are here. Kitty, the oldest, is babysitting for a French family in a chateau near Paris, Jonathan* is a junior counselor at camp, and Steven is visiting his other grandmother in New Hampshire.

I enclose some of Andy's snapshots of the garden in early spring. As you can see, it isn't a garden—no plan, no style, no proper arrangement of colors—but at least the pictures may give you the feel of the land in a cold, late Maine spring. Everything is very different now. The picket fence hardly shows for the flowers, the grey windbreak is covered with the blossoms of Mme. Baron Veillard, Jackmarie, and Mrs. Cholmondley, and on the little terrace, the hybrid roses are full of bloom. We lost one of our big Balm of Gilead trees (*not* the coon tree) in a fierce wind and rain storm and Andy has made a most ingenious birdbath from a section of its big trunk, into which he poured cement. This bath is not on the terrace but as we sat there yesterday, we could watch two song sparrows and a yellow warbler take their baths under the pear tree.

*Son of Nancy Angell Stableford and Louis Stableford.

Even if I can't garden, I can enjoy the flowers in a maddeningly remote way. My first water lily is in blossom in the pasture pond, for I did go ahead and get Andy and Henry to plant two hardy white lilies in a tub there in June. Today, my first-ever hardy cyclamen is in bloom under the Persian lilac. It is enchanting and a triumph as I have failed so often with them. I finally raised this one indoors last winter and set it out this spring. I don't even know the variety, for the tag is lost. It has pink blossoms and variegated leaves. Everything else is at sixes and sevens—iris needs separating; one long perennial bed is too crowded; one is too skimpy thanks to winter losses. It has been a year of frustration. Andy finally sold our beautiful Herefords and there goes my source of manure. Oh, dear, we are crumbling badly! But just writing you gives me hope and I am determined that I shall get back to normal again. We really feel encouraged.

I do earnestly hope that your life is better than it was. I hardly dare ask for your mother.

Ever affectionately,
Katharine

AUGUST 10 [1961]

Dear Katharine,

I cannot tell you how happy and relieved I was to have your letter this morning, for I knew, when I didn't hear from you, that you were ill again. [. . .]

I think it would be better to send the Lenten Roses in the spring, as they will keep growing here all winter, and be that much ahead. There are plenty of them as they seed abundantly when they are once established.

Your cyclamen must be *neapolitanum* as that is the only one that would be in bloom now, I think, except *C. europaeum* which has entire and perfectly plain leaves. Mine hasn't bloomed yet—I only hope that Shelby* did not grub up the whole patch—I turned my back for a minute, and he had out the clumps of *Cimicifuga* that were just getting well-established after five years.

Thank you for the pictures. I love them and you and the children, but how you get work out of children I shall never know. Chip did help me rake leaves once when he was imbued with the good deeds of Cub Scouts.

My garden has been lovely this summer. We have had rain every few days, which is unheard of, and very few days over ninety-five, so things have not been scorched and blistered as usual, and there have been no high winds and beating rains to batter things down.

My typing seems to be worse than usual. My nerves are all shot (as Bracelen Flood used to go about muttering when he was three . . . quoting a *New Yorker* cartoon of a laborer drilling in the street). My brother [in-law] sent the termite man over to go under the house, and of course they always find termites, and they have been drilling or hammering all morning under my studio. They finally left, but said they would be back at eight in the morning.

My mother still goes downhill slowly and miserably. Fortunately the nurse situation is marking time at present. Mary finally got over the effects of her automobile accident, and seems well. Ivey and I are in a sort of truce.

I can't tell you how happy I am to have your letter and have you sounding so much better. And I do love those pictures and the flowers against the beautiful fence.

Affectionately,
Elizabeth Lawrence

*"Shelby" must have been someone EL had hired to help her in the garden.

[AUGUST 1961]

Dear Katharine,

Mr. Ranger says he is looking for a book for you by Richardson Wright on the American seed trade. He wonders if you mean *The Story of the Garden,* which I have—it has a few pages on "The Initial Nurserymen" in the chapter on "The Rise of American Gardening." Would you like me to send it to you?

Aff,
Elizabeth Lawrence

AUGUST 25, 1961

Dear Elizabeth,

Many thanks for your offer to lend me Richardson Wright's *The Story of the Garden,* if that is the title. [. . .] Unless it's too much bother I would be grateful if you would mail me the Wright book c/o *The New Yorker* to get there about Sept. 11. [. . .] Your other suggestion of the Hedrick book [*History of Horticulture in America to 1860*] sounds much more to the point and I shall try to have Mr. Ranger find me that book.

Sometimes I wonder whether I'm not foolish even to pursue garden reading and especially to have these piles of catalogues keep arriving when I can't really write about them but I hesitate to cut off the flow, burdensome as the catalogues are except for my personal use, lest I could never start the flow coming again. I shall perhaps know better how to plan after this next set of tests, though I really doubt it. [. . .] the only thing to do, I've decided, is to assume I shall suddenly turn up well again. And this is the reason for reading the books.

[. . .]

I *am* stronger and better in many ways. Meanwhile, to get the vegetables frozen! We raise our winter supply, of course. I could go on and on but I shall not and I should not have written all this. On the whole, with the exception of measles in one household, my three young families are thriving, and all our anxieties have been what one might expect in any big family.

I look forward to planting the hellebore next spring. I'm glad your nurse situation is steady but I sorrow for your day by day sad situation. It's hell to grow old, so I feel for your poor mother. No answer expected.

Much love,
Katharine

[SEPTEMBER 1961]

Dear Katharine,

I haven't caught Richardson Wright in any inaccuracies, but shouldn't be surprised to find them. What he does do is to lift, almost verbatim. I suppose he thinks his readers won't know his sources. But he does provide little bits of information here and there. I never did like him, but his friends are devoted. I am one of the few friends who could resist him—but there are a few who were not amused by his rudeness. Once, when I went to Alabama to lecture, one of the ladies confided, "So-and-so insisted upon having you, but *I* wanted Richardson Wright."

Please don't let the medical prognosis shatter you. I have suffered through so many brain tumors that didn't exist—incurable cancers that didn't exist. [. . .] You have enough to undo you, and account for everything. I was brought up on my great-grandfather's saying, "Medicine is not an exact science"—though they now try to pretend that it is.

My cyclamen is not out yet—but has a bud—*Leucojum autum-*
nale is in bloom—a tiny snowflake on a hair-bell stem.

Love, cheer, and sympathy
Aff,
Elizabeth Lawrence

SEPTEMBER 27, 1961

Dear Elizabeth,
Under separate cover I am returning the Richardson Wright
book with many thanks. I have only read in and about it but shall
use your other history, which I have ordered from Mr. Ranger.
How right you are about the brain tumors that don't exist!
At last, after a gruesome arteriogram, we know that I don't have
a benign tumor as the doctors felt quite sure, but instead they
turned up what probably is the root of my trouble—an occluded
artery in my neck which prevents the blood from reaching one
side of my brain. I leave on Friday for Rochester, New York, and
the Strong Memorial Hospital, presumably to have an operation
[. . .] so please keep your fingers crossed for me, and consider
that this report is good news. I *hope* your news is good.

Much love,
Katharine

[SEPTEMBER 1961]

Dear Katharine,
I do consider your news good, though I am distressed to find
you still in the hands of the doctors. I hope by now all is well. You
have been in my thoughts and prayers.
We have been having October's bright blue weather all of September, and I could not get about with the hose in time to keep

some things from drying up. The leaves are fading without coloring, but the Korean daisies and the British Soldiers (*Lycoris radiata*) are fresh and gay. If you haven't the Korean daisy I must send you some, sometime.

I enclose a butterfly lily, hoping that the scent will linger until it gets to you. It always delights me to have such a tropical scent and such an exotic flower blooming in the garden after the furnace is needed to keep the house warm.

Later

I thought this had been sent but found it unfinished along with an already addressed envelope—when I was searching my desk for scotch tape. My filing system has completely broken down, and I am in confusion and despair.

I send the unfinished letter along with a fresh butterfly lily, and more love.

Affectionately,
Elizabeth Lawrence

OCTOBER 18, 1961

Dear Elizabeth,

I have been long in thanking you for your note and the enclosed sweet spidery butterfly lily. I've been to Rochester and had the operation and have survived, although I went into shock and almost died in the recovery room after it. I was there for hours with a very low blood pressure but a transfusion brought me back. I'm in New York now on my way back to Maine. The operation was a success, supposedly, and although I still feel quite weird, at least I am no longer dizzy. Whether I get over the headaches enough to be able to write and to garden is still an open question. [. . .] My plan is to get home and not even *think* about garden catalogues or books for a month. If eventually I find I can't write as well as I did before, I don't want to do it at all.

[. . .]

Maine has had frosts and snow so I suppose the garden will be bare. The *Strelitzia Reginae,* which last year at this time was full of flower stalks, has none. I've neglected the feeding.

Much love,
Katharine

[DECEMBER 1961]

Dear Katharine,

[. . .]

You need not worry about being able to write whatever you want to, when you feel like undertaking it. Anyone who writes a letter like yours can write anything.

I enclose a flower and a leaf of *Cyclamen neapolitanum* and of *C. europaeum.* I am afraid the flowers will not be fresh enough to show any difference in form or color, but the leaves are distinct. The leaf of *C. neapolitanum* is the first, and does not show its mature size and marking.

[. . .]

I hope you are back in North Brooklin, and that the headaches are gone, and Andy all right.

With love and all good wishes,
Affectionately,
Elizabeth Lawrence

[DECEMBER 1961]
Merry Christmas from Katharine and E. B. White

Dear Elizabeth,

A real letter to you, with thanks for the hardy cyclamen samples, has been one of my projects for weeks. In fact I dictated a letter to you ten days ago but it sounded so unlike me that I didn't mail it. I've been having a bad time so far as health goes but now I do have two or three days of feeling well before there comes a setback. It's just a matter of patience and time, I guess. My *C. neapolitanum* bloomed nicely in October; it has been mislabeled *europaeum*. On Dec. 11 I picked a bowl full of Clear Crystals pansies—blue, mahogany, and red—so you see our fall has been wonderfully prolonged. Now we are under snow. The Christmas rose has no buds and looks ill. Perhaps this isn't the climate for hellebores?

Much love to you and a happy New Year. I hope your mother is no worse.
Katharine

[DECEMBER 1961]

Dear Katharine,

The postman has just dropped your card through the mail slot. Your writing on the envelope was a welcome sight. [. . .]

I feel sure that the hellebores will love your garden, but it does take them time to get settled, and they often go backward instead of forward the second year.

When I send you Lenten roses in the spring, I shall send you a start of my cyclamen. I thought my yard man had demolished most of them when he ripped out the long runners of *Robinia Kelseyi,* a lovely thing that I should never have planted in a small garden. Each year I thought I would wait until it bloomed one more time before getting rid of it, and then I hadn't the heart to do it. And now I find that lots of the cyclamen is coming up. I even found a seedling in another part of the garden.

This has been a mild before-Christmas winter. More than a dozen things were in bloom in my garden yesterday, and even after ice in the bird-bath and a beautiful white frost, the snowdrops are unharmed, and so is the wintersweet and the clematis and the one little crocus that the chipmunks have spared.

I have been getting letters from all over the country about the things in bloom in December.

[...]

I do hope you will continue to feel better.

Aff,
Elizabeth Lawrence

Part Two

"A TENDER LEAF OF HOPE"

1962–1968

Sometimes, in January, I find something new in bloom every time I go into the garden and even when there is no new flower, I find a tender leaf of hope.

Gardens in Winter, ELIZABETH LAWRENCE

The letters in this section reflect a seasoned friendship that survived personal difficulties, dashed hopes, and long silences, but also included triumphant recovery. Elizabeth's book on winter gardens was finally published; Katharine was able to finish another column. Each woman praised the other's achievement with more open expressions of affection, and, often, humor lightened their days.

Then during the winter of 1963–64 Katharine was hit with her most debilitating illness, an outbreak of a terrible skin disease. For three years she was unable to submit a single garden column. Elizabeth's mother continued to decline, and her death in the summer of 1964 left Elizabeth, now sixty years old, living alone for the first time. The letters, however, show a resilience that enabled both women to keep hoping to do new work and to make plans finally to meet each other in person. That occasion took place at lunch in New York City in April 1967, a "nervous moment" that apparently was in some way disap-

pointing. Afterward, there were months of no letters. When they began writing to one another again, however, they glossed over the silence, and their conversation in letters seemed to take on increased intellectual energy, even as their physical energy waned. Katharine had fun writing a long and lively piece on the history—and sometimes the absurdity—of flower arrangements. Elizabeth had important new publications, each of which she credited to Katharine's having spoken so highly of her in her New Yorker *pieces. It was good to be recognized, Elizabeth reported; even her rector had read about her in Mrs. White's column.*

JUNE 5, 1962

Dear Elizabeth,

I have been thinking of you even though I haven't written and I am worrying about you, too, for fear, in the months I haven't heard or haven't written, your mother might have become worse. I do hope that all goes well with you and hope, too, that you are getting enough freedom of mind to work on your next book.

If I had had time, I would have preferred to ask you your impression of Buckner Hollingsworth's new book.* I have just given it a short review in an "Upward and Onward in the Garden" piece that will come out in *The New Yorker* this week. Buckner is an old friend of mine, was in college with me at Bryn Mawr, and of late years we have been corresponding. The horror to me is to have to review the book with less than great enthusiasm. This horror, in case you don't know about her, is compounded by the fact that she is now practically totally blind. I really did not think that the book was a very good book, but having made so much fuss about receiving a review copy and thinking it had some merits and would be of interest to many, I felt I had to write about it, rather than not reviewing it. Friendship, or blindness, can't enter

Her Garden Was Her Delight (Macmillan, 1962).

into honesty in reviews. But I did have the horrors and if I have done her, in your opinion, an injustice, I would be dreadfully sorry. I detected many small errors in fact but made no mention of them. What I'm suffering over now is whether it would have been kinder to skip a review entirely. Maybe if I had read it alongside Geoffrey Taylor, I would have liked it better. One of my problems was that she sent me the proofs of the Gertrude Jekyll section and asked for my comments. It was shot through with errors of fact which I pointed out, and I think some of them are in there, at least by omission, still. She hates the woman, and I don't, which is another problem. Therefore, it was embarrassing to me to have Buckner in her acknowledgments thank me for having helped her on that particular chapter. But such is life—if one is an editor, reviewer, or even a writer with opinions, one is bound to hurt people and make enemies. I daresay that Mr. Burpee will refuse to send me his catalogue from here on out, just as that crazy rose man in Oregon* did. Anyway, as you will see, the piece this time has almost no gardening information in it—far less than I had intended because the deadline was suddenly moved up a month. [. . .] It was a dreadful effort to get anything down on paper and I persisted, perhaps only to prove to myself that I could. I am ever so much better than I was, but still have my bad days and my strength does not last very long—either at my desk or in the garden. We are having a bad drought, nevertheless have had beautiful bulbs in flower. I was also pleased that the Lenten Rose survived the winter and bloomed.

I am wondering what you are writing your next book about. I look forward to it eagerly.

So far this has been a dictated letter as you can easily detect. [The following is handwritten by KSW.] My dear daughter-in-law [Allene White] comes in one morning a week to help Andy

*Roy Hennessey.

and me on letters and typing. I have a whole year's work to catch up on. We went to Florida for two months and these warm weeks worked wonders for me; instead of being an invalid with breakfast in bed and a whole afternoon of sleep, I'm now back to being up and around all the time, though I still can't write well or easily or really bear down on desk work. This was why, when my *New Yorker* deadline was moved up, so the piece could run before the long Rachel Carson series on poison sprays, etc., I couldn't cover half what I had intended to. Of course I had to skip spring catalogues entirely as I was not well enough to turn in a piece by Feb. 1st, so what it mostly turned out to be was the usual *New Yorker* memory piece stuff, which I had not intended to preempt the news on catalogues.

By the way, don't miss those Carson pieces. They are part of a book and too long for a weekly magazine, but the facts she gathered ought to stir up a hornet's nest among the chemists and horticulturists. (Our county agent sends us weekly bulletins about spraying the weeds in our lawn with dieldrin. This kills off all robins, who die in convulsions after eating the worms that have eaten dieldrin and chlordane. And we have almost *no* bees this year—all killed in the blueberry barrens, by the poison dusts and sprays.) The Carson series starts in the issue of June 15.* I know you will want to read it.

I've just finished the biography of "Elizabeth" of the German garden, by Leslie de Charms. I wish I'd read it before I wrote even that paragraph about her a year and more ago, but I enjoyed the book greatly.

This letter is dull and already too long. I will only add the item that my hardy water lilies did survive the winter in our shallow pasture pond. Whether they'll survive our dachshund is another

---

*Carson's *Silent Spring* was first published in three installments in *The New Yorker*, beginning in the June 15, 1962, issue. The book was published by Houghton Mifflin in September 1962.

matter. Whenever he gets hot he goes off by himself and swims in the pond. Andy saw him emerging from one such lonely swim this week bearing proudly in his mouth a lily pad. Or it could have been a lily *bud*. It's our own fault; when he swims with us at the shore we throw sticks for him to retrieve and I suppose habit made him feel he should bring back some trophy. I see little hope for *Nymphaea odorata*!

I can't help wishing that it was *you* who had written about the women gardeners.

Affectionately,
Katharine

P.S. Our dear Mrs. Freethy, the friend and neighbor of thirty years, who had been our cook for the past eleven years, died last month. Her illness and death were one of the reasons I didn't get going faster on writing that garden piece. We are still in a state of turmoil domestically. And in the garden it's the same. The boy who cut our grass and lugged water for the past three summers is now in the Navy, learning to be a submarine electronic engineer. Time and friends grow up or pass too fast at my age.

[JUNE 1962]

Dear Katharine,

I was so happy to find your letter in the mail. I have kept up with you through Mr. Ranger, who wrote that you were home, and better, and doing another "Onward and Upward." *The New Yorker* came the next day, and the piece is wonderful. I took it to Hannah Withers who was equally pleased, and is even more indignant than you over Mrs. H's [Buckner Hollingsworth's] portrait of Miss Jekyll. I feel sure that most authors would consider that you had given *Her Garden Was Her Delight* a very good review. [. . .] We both think Mrs. H. would have done a better job to leave Miss Jekyll and Mrs. Loudon out, and to have put in two other American women—Mrs. Wilder, for example. Hannah was so pleased over your devotion to Hedrick. [. . .] She said, "That's what I like about Mrs. White, she likes all the books I like."

[. . .]

My mother continues to go downhill very slowly. She gets more weary and I get more depressed. I am not taking on any new clients for a while, but I have to help old ones, and friends, and that and the garden and my column and the nursing leave me little time or strength to concentrate on writing. I don't see how you do what you do . . . or rather I do see. You are better disciplined.

Mary's husband, who is as good as she is, has been helping me in the garden when his boss-man doesn't require him on his afternoon off, but I can't turn him loose, and even standing beside him could not prevent his pulling up a hellebore—a rare one—that was just getting established. Mary was in *another* dreadful accident, and no one knows how she came out of it alive. A Davey Tree truck, a heavy one, ran into her while she had stopped for a light, and threw her into the path of two oncoming cars. She says a voice said "Mary, move over," and she did and that was why she wasn't crushed between the seat and the wheel. But she was in the hospital and at home for weeks and weeks, and then had a bad time getting adjusted to work again, and still has trouble with her back and leg. She has a very fine Negro doctor who encourages her to go on working, but she goes to pieces and so do I. I still do a third of the nursing [. . .] as I can't afford to have a third nurse all the time, and have found no one else who is willing to take over for a short time. They come by the week, or not at all, and are above filling in. Ada lived nearby, and had a car, and was an old friend, so she was glad to help me out. So I truly sympathize with your loss of Mrs. Freethy.

I was so interested in what you said about bamboos.* Would you like me to send you a root of mine? It is the one that Elsie Hassan grows in Ohio, though the government people said they could not name it for me. Elsie says hers has come through that zero weather last winter—though, of course, it suffered.

[. . .]

My book is a sort of medley—more of the same—about my friends in person and in books—especially "Elizabeth" [von Arnim] of whom I have written so much in my column as well as in my books. No one else has ever written of gardens as she has— it must have been hard to be her child or her husband or servant, but they all seem to have adored her. It was only her lovers who got the upper hand.

[. . .]

I am a non-sprayer. Too lazy, and using poisons scares me stiff. We find dead and dying birds every summer when the DDT wagon makes its round. But we also have fewer flies and bugs.

Let me know if you still want your hellebores. And if you know how hardy the chinquapin rose is. But don't bother to tell me, if the answer is no.

Aff,
Elizabeth Lawrence

JUNE 25, 1962

Dear Elizabeth,

I always feel at peace if *you* like one of my garden pieces, so your letter was a great comfort and joy, except for the depressing news about your mother. I suppose you may soon have to make the agonizing decision whether or not to put her in a nursing home or hospital. I went through that particular hell when my

*In her 6/9/62 column, KSW discussed the hardiness of bamboo in cold climates.

ninety-two-year-old aunt came to live with us for good, after my sister, Rosamond, who lived in Sarasota, died. [. . .] I do feel, though, that it is wrong for a younger person to lose her health and stop her work in order to care for someone who no longer gets anything out of having the younger person there. This probably is not so yet with your mother. Anyway, I am so sorry, dear Elizabeth. Every case is different and please do not think I would presume to suggest what you should do.

[. . .]

I would love to have the hellebore plant or plants if you can spare it or them. I don't think I should try bamboo this year—not until I figure where to put the thicket. I've recently discovered there is a clump just down the road hiding an outhouse, so perhaps I could get my root from there early next spring. The garden was a mess when I left—no rain just when we were transplanting annuals. I dread going back to it especially as I seem to have picked up sciatica in New York and will find working in a garden difficult.

[. . .]

Affectionately,
Katharine

P.S. I hope you're reading the Rachel Carson pieces, grim as they are.

JULY 3 [1962]

Dear Katharine,

I put the little Nandina seedling in with the hellebores, and a nice root of Ivy Fleur de lis that came up with the Nandina.

Promise you won't bother with these if they come at an inconvenient time. More will be forthcoming.

I remember you said you wished Mr. Ranger wouldn't bother

you with ideas—so I try not to—but Ellen (Flood) sent me such an interesting brochure on organic gardening. It costs a dollar —but I'm sure he'll be only too glad to send it free—and comes from the Brookside Nurseries, Darien, Connecticut. Ellen went there to a demonstration, and was entranced with everything but the garbage compost. She says it *does* smell.

I wrote about *Silent Spring*, and I shall write again. I am also trying to see that everyone reads *The New Yorker*.

Thank you for your sympathy and concern. I am getting on better. I may come to the nursing home, as we continuously go beyond our income this way—but it would be much harder for me to have my mother there. My sister has taken a job for next winter, as she has two children in school next year. That will make it difficult, too.

I hope you are better. I know I had more to say, but I can't find your letter. I didn't file it, and there is no telling what pile it is under.

Aff,

Elizabeth Lawrence

P.S. Fuzz says she will mail the plants for me.

JULY 13, 1962

Dear Elizabeth,

[. . .] The plants arrived in perfect shape and by some miracle Henry and I got them into the ground on a foggy, cloudy day. They've been watered constantly since then and look well. We are in the midst of what the paper calls the worst drought in ten years. Every time I water, I wonder whether the spring, which has never failed, will fail this time. We don't dare water the big vegetable garden so the peas are drying up on the vines and nothing grows. Mostly it's been sun, sun, sun but also we're way behind because the spring was so late.

I put the Nandina against the east side of the gray-shingled garage and shop. I fear it may not winter here but it will be fun to try it and with winter protection I hope it will live. It is wonderful to have the Hellebores, and the Ivy fleur de lis now growing in a big terra rossa pot filled with petunias on the terrace; I shall bring it indoors next winter. I'm ignorant on ivies. This one would not be hardy here, would it?

I cherish *ideas* more than anything, especially from you. What I said about Mr. Ranger must have been written in a pet when he sold me on buying an expensive book on old roses, which turned out to be only one in a series of which the remainder is unavailable. [. . .]

This is a poor letter but I'll send it for there may be no chance to write a better one.

Ever gratefully,
Katharine

NEW YORK
AUGUST 6, 1962

Dear Elizabeth,

[. . .] Today [Andy] turned in the page proofs of his fall book.* Working on them has been what I've been doing mostly. My hopes of doing a brief garden piece for late August or early September have been defeated and I suppose the garden itself has suffered by my absence. When I left home your plants all seemed to be doing nicely. The only garden news I've had is that our biggest, most important clematis vine on the terrace windbreak shows sign of "clematis wilt." What *is* clematis wilt? And what does one do for it? This is our third attack in this location. The first time it struck, I dug up the vine, burned it, and changed

---

The Points of My Compass (Harper and Row, 1962), a collection of *New Yorker* essays from the preceding seven years.

the soil. Then I read in one of the reference books that all one needed to do was to cut off the vine at the ground and it would come up again. So I did this earlier this year on a new vine that turned brown. Now it looks to me like something contagious. Is it a fungus? I can't remember. Or is it another name for nematodes, or what? Maybe I'd better just get home fast and apply sugar or a nice sweet rice pudding! [...]

I met Mary Ellen Flood in the halls yesterday, looking thin and pretty and happy. Nice to see her.

Aff'y,
Katharine

P.S. Home—And a quick look at the gardens makes me realize how badly they have suffered from two summers of neglect. The long north border has very little bloom. But the sun has been absent for two and a half months.

[AUGUST, 1962]

Dear Katharine,

I'm sorry the plants came in the drought. They left in cool, showery weather. I didn't suppose you were ever dry or hot. Don't fool with them. I can always send more in the fall—I don't expect the nandina to live—but I love to send things North. That is what we had—but I don't want to worry you. I doubt whether the ivy is hardy—but if you want to try it, I can always send more.

Elsie Hassan says that only one miniature rose has proved hardy in Ohio—*Leprechaun*, I think—so they are not likely to be hardy with you.

Joseph Mitchell's sisters were here last week. Linda Lamm says she bought *Her Garden Was Her Delight* after reading your review. They came to their niece's wedding. Each bridesmaid carried an enormous, *absolutely perfect* magnolia. I don't know how they did it. Magnolias turn brown if you even *look* at them.

[. . .]

Aff,
Elizabeth Lawrence

P.S. Linda loved the "Onward and Upward."

We get sprayed regularly with DDT—our small lot, 225′ deep, gets it *twice*, front and back in one night. I have all the symptoms of DDT poisoning: "extreme irritability—great distaste for work of any sort—a feeling of mental incompetence in tackling the simplest mental task—the joint pains are quite violent at times." I forgot to look in *The Gardener's Bug Book* to see about the clematis wilt. If you want to fumigate there is a whole paragraph—Nemafume, Dowfume, Soilfume, etc.! I thought you would be interested in the sugar cure—see page 3. Please return the Bulletin for my files. I try to join a new society each year, to write about in my column. The Boxwood Society is the newest! *The Daffodil Year Book* is excellent. Some of the best people are writing for it.

AUGUST 11, 1962

[Dear Katharine,]

The wilt is caused by a nematode, and as far as I know there is nothing to be done about it, that you have not done already.

The thing is, good culture-healthy plants don't succumb. [. . .] My system is to grow only what shows.

I hope the luck has now changed. I know how you feel about the garden.

Aff,
E.L.

AUGUST 23, 1962

Dear Elizabeth,

I was very much interested in the sugar nematode control and have sent the Daffodil bulletin to the office to have this section copied for me. It ties in with clippings I have from the *Times,* which I was saving as a follow-up on the rice pudding anecdote in case I ever get these garden pieces into a book. (This prospect looks more and more remote.) I also am interested in trying sugar on my own vines. When the copy is made I shall promptly return the bulletin. In any case I can't complain too much as two Mme. Baron Veillard vines are in full bloom and Mrs. Cholmondley has just stopped flowering. The Mrs. Robert Brydon vines with its little pale blue flowers are in wild bloom but one of them and a Montana have to be uprooted, together with everything else in one third of my south bed by the house, so we can put in a new plastic pipe to our spring to replace the 330 feet of copper pipe that has been four-foot underground for over thirty years. (The hazards of life in the country!) There's a strong suspicion that we are drinking too much copper for our own good and our water turns aquamarine the instant one uses soap. Even the highway has to be torn up for the pipe and I can see that all our extra resources are going to have to go into this disagreeable project instead of into new wallpaper and chintz so badly needed for the living room.

I worry about you and DDT. I took your note on your symptoms as humorous but perhaps you meant it as deadly serious. I admit to most of the same symptoms. [. . .]

Aff'y,
Katharine
[. . .]

P.S. I have a quotation from a letter received today from Mrs. Lockwood de Forest: "How about working into a garden piece some time a despairing wail at the death of good horticultural writing today in this country? Elizabeth Lawrence shines out like a planet; I know of no one else!" How true, I say, and I hope I can say so sometime. *You* can't! I am also fascinated by the discovery that the Encyclopedia Britannica in our old 14th edition seems to have entirely skipped mention of England's great horticulturists and horticultural writers. I haven't made a very thorough check yet but I have it in mind to for the future. I couldn't find the Loudons or Wm. Robinson or some of the plant explorers. Possibly the newer editors have caught up on it. Haven't checked that yet either.

[SEPTEMBER 1962]

Dear Katharine,

[. . .]

I am distressed to hear your ills added to. *I* should never complain, being just no-account. I can't blame my aches and pains on DDT—or my laziness—I had it all before the sprayer went round. But I was told that the death of some children in the eastern part of the state was due to the poison that the farmers sprayed—or dusted.

I also noticed the absence of horticulturists in one old *Britannica* (the eleventh ed.). When I looked up Parkinson, there was no John—but there was a paragraph on Parkersburg, West Virginia (where my grandmother lived), including the fact that it was the see of an Episcopal bishop. Devoted as I am to the memory of Bishop Peterkin, I would rather read about Parkinson.

[. . .]

I hope this will find you better.

Aff,
Elizabeth Lawrence

OCTOBER 3, 1962

[Dear Katharine,]

I have at last got the long-sought Bailey, *How Plants Got Their Names*—and find it very disappointing. The list of specific names I have already in the Cyclopedia, and the text—much of it out of date—is not what I thought it would be. If you haven't found a copy, I'd be glad to let you see mine. [. . .]

[Aff, Elizabeth Lawrence]

NEW YORK

OCTOBER 13, 1962

Dear Elizabeth,

I feel guilty about that Liberty Hyde Bailey book on plant names. I didn't realize you also wanted to have it or I'd have told you that I found a copy many months back and found it as disappointing as you did. I could have sent you the book. I'm right where I was, just as you are.

We are here in New York for the same dreary old reasons of health—mostly mine this time—and more tests, tests, tests. After last fall's operation I slowly improved up to June, then slowly and lately not so slowly, ran down hill, with some manifestations disturbingly like those I had before the artery block was removed. It may not be that, though. I'll let you know how it turns out. In any case I haven't even been able to think of writing a garden piece or getting to work on that mythical book. I ought to know soon whether I ever can and if I can't, it will be a job to throw out all the stuff I've been saving. Any really good tidbits you will have, if you want them. [. . .]

I came off having planted only my daffodils, hyacinths, and little bulbs. It was too warm and early to put in tulips and I'm hoping to get home in time to do that. Both your hellebores were doing well—also the nandina. Henry and I (I merely sitting and pointing) remade one long border entirely and thinned out the other. Our next to last day at home Hurricane Daisy, combined with another storm, hit us and we had terrible destruction, especially around the spring which is our water supply. We weren't in the eye of the hurricane but it did more damage than either of the two hurricanes that hit us squarely. Much of the summer had been devoted, at great cost, to changing the 300 feet of pipe to the spring, with a backhoe causing much upheaval of soil and ground, so the three hackmatacks that were uprooted in the woods leaving huge holes filled up with surface clay, silt and mud, and the water when we left was unusable—black mud. What a mess! We hear that it is clear again and it has been chlorinated but now we must reforest, to hold the soil and the precious rivulets of water. Two weeks earlier we had finally managed to get a Bangor tree surgeon to come and tend to our lawn trees and at that time we'd had to make the heartbreaking decision to cut down the two ancient Balm of Gilead trees which were the chief beauty of the house yard. One was the coon tree.* It proved to be a hollow shell from top to bottom and it's lucky we did cut them both for the big wind would surely have laid them low, bashing in our roof or perhaps hitting a passing car on the highway and killing someone. As it was, a big limb was taken off our lawn oak. So now we look denuded—a row of maples and the oak by the hedge and road are left and two elms close to the house. We must plant trees later to take the place of the Balm of Gileads and are disputing about what sort of tree to plant. Andy wants B of Gs again. I rather favor maples or oaks. Whatever we choose must be something native to Maine.

I have a copy of Andy's new book [*The Points of My Compass*] for

---

*EBW wrote about the coon tree in a June 14, 1956, "Letter from the East" and returned to the subject in March 1962 to report that "the coon tree is still in business." Reprinted in *The Points of My Compass.*

you, so don't buy it. I'll send it along when we get home and he will write in it. It's due to be published this coming week. He dreads the reviews.

Much love,
Katharine

[DECEMBER 1962]

Dear Katharine,

I value your love as much as the book. Your affection has a quality that always touches me. I wrote to tell you that you must never let loose your notes and that I feel the book will go on with the new year. I was so relieved to see the Maine postmark, and hope you are safely out of the hands of the doctors.

I will mail this in haste for fear, like the last, it will not get mailed. I get more and more confused. The last crisis was the nurses—first one, then the other, and my sister's illness. Now that she is working, I not only haven't her to fall back on, but she falls back on me. Our family is like yours—we *all* struggle together.

I hope you are enough better to have a good Christmas.

Aff,
Elizabeth

SARASOTA, FLORIDA
JANUARY 25, 1963

Dear Elizabeth,

We're here at the old Sarasota address, and have been for nearly two weeks—two nightmare weeks, really. Andy has been so sick that he has had to turn over his backed up correspondence to me and has asked me to thank you for your note and the clipping from the *Charlotte Observer.** He was very much pleased by them both and by your reference to *The Points of My Compass*. He is happy that you like "the *little* book."† He would prefer to thank you himself for telling him so.

[…]

I am praying that the dreadful freeze Florida had did not destroy your precious trees, shrubs, and tender flowers. Here the destruction is terribly sad—I especially mourn the hibiscus, the coconut palms, and the Australian pines.

Affectionately,
Katharine

P.S. Later—Now the *new* cold weather. You must be in despair over your garden. I mourn for you. […] I'm praying we can stay here, for, cold or not, it is better than New England—for me, anyway.

MAY 17, 1963

Dear Elizabeth,

[…]

As we arrived last week, the first flowers I spotted in bloom in my south border were two Hellebores; one was the Christmas rose, and was, I guess, my old one, only now able to blossom because of last winter's many feet of snow. A beautiful chartreuse and white one must have come from you. Is it the Lenten rose or another kind, I wonder? Two others you sent me are alive but not blossoming. Your charming little ivy is now quite a plant

---

*In her column (1/6/63) EL, who had cleared out a nest of sparrows from under the eaves, reported that she found it "comforting" that EBW had written about his enemy the fox in *The Points of My Compass*.
†*The Elements of Style* (Macmillan, 1959), EBW's revised edition of the forty-three-page writing handbook by William Strunk, Jr., his Cornell teacher, whom EBW remembered in his introduction as having admonished his students, "Get the *little* book!"

having been tended all winter in the house and I wish I knew its name. As for the Nandina, I thought it had died but a second look showed it there, cut down almost to the ground, but sending out new pink shoots. By the looks of it, it should never have been cut back so drastically. The absentee gardener is no gardener! [. . .]

I received through the New Yorker's clipping service your review of *The Great Flower Books* and thought it was awfully good. I only wish I had done as well. It was noble of you to mention my having written about the book earlier but utterly unnecessary. [. . .]

We had a couple inches more snow on May 13th, since our arrival, but on the whole I think things have come through pretty well. My daffodils are a glory right now and hyacinths and some of the early little tulips are in bloom but the rest of the landscape is still fairly wintry. Scillas still blossom.

I haven't been able to write a word this winter. My dear daughter-in-law is helping me write this, because I have bursitis in my right shoulder added to my other troubles. Probably I'll never write another garden piece but I have not quite given up yet, nor tossed out all the files. I do think I've lost ground but not on one big point. I fooled the vascular surgeon who thought I would need an operation on my blocked femoral artery in my left leg this spring. Instead I rerouted myself and walked so faithfully while in Florida that I have less pain walking and can walk further than last fall. However, the same thing is now starting in my right leg. The arteries to the brain still flow well, thanks to that operation of nearly two years ago, but *I* find my brain doesn't work as well as it did. Not that I can't think clearly or remember but I can't keep at writing for any length of time or write *well*. This may be nerves entirely and then again it may not be. I have too many anxieties just now to be sure.

Katharine always enjoyed visits from her children and grandchildren. Here are two who lived just down the road, Martha and Steven, children of Katharine and Andy's son, Joel, and his wife, Allene. Katharine loved baseball, and sometimes she took her turn at bat.

Katharine's front yard border supplied the flowers that she arranged for the house, a "magic show" Andy described in his introduction to *Onward and Upward in the Garden*.

Katharine White in a 1940s photograph that was later used to publicize *Onward and Upward in the Garden.*

Joseph Mitchell, native North Carolinian, *New Yorker* writer, and friend of Katharine White and Elizabeth Lawrence, in 1993. Elizabeth designed a garden for Mitchell's sister in Wilson, North Carolina.

I do hope your complex household and *your* great anxieties are not preventing you from working.

Affectionately always,
Katharine White

P.S. Do you know Peter Taylor—a writer I admire? He is moving to Greensboro and will next year teach at the U. of N.C. but only a little, and have his mornings free to write. He is a person I like as well as admire, and he has been weighed down by too much teaching to write as much as he should.

MAY 1963

Dear Katharine,

How happy I am to see your handwriting on the envelope. I have worried about you, and wanted to write to thank you for suggesting that I do the [Gertrude Jekyll] anthology for Miss Parker,* but I am always afraid to write for fear you will tax yourself trying to reply. I couldn't do the anthology, but Miss Parker is doing it herself, and it will give me the greatest pleasure, as you know, to do the introduction.

The chartreuse and white hellebore is the Lenten rose, Mr. Krippendorf's hybrid. I am so pleased that you got such a good one as there is great variation, and some forms are rather washed out. I hope the other two do as well. I'm sorry I don't remember which Ivy I sent, but I enclose Needlepoint and Fleur de lis as the most likely. Don't you think it was the cold, not the gardener, that cut back the nandina, but if it is root-hardy it will be good for foliage, and it wouldn't berry anyway.

[. . .]

My morning was completely wasted by a woman who arrived

On Gardening (Scribner's, 1964). Elinor Parker was the unnamed editor. Reprinted as *The Gardener's Essential Gertrude Jekyll* (David R. Godine Publisher, 1986).

and asked to see the garden. I told her I was working, but she stayed more than an hour. I gladly gave her plants, addresses and information, but could not but grudge the time. I often think of Miss Jekyll's pathetic preface to *Home and Garden,* in which she begs people not to come to see her. She was so severely and un-justly criticized for it. But at least Miss Jekyll had a big place and all those devoted servants to protect her, and I often look up and see some stranger outside my studio window waving gaily.

I don't know Peter Taylor, but would like to if you admire him, both personally and to read.

I must stop, as Elizabeth* is ready to get Mother up. I was cheered by your escaping the operation, and hope that the next report will be that you are able to write. I am sure that you imag-ine that you don't write well—I need only your letters to prove that, and you have plenty of company among those who find they cannot keep at it long. I, who am in rude health (except for aller-gies, rheumatism and trouble with my eyes) feel exactly as you do —both ways.

I hope E. B. is better, and tell him in my war with editors I comfort myself with the Little Book.

Aff,
Elizabeth Lawrence

[DECEMBER 1963]

Dear Katharine,

    [. . .]

Things go along sadly here. Poor Ivey had to give up, and I had to get used to another nurse, but I am glad to have anyone who is faithful—she is—and colored nurses are so kind.

    [. . .]

---

*A nurse who came to help EL after Ivey and Mary had retired.

I have finally finished the book I have been working on all this time—but it still has things to be done to it. I miss "Onward and Upward," and so does everyone else. Please get back in print.

Affectionately,
Elizabeth Lawrence

NOVEMBER 18, 1964

Dear Elizabeth,

The publishers have sent me a copy of the Gertrude Jekyll anthology. I have not had time to more than skim the selections but I read your graceful preface with delight in every word of it. It is such a pleasure to have a really informed appreciation of Miss Jekyll [. . .] and I was charmed by the writing and marveled at how much you had done in so few words. At only a quick glance I found myself slightly disappointed by the anthology itself, wishing that more could have been included. Somehow the drama of *Wood and Garden* and *Home and Garden* got lost and I would gladly have settled for smaller print, a less handsome book, and more Jekyll text. Also pictures of Miss J and the Munstead garden. But this may be unfair. I take it that you did not make the selection? It would be dreadful for me to write this if you had!

The past year has been such a nightmare for me and my files are in such disorder, thanks to my bad health, that I have no idea when I last heard from you or when I last wrote you. My last *filed* letter from you is May, 1963! I also have very little memory of 1964 because I was so sick for much of the year and taking so many drugs. I only know now that I seem to know nothing about you— not even whether your mother is still alive. I can only pray that she is better and that you yourself are as well as you sound in that preface and hope that life has not been too hard and too sad for you. Will you write me just a word on this so I'll know before we start South from New York around Dec. 10? We shall be heading for Beaufort, S.C., where we expect to spend five or six weeks in a boarding house (though in a cottage of our own) to stay till the end of January when we go on to Sarasota again and (we hope) for two months in the same rented house there. [. . .] (I have promised Andy and my doctors not to send a single Xmas card or wrap a single gift.) But I believe the whole trouble got set up by the shock of Kennedy's assassination, a year ago this week. I still can't bear a world without him.

There's just a chance—I admit a rather dim chance—that I shall drive with Andy to Beaufort and that if I should, our journey might take us rather near Charlotte. If it were cold or snowy, we'd go the shore route. If we did, though, happen to be near Charlotte and could drop in for a brief call, would this be at all possible for you?

[. . .]

I probably did tell you what happened to me but I'll repeat in case I never did. Two days after Xmas I burst out with a weird and dreadful dermatitis and was flown to the N.Y. hospital where I stayed two weeks in January. The skin trouble was misdiagnosed then, was suppressed with a cortisone drug, and I eventually got to Sarasota the end of January. After four icy weeks there I was flown back to the hospital and incarcerated for nine weeks more, with special nurses around the clock and very high fevers and a very tortured time of it. This time they discovered what the trouble was—a rare skin disease with a horrible name [subcorneal pustular dermatosis], known mostly in Europe. But the correct diagnosis did little good for the only cure is sulfa and I am allergic to sulfa. They gave me some just the same and induced a real drug allergy this time on top of the other trouble. I blistered all over and lost my entire skin. The worst thing, though, was the huge doses of prednisone (cortisone) which were worse than the dermatosis. I have had every conceivable bad side effect. [. . .]

Elsie [. . .] is now, alas, in a nursing home outside of the city.

[. . .] Every bit of my time and strength has had to go into getting her house emptied and her books, papers, and family possessions dispersed except the ones she has with her at the nursing home. She is at least still surrounded by the best pieces of old family furniture.

[. . .]

My garden was neglected yet full of bloom. Your hellebores all lived—two bloomed beautifully. Even the nandina, which I thought was winterkilled last year, came back. It's not only flourishing; the drought this fall will be bad for everything. We buried the terrace hybrid roses today but up till then I've had roses to pick every day. A frostbitten pitcherful is now on the living room table. Up till two days ago we had Nelly Moses clematis in bloom. But tonight we have snow.

Are you—I hope—writing a book? Forgive this far too long letter (those drugs!) and it's also too full of my own troubles. I haven't time to do it over so I'll send it along, for better or worse. What I really want to know is how *you* are, and your mother.

Affectionately, your unknown correspondent
Katharine

[NOVEMBER 23, 1964]

Dear Katharine,

Your letter has just come and I hasten to assure you about the anthology. Miss Parker wrote that you had suggested that I do it, but I told her I did not have time, so she did it herself. I agree with you on every count, but this is between us; I am so pleased to have *any*thing of Miss Jekyll's back in print. I am so grateful to you for suggesting that I do the introduction as nothing has ever given me more pleasure. I think (and hope) I wrote to thank you at the time.

The last time you wrote to me was just after Mr. Kennedy's

death, and we think alike about that too. I did not know you had been so ill, but I was afraid you were not well when I did not hear from you. I was not waiting to hear in order to write, but I knew that if I did you would feel you must answer, and I did not want to add a grasshopper to your burdens. I do hope you will come this way on your way South, and I hope you can spend at least a night with me. My mother died this summer, and I'm all alone, and have a guest room and bath all ready for you. Also room for the Cooks if they are along. I didn't quite understand about them.*

I am going to stop so I can mail this as I go out to do an errand, and I'll write to *The New Yorker* too, in case this misses you.

Aff,
Elizabeth Lawrence

NOVEMBER 24, 1964
Tuesday (I *think*—as Caroline Dormon says)

Dear Katharine,

I wrote so hurriedly yesterday I am not sure what I said, and what I left for this letter. I am so distressed by your illness and your sister's, and as you know, no one can sympathize with you more over your sister's being in a nursing home, but it sounds as if she were very fortunate in the one she is in, and perhaps she would not know it if she were with some of her family. The same thing happened to my great-grandmother, who would say over and over, "Please take me home," and would not believe us when we told her she was already there.

I am so glad you are going to Beaufort. I think it is (or was?) the dearest part of the Low Country, and I love all of the Low Country. I have always wished I had been born there in one of the sleepy little towns that my father's people came from. We almost

---

*The Whites usually employed a Maine woman to do the cooking and housekeeping in Florida, and this year Ethylyn Cook and her husband were joining them.

went to Beaufort to live once, and were always sorry that it didn't work out. The Lawrences came from Hilton Head and some of them are buried in the churchyard at St. Helena's. My father said it gave him a shock when walking among the graves to find his name on one of them, but then (he said) he looked again, and found "Wife of" written above it, so he felt better.

I had written Miss Parker to ask if she had sent you a copy of Miss Jekyll, as I wanted to send you one if she hadn't. I was waiting to hear, and then I meant to write to tell you that I had been rereading your *New Yorker* articles, while searching for what you had said about Miss Jekyll (and found I remembered correctly that it was you who first suggested the anthology), and was impressed anew by how good they are. I do hope you will soon be well enough to get back to "Onward and Upward" and the book. I was interrupted here by the postman with a large carton of plants from Heatherfells, with rare hellebores, and *Adonis amurensis* for which Mr. Krippendorf and I searched for so many years. I have only one plant of the *Adonis*, which he sent me when we first came here, and then we could never find another source. (Mr. and Mrs. Krippendorf died this spring, within two weeks of each other, and not long before my Mother's death. They were all about the same age.) Just to think of putting plants out in this welcome but chilly drizzle makes my poor old bones ache.

Thank you for the garden notes which are always valuable to me. Hearing that the nandina had survived reminded me again of the lavender I saw on the coast of Maine. My files are my main problem—mostly on the floor—but I still manage to keep these valuable notes in place.

In case you did not get the letter to No. Brooklin, I am here alone, have room for you and anybody who is with you; will do my best to give you nourishment, though I have not got that department very well organized. My mother always looked after the kitchen. I am the bartender. Anyway I can imagine nothing nicer than having you stay with me as long as you will. Or will be grateful for any amount of time. Only let me know so I can give you a bowl of soup, at least.

Aff and love to you both,
Elizabeth Lawrence

[DECEMBER 1965]

Dear Katharine,

Next to getting the children safely home out of the air and off the highway (Fuzz is at the University of Colorado, and Chip has just got his commission in the Navy, and is on his way to the engineering school in California, and he *hopes* his next assignment will be Viet Nam), finding "Onward and Upward" again in *The New Yorker** has done the most to make my holidays happy. Caroline Dormon had just written to ask me whether the address of "darling Katharine White" is the same, as she wants to send you a review copy of her new book, *Natives Preferred,* and I had told her I did not know whether you were well enough to do any writing. I shall hastily send her the joyful news. It is a splendid piece. I loved reading about myself,† of course, but I loved every bit of it, and I looked and read all night. And I didn't know about *Garden Spice* and *Wild Pot-Herbs,* though Evelyn Way,‡ who teaches Latin and Greek at the University of Mississippi, had told me about the plants of the *Georgics.* I didn't find it dull, and I think Miss Abbe§ does appreciate the poetry (because of her translations) but I was somewhat disappointed as I was expecting something more

*After an absence of more than three years, KSW had resumed her garden piece in the 12/18/65 issue.
†KSW praised EL's introduction to *On Gardening* and compared her favorably to Gertrude Jekyll.
‡Sister of EL's brother-in-law.
§EL reviewed *The Plants of Virgil's Georgics (CO* 10/31/65) and praised its woodcuts by Elfriede Abbe, an illustrator in Cornell's Department of Botany.

scholarly, something like Martyn's *Virgil*,* but brought up to date. What I *do* like about it is having an index (which the scholarly works have not) and being able, when I want to know what Virgil said about a plant, to find the information I want without having to scramble through the whole of the *Georgics*. I wish she had done the *Aenaeid* and the *Georgics,* too.

Hannah Withers is as delighted as I am, and we are setting out for the bookstore. I am afraid you are going to prove to be very expensive reading.

I do hope you are as well as your writing sounds, and that you and E. B. are coming my way. I have lots of room and would love to have you stay with me.

Aff and with best wishes,
Elizabeth Lawrence

SARASOTA, FLORIDA
JANUARY 4, 1966

Dear Elizabeth,

Of all the letters I've received on my garden book review, yours, as always, meant the most to me. You were a dear to take time to write in the midst of the busy holidays that you had liked it. It was a poor thing in many ways and it made me miserable to read it in the magazine, if only because of a few passages that were bollixed up due to proof corrections by long distance phone (bad connections, etc.) while we were en route South. [. . .] The piece was of course not up to the earlier ones, but it was in a way a triumph for me to have done it at all after these years of silence and was only arrived at by terrible effort, an effort which I know only too well shows plainly. But I hope to go on and even to get at that book, once I write a few more chapters. So if dear Miss Dor-

---

*John Martyn had edited *The Georgics of Virgil,* in Latin with an English translation, first published in London in 1741.

mon wants to send me a review copy of her new book I would love to have it. I can't promise it will ever get reviewed but at least I hope it will. Lots of publishers and authors had to wait years for the books I covered in this last piece to be reviewed. A garden article devoted only to books isn't a good idea but I had this accumulation and in my rusty state and with my capacity of work at a typewriter limited now to a very short span, a review of books seemed the easiest way to start again, because I could do it in short takes.

I'm unhappy if I have done Miss Abbe an injustice on her book about the *Georgics.* All I meant was that I had hoped for some general sort of comment on Virgil's feeling for the natural world, and a more literary approach, or even a complete new translation with botanical and poetic comment instead of a series of translated excerpts relating only to plants. I can see it is very useful to a scholar like you who knows the *Georgics* well; I do not. I had a lot of Latin at school and took an extra course the year I stayed out of school before going to college, but at Bryn Mawr I switched to Greek. I should have shut up on Virgil.

We left home November 29 in a snowstorm and made our way south, avoiding NYC and travelling by slow stages, stopping off at my daughter's in Easton, Pa., for two nights and again for two nights in Yemassee [South Carolina] with our friend Joe Wearn. [. . .] Joe's wife [Susan Lyman Wearn] was my best friend in Brooklin, where the Wearns summer, and was a friend of my school days in Boston. We had Christmas with them last year in Yemassee. This last May, when they returned to Brooklin, she died of a heart attack the second day they were there. It was a dreadful shock and loss. She and Joe had been coming for dinner with us that very night. Thus this visit to Castle Hill Plantation was sad, but we were glad we stopped. Each time we make the drive South I long to stop over in Charlotte but the drive is now

so hard on Andy that I hesitate to ask him to add the extra miles.
[. . .] But someday we may surprise you and make it. I feel I
know little about you and your life and fear your mother may
have died. Perhaps you told me this but I don't have your letters
here and much of the past year is dim in my memory because of
all the drugs I still have to take for my various disabilities.

I think of you as my guide and mentor in any garden writing I
do; you are wrong about my knowing a lot—I'm frightfully ignorant on gardens. I want to ply you with questions but hesitate to
bother you, but I shall even so and if you have time maybe just a
postcard or two would be a great help. The first is to ask whether
Lynn Ranger of Lynn, Mass. (if that is his name and his address),
is still alive. [. . .] His notices and lists have stopped coming and
I miss them.

My next question is to ask whether you happen to know the titles of any good recent books on flower arrangement. My next
piece, if it ever happens, just might be an irreverent one on modern flower arrangements and modern flower shows. [. . .] I have
of course Miss Jekyll, and a pile of other old books I think might
be useful, including ones on Japan and Zen, etc. [. . .] These
books are set aside in Maine to be mailed to me if I feel up to tackling it once I get through income tax and seed orders and family
visits. But I have more hope of doing it here than at home where
domestic help is now scarce and where cartons and cartons of
family papers that come to me from my sister remain to be sorted
for university libraries, plus the balance of Andy's papers for Cornell. He can no longer do this as the old letters give him asthma.

On the other hand, perhaps I should first write a catalogue article again. I haven't decided. (Any names of interesting catalogues would be welcome.) And still, on the other hand, perhaps
I should first attempt the fill-in chapters on the garden and family locales of my life, which I may intersperse with *The New Yorker*

pieces for a book. Life is too short. I am eager to hear what you are working on. Forgive this overlong letter and do not bother to answer except on postcards. We hope to be here till mid-April.

Affectionately and gratefully,
Katharine

FEAST OF THE EPIPHANY [1966]

Dear Katharine,

How wonderful to hear from you. But before I go any further (or I may forget) please tell E. B. that not only my niece, Fuzz (now called Elizabeth), but the new generation (just beginning to read real books for themselves, eight years or earlier), put *Charlotte's Web* first, and also love *Stuart Little*. [. . .]

My mother did die, on the last day of July, 1964. And I am sure that I did not tell you.* I didn't mean not to. I just didn't happen to write at the time, and then I forgot. I still have not recovered from those long years of her illness and worrying whether Mary and Ivey would get back and forth in the sleet (Mary had three terrible automobile accidents while she was with me), and I am very slow to adjust myself to living alone, as I was brought up never to enter an empty house, and never to stay in one alone, even in the daytime. And at present, with the outbreak of burglary, and right in our neighborhood, and the papers so full of it that you can't pick one up without seeing the headlines, and that splendid story by Truman Capote† (in *The New Yorker*—I haven't read the book) which was so good I read way into it before I found I'd have to stop, or go to the old ladies' home. Well, anyway, I found that I'd rather live alone than take someone in. I could not do it if I did not have my sister next door.

*EL wrote KSW of her mother's death in her 11/23/64 letter.
†Capote's "nonfiction novel" *In Cold Blood* about the murders of a rural Kansas family was first published in *The New Yorker*, based on the author's six years of interviews with the convicted killers, two young drifters.

Now: questions: Mr. Ranger is very much alive (though his wife died), and has been diligently searching out books for me. He wrote some time ago to say that his son was coming here to live, and asking me to put him in touch with the Quakers (which I did, after a good deal of research—couldn't find them under Churches, so I called the Quaker Chemical Corporation, who were baffled by my question, but finally said they had no religious connections). Fortunately, my sister is rather bright, and told me to look under Friends. So I did, and found they meet at someone's house, and if that number doesn't answer call another. Neither answered. Ever. But I sent the address, so I told him to tell his son to call me, but he never did, so I guess he didn't come. I was eager to meet him after reading Mr. Ranger's Christmas letter about his family (years ago).

Do you know Elisabeth Woodburn, Booknoll Farm, Hopewell, New Jersey? If not send for her splendid *Gardening Books,* catalogue 165 (free). (Elisabeth with an S is even more frustrating to me than Katharine with an A.) Unfortunately you have come to the wrong person for books on flower arrangement. I always knew I could arrange flowers better than anyone else, and have read very few (and never got even honorable mention in a flower show.). I consider that Mrs. [Annabel Whitney Baggaley] Hine said all there is to say in her first book: *The Arrangement of Flowers* [1933], and that all else is poppycock. I like M. Preininger *Japanese Flower Arrangements for Modern Homes* (1936) (and would like it even better for houses), I dislike Mrs. Cary,* and loathe Mr. Conway.† My idea of reviewing is that other people may like books I don't like, so I do some arrangements now and then, simply quoting to give an idea what the book is like. One I did was Julia Clement's *Fun without Flowers* (I loved what she had to say about grasses, made a list, looked up sources, and still hope to grow

*Katharine T. Cary, *Arranging Flowers Throughout the Year* (Dodd, Mead, 1933).
†J. Gregory Conway, *Flowers, Their Arrangement* (Knopf, 1940).

some), and another was *Design for Flower Arrangements* by Dorothy Riester (1959). I can send you all these if you like, as soon as I can get to the P.O. I cracked my knee coming out of the liquor store, and cannot drive the car. They say it is nothing, and will give no trouble, but I feel chronic bursitis is just waiting to move from shoulder to knee.

[. . .]

I *still* think your *New Yorker* review one of your best, and the proof of the pudding is in the eating: our little bookshop in the mall told Hannah that their phone rang all day for days asking for the books you wrote about.

[. . .]

I am not working on anything at present (except my column, of course). After my mother died I had to try to get the house and garden back into some sort of order, it had all gone down so, and the kitchen had to be entirely done over. The estate is *still* not settled, though such a simple thing, just my sister and me; however the complicated ones ever get done I can't imagine. There is still some property in West Virginia left over from my great-grandfather's day, and correspondence about that seems endless. I want to write a book about children and gardens, taking Miss Jekyll's title, and writing about children I have known. But I can't find a publisher who is interested in the kind of book I have in mind. I have been collecting material for years, but when I sketched out my ideas to Miss Parker, she said she wouldn't be interested in even *looking* at the manuscript of anything but a how-to-do-it. I was completely discouraged, as she is the most satisfactory person I ever worked with.

[. . .]

How *do* you type so perfectly? I hoped I'd do better with a new typewriter, my old one was thirty years old, but I find it doesn't help a bit. I tried an electric one, but couldn't use that at all. I couldn't think while it stood there purring.

I have just been for a tour around the garden, and the air smells like spring (sweet olive) though it is cold and dank, and I picked the first Lenten rose, but that will not impress you now that you are in Florida. By the way, do you know Dr. [Henry] Nehrling's books? *My Garden in Florida*? [...]

I hope you continue to improve and write. I can hardly wait.

With love to you both.

Aff,
Elizabeth Lawrence

SARASOTA, FLORIDA
JANUARY 15, 1966

Dear Elizabeth,

That typing on my last letter was not mine; it was that of dear Mrs. Barbara Rupprecht, who helps me out here a few hours a week. You should see my typing and handwriting, both of which have degenerated! I never was a good typist but now I type only the letters to my children and drafts of my articles, which then usually have to be copied.

I am so sorry about your mother's death and send you my belated sympathy. I know your feelings must have been mixed about her death, since one can't help taking some comfort that anyone one loves has been released from half a life or from suffering, but even so the loss and the awful gap left by the death of one's parents, no matter how old or how ill they were, is hard to bear. When my Aunt Caroline died at 93, I felt that there was no one left in the world in whose eyes I could do no wrong no matter how badly I behaved. She was really my mother—brought me up from the age of six and lived with my father all the rest of his life, too. To lose children or husbands or wives must be unbearable, but in a somewhat different way. I sympathize with you, too, in the difficulty of learning to live alone. I'm not sure I could do it, now.

[. . .]

You are good to offer to lend me some of your books but there are several reasons for your not doing so. It may take me years to produce anything and if I did, every book I mention has to be shipped with my piece to *The New Yorker* for our Checking Department. [. . .] Mostly, though, the piece I have in mind would be memories of flower arranging from the past and the trends and changes with some scattered and crazy notes I've made at many flower shows. I, too, have never won a prize at our local show in Maine except for houseplants or specimens and of late years I haven't bothered with it. Once I did a parody arrangement, making it as hideous as I knew how to and as exaggerated. None of the local judges even recognized it as a parody, and considered it quite seriously. The Sarasota Flower Show is something—always based on a very fancy theme. I dragged poor Andy to a show one year in the huge Municipal Hall they hold it in here, and as he entered the vast building, he looked around and said: "But where are the flowers?" He was right; few flowers and a huge array of "accessories."

[. . .] I wish I could subscribe to the issue or issues a week in which your column appears, for the pleasure and the information it would give me. I now even forget what paper it is in—the *Raleigh* what? If it appears on Sunday only, maybe they would permit me to subscribe just for that.

As for your book, I am outraged that your suggestion was turned down by Miss Parker. [. . .] I suggest that you write the book anyway and send it to old Alfred Knopf, who very much likes well-written garden books that are not how-to-do-it books, or to Macmillan ditto, or to Random House. The latter (Bennett Cerf) now owns A. A. Knopf but Alfred and Blanche Knopf still run their own show. Or if you felt you couldn't write the book without first asking whether the idea pleased the publisher, write to these houses and all the other general publishing houses. Mr. Knopf for years pursued me to make my *New Yorker* pieces into a book, but he's given it up since my long silence and I guess has decided I'm too old and ill to do it, which I probably am. Anyway, he is a friend, and if you write him, you may say I suggested you ask him about this book. Mrs. K. is not the gardener, it is Mr. K. Your outline sounds like just the book *I* want most to read and you can tell him that. Please, please don't be discouraged. Andy and I think, though, that the best thing to do usually is to write the book *you* want to and *then* submit it.

[. . .] I'd like to read [Nehrling's] book on Florida gardens but hardly dare to, as it would make me want to own a house here. I do half want to, but both of us feel that even if we could afford it, which we probably can't, it is just too much to own and run two houses. We've come to the time when we want to simplify rather than expand. It's hard enough even to get out the seed orders for Maine. I must get back to my Harris vegetable order and stop this ramble.

Affectionately,
Katharine

[JANUARY 1966]

Dear Katharine,

I hope you won't be discouraged by my return-mail answer, but I cannot bear to let your kind letter get immersed in the pile of unanswered mail, notes of tetraploid daylilies, Alze Lee's* social security form (I've totted it up, but can't find her social security number) and the unfiled papers and letters that litter my desk.

*EL's occasional housekeeper.

I appreciate your sympathy, and, as you say, it is a bad feeling to find there is no longer an older generation behind you.

[. . .]

I enclose some gems from my collection of flower show programs. Do not return! I gave up judging long ago, but the last time I did, the president of the club took me aside and said, "Do see that Mrs. Jones gets a ribbon. She's going to have a baby."

It is the Sunday *Charlotte Observer* that I write for. It is very expensive and wouldn't be worth it, as I have to do so many local things—even flower arrangements which I don't attempt to evaluate. I describe them, and quote the judge's notes.

You all (meaning you two) are a great comfort to me. I entirely agree about writing the book and sending it on afterward, but it is getting to be very hard to get a finished manuscript published. Harper did my last book, but just after that they merged with Row. Mr. McAdoo, who worked with me, has been moved from the Outdoor Books, and there is a new Pharaoh.

The next morning

I stopped here to look in Exodus to see whether I had spelled Pharaoh right and was so entranced with the judgments that follow the commandments, that I never got back to this. What do you suppose they mean by "Neither shalt thou countenance a poor man in his cause"? I must ask B. Y. Morrison, who is a Presbyterian and knows everything.

Not only do they (to go back to the publishers) want only how-to-do-its, but they don't want anything local or personal. And "Don't bring in so many different gardeners, and don't mention one person too often, especially Mr. Morrison." "Leave out Tingle. Too local." Tingle being the only nursery left (since Kohankie went out of business) with an extensive list of trees and shrubs. And when the galleys arrive, your style has been "updated" by having "Actually" and "admittedly" thrown in at intervals, and instead of "Pliny says," "Pliny has this to say." . . . Also as the manuscript goes through the mill, it goes through various hands, and each pair strikes out more of your style, and adds more journalese. All this is put back into the original (with tears) in the second galley, but when the book comes out the journalese is still there. As Mr. Russell* said to Eudora Welty, "There are no publishers, anymore—just book factories."

[. . .]

When I first talked to him (the editor) about doing the column, he said, "Remember you are not writing for Dr. Mayer." But I do write for Dr. Mayer, and a large part of the letters I get are written in pencil by farm women who say, "Please tell me where to get seeds of the pocket melon, I haven't seen it since I was a girl." Or a telephone call from our old Mary, "Miss Elizabeth! You know that plant you wrote about and you didn't know what it was? I got that plant!"

Although I agree about the books, my rock garden book took some five years of my best writing years, and of course all my life up to then collecting the material, and it is still on the shelf. Not Salable. Too local.† It covered only half of the United States, and that half was Southern. And mentioned too many gardeners, all of whom had generously sent me notes on their soils and climates and the plants they could and could not grow. All that sort of thing should be put in tables. No one cares what Mr. Morrison grows in Pass Christian.

The same thing has happened in England. When I asked Clarence Elliott for permission to quote one of his letters to Mr. Krippendorf, and told him how I missed his pieces in the *Illustrated London News*, he wrote that he was sacked because all they wanted was howtodoits and he was too old a leopard to change

---

*Diarmuid Russell, Welty's longtime literary agent.
†*A Rock Garden in the South*, edited by Nancy Goodwin with Allen Lacy, was published posthumously (Duke University Press, 1990).

his spots. I expect this old leopard to be dropped from *The Observer* anytime, which will be very sad, for I love doing the column, and so far, with that one exception, have been able to say what I want to.

I didn't mean to get started on all this, but just to thank you for your suggestion and kindness. So, having found Alze Lee's social security number I must get back to my checkbook.

Aff,

Elizabeth Lawrence

P.S. You are so right about two houses. Don't be tempted.
[. . .]

SARASOTA, FLORIDA
JANUARY 17, 1967

Dear Elizabeth,

At this late date I suddenly remember that one of your last winter's letters spoke of a new book by Caroline Dormon. I haven't your letter here but I seem to remember that you said she was tempted to send me a copy if I wanted it, and I said of course I did very much want it but would send and buy a copy. Well, I never did send for it because of domestic misfortunes. You gave me the address but now I forget it. Is it still Claitor's Book Store and, if so, is the address what it was way back in 1960 when I reviewed her other book? [. . .] This forgetfulness of mine makes me furious, for I missed a wonderful chance to mention the book, if it is about wild flowers, when I reviewed the first volumes of Rickett's huge new *Wild Flowers of the United States* in last December 10 issue of *The New Yorker*. The trouble was that I was deep in writing that flower arrangement piece, which is giving me great difficulties, but put it aside to do "The Million-Dollar Book" plus

The young Elizabeth Lawrence

Elizabeth's crowded perennial borders in her garden in Raleigh, North Carolina.

Elizabeth and her spaniel, Mr. Cayce, posing on the steps of her Raleigh garden. Katharine liked this photograph of Elizabeth as "a real garden nymph."

my meager stored-up baby memories of Charles S. Sargent.* Bill Shawn wanted the review to get in before Christmas and it was done in a wild rush—for me (two months). Some errors got in because of this—"Charles" instead of "Alfred" Rehder et al.— mostly because I had to correct proofs by long distance phone while driving South.

How *are* you? We had a miserable year of '66 what with many family, health, and domestic problems, and 1967 is starting out even worse. [...] I am under pressure to determine finally whether these articles will make a book and get at it before I'm too old. (Age is pressing down on me. I hate it!) The very old ones make dull reading and must be fixed, and several new chapters, of memories and backgrounds only, must get written. My first task, though, is to try to whip "The Flower Arrangers" into shape if it is possible in order to salvage months of work. It is too tough a subject for me and I've got in too deep—in fact, as deep as the 14th century B.C.! I also sound preachy about the modern trends. But I get no time for writing as I must first keep this wobbly household together, get Andy well, and spend most of my working hours on his reprint requests and letters from readers, and on my own occasional *New Yorker* work.

I do hope you are writing a book and are in good health. I am reading Tyler Whittle's *Some Ancient Gentlemen*—a garden book written with delightful style and humor—just like your writing. You are my candidate always for an American who writes on gardening subjects as well as the English do.

Affectionately,
Katharine

---

*The December 10, 1966, review, "The Million-Dollar Book," included KSW's memories of having grown up in Brookline, Mass., near the estate of Professor Charles Sargent, who developed Harvard's Arnold Arboretum.

[JANUARY 1967]

Dear Katharine,

You must think me perfectly horrid for not having written at once to tell you how delightful your piece in *The New Yorker* is. The minute I saw it I laid it aside, but before I could read it I was side-tracked, and it was drawn back into the pool of *New Yorkers* that stay in stacks for weeks and months, and I spent several nights in vain going through various ones in search of it.

[...]

I expect Caroline was ashamed to send *Natives Preferred* to you because of the numerous and glaring [errors] due to Mr. Claitor's being inexperienced and too hurried, and its being an author-to-publisher job. I should have seen to it that you had a copy. The book is $5.00. [...] Wouldn't you think there would be *some* publisher in this whole country, who would accept Caroline as she is, and appreciate her knowledge, talent and character—before it is too late, which it almost is.

I was so interested in what you say about common names.* I have made a list in the back of *Hortus II* (whose selling point was that you could find any plant by its common name) of those that were left out. They don't list gallberry, sweet alyssum, or love apple. It took me years to discover that the myrtle tree someone asked me to identify is *umbellularia.* For wild flowers Britten and Brown† is a treasure of country names. They seldom fail me. For Marsh Marigold they give twenty-eight old English and local American names, and Mrs. Grieve‡ gives some they leave out—but her book is the worst of all for finding things, as it is impossi-

*In her 12/10/66 review, KSW discussed the need for authors to identify plants not only by botanical nomenclature but by flower families and common names.
†Nathaniel Lord Britton and Addison Brown, *An Illustrated Flora of the Northern United States, Canada, and the British Possessions.* (Lancaster Press, 1943).
‡Maud Grieve, *A Modern Herbal* (Hafner Publishing Co., 1959).

ble to know what she will list them as, and there is no Latin index—and I never find what I want in the index of country names.
For example, how would you know that you must look for May
apple (not in the index) under Mandrake, American?

As for errors, I find the writer is often the only one they offend.
I simply read "Alfred" for "Charles" (having known no other
Rehder). And speaking of Alfred, that is a loss I have never got
over. [. . .]*

Would E. B. give me permission to quote "The Deserted Nation"† in my column, or should I ask *The New Yorker*?

[. . .]

In Sarasota it will not excite you to hear that the Algerian Iris,
Crocus imperialis (the loveliest of all species), and little pale yellow
tazetta, that came to me from California as Bathurst but they say
it is not, have been in bloom on the sunny side of the house for a
fortnight, in spite of continual white frosts and ice on the garden
pool. But this morning the sleet is small and sharp.

I am sorry to hear of your trials and illness. I can get along,
though not the way I'd like, with the minimum amount of help I
can get at present, but I wonder how long I will be able to. I have
pretty well got over the operation I had on my shoulder last
spring, and have got the use of my arm, but it did not, as the doctor hoped, do away with the pain in the back of my head. Darvon
has helped a lot.

At the present moment I am not writing anything but my column, as my niece and namesake, Fuzz, but now called Elizabeth,
is graduating next week (we hope) from the University, and is
being married the fourth of March. As I am having the wedding

*Alfred Rehder, author and colleague of Charles Sargent at the Arnold Arboretum, died
in 1949 at age eighty-six.
†EBW's poem calling attention to the deaths of eagles from pesticides had appeared in
The New Yorker (10/8/66).

breakfast in this small house, and people in and out for days, I shall have to spend most of my time from now until then getting work in progress put out of the way in some place I know, and can have access to. I don't know where it is going to be. Every closet is bulging already, and under my studio couch is a box of unfiled clippings and papers, and another of Baring-Gould's *Lives of the Saints* lent to me for a book I've been working on for years on flowers of the church.

[. . .]

I am glad you are being pressed to gather the articles into a book, and add memories which I love and which are like to snow-flakes on the river if they are not caught and put on paper. You must have total recall. I never remember anything but emotions. It is frustrating.

With love to you both. I am thankful for your writings. And letters.

Aff,
Elizabeth

JANUARY 27, 1967

[Dear Elizabeth,]

Andy gladly gives *his* permission for you to reprint "The Deserted Nation" but you will have to write to Mr. Harding Mason, *The New Yorker,* to get the magazine's permission. [. . .]

Andy is delighted that you want to use the poem. (The eagle live nestling count is down shockingly in Florida also this year.) I would simply ask Harding Mason to write you yes except that I'm away from my letter files and can't be sure I know the name of your newspaper. *The New Yorker* has to know that. So you write, and I'll write Harding Mason.

I didn't know about your operation. I'm *so* sorry. I'll answer your letter properly in a few days. Meanwhile I thank you for it.

Affy,
KSW

P.S. Andy is honored that you want to use the poem.

[FEBRUARY 23, 1967]

Dear Katharine,

I am sorry to hear from you the trouble of writing to *The New Yorker* and me,* and distressed not to be able to quote the poem. I know [the book page editor of the *Observer*] would not accept the conditions. He always changes the lines of poetry to fit the narrow columns—and would likely as not leave out "Reprinted by permission _." He has never yet done anything I asked. But even so he does less harm than editors of books and garden magazines. Once he did leave the Mr. off of Morrison, but when I wrote to apologize, Ben said not to worry, it didn't make him feel at all like a butler. I miss Ben so, I can hardly bear it.† And at least the newspaper editors don't have time to improve manuscripts by a good sprinkling of admittedly, actually, and so and so has this to say. Do you remember the dowager in one of Angela Thirkell's novels who said to the earnest but illiterate young vicar, "It is pronounced 'actually,' and it isn't used often."

With love to both of you and I hope you are better.

Aff,
Elizabeth Lawrence

*KSW and EL exchanged a number of letters despairing of the requirements imposed by *The New Yorker* and the *Charlotte Observer* to reprint EBW's poem. KSW wrote a strongly worded letter to Harding Mason at *The New Yorker*, concluding, "If I were a person like Elizabeth Lawrence, I would pay no heed to your letter."
†Benjamin Y. Morrison died in 1966.

P.S. I am going to Philadelphia in the middle of April to the daffodil meeting, and afterward to New York to spend a few days with Ellen Flood. I'll let you know when, in hopes that you will be there.

Dear Elizabeth,

[. . .] The only requirements, if you use the whole poem, are 1) to print the whole thing, subtitle and all, and 2) to give the author's name and *The New Yorker*'s, either in your own text or at the end of the poem, or as a footnote with asterisk at the end of your piece, "Copyright *The New Yorker,* 1966." *All* newspapers know they have to do this with copyrighted material where a full poem (however short) or prose of any length beyond "fair quotation" is used. The reason, of course, is that if printed without this protection, anyone can lift it from *The Observer* and the copyright becomes lost to the author, who may someday want to use the poem in one of his own books. Once in a book, Andy's publishers demand and get reprint fees unless he asks for an exception to be made in special cases. Scores of Andy's *New Yorker* "Comment" paragraphs have been picked up by newspapers all over the country and reprinted with permission. Also many of his poems. [. . .]

This still can't be more than a business letter but I am anxious to hear much more about your operation last spring and the pain in the back of your head. That is really unhappy news and I *am* so sorry. After the wedding you must tell me what happened and what the operation was. Because of my old spinal fusion and a back put together with two screws, I am very sympathetic to those in pain. [. . .]

I shall be in New York in April but I don't yet know when. It would be thrilling for me if we could meet at last. Let's keep in touch. More later.

Affectionately,
Katharine

[MARCH 1967]

[Dear Katharine,]

Mr. Mason was clairvoyant when he said, "Don't give up, even if the lines have to be triple-turned." The format reminds me of the mouse's tale—"Your tail is a long one, Alice said."

But Mr. Mason's faith in the *Observer* was justified as to author and copyright. My telling Mr. Heffner* to return the manuscript if he couldn't comply seems to have been effective.

Thank you and E. B. for letting me use it, and forgive me, please, for causing so much trouble.

[Aff, Elizabeth Lawrence]

P.S. The piece was entitled: "Wildlife and Pesticides." Their headlines ruin my Sundays.

MARCH 2, 1967

Dear Elizabeth,

That's a fine column—never mind the headline. Andy and I both thought so, and the statistics and scientific facts you quoted are appalling. The poem looked fine, but I still think it was silly of Mason to insist on the name "E. B. White" *after* the poem when you had given it just above. Not happy for an author like you or even for the writer of the quoted poem. [. . .]

I hope you haven't lost any of your precious plants in this re-cent severe weather, but I'm sure you lost all your blossoms. A

*The editor of the Sunday *Charlotte Observer.*

friend in Yemassee, S.C., writes that every camellia bloom and every other flower were frozen. Here it went down to 29 degrees one night.

Don't forget to tell me your New York dates and address when you know them. Andy sends his thanks to you for the clipping, for what you wrote, and for wanting to use his poem.

Affectionately,
Katharine

MARCH 19 [1967]

Dear Elizabeth,

[. . .]

Re: Mount Vernon,* I was glad of the material sent me and passed along some of it to our Maine Congressman with a letter, acknowledged gracefully if, as always, non-committally. Response from the White House this time was from a secretary who said Udall† was working on the neon-signed motel, twenty miles from Mt. Vernon. Not a word about Piscataway Park, so she misses the point. I'm writing this secretary again about the August 7 deadline on the Congressional appropriation saying maybe Mrs. J. would be a better persuader for action than anyone, though I knew it was up to the House of R. Lady Bird was too busy planting dogwood with the governors' wives I guess. This is about all I can do.

Aff'y,
Katharine

---

*EL's column "Mount Vernon" (*CO* 2/20/66) discussed George Washington's original plans for gardens and urged her readers to use Washington's birthday as an occasion to write to their congressional representatives about securing additional land for the park along the Potomac. KSW was so "stirred up" by threats to the view from Mount Vernon that she wrote Mrs. Lyndon Johnson, as well as her Maine congressman.
†Stewart Udall, President Johnson's Secretary of the Interior.

NOVEMBER 16, 1967

Dear Elizabeth,

The flower arrangement pieces, on which I owe you so much for your help, have finally been published in the November 4 and 11 issues of *The New Yorker*. (I turned them in, in July.) I can only pray that the Garden Club passages or any part of it do not offend you or too many of your friends. I expect wrathful letters but I *had* to say how I felt, no matter how many friends I lose in the North or South. I can see no way in which you could be identified as having sent me the local flower show programs from your region and purposely did not mention your name for this reason. The articles are too long and I guess many will never finish reading them. This is what age does; it makes one long-winded. [. . .]

I have written so many letters to you in my mind since last spring that I now have no way of knowing whether I ever did really write you to say what a great pleasure it was to meet you and Mrs. Flood and how much I enjoyed that luncheon.* It is very bad manners that I never wrote her or you if I did not. My only excuse is that we've had a *miserable* summer full of many problems—family, domestic help, dreadful weather, poor health. [. . .]

Meeting you in person at last—you who have been my guide and mentor and my envy and admiration because of your knowledge and your wonderful books and writing—was a nervous moment for me so if I acted jumpy, I hope you can forgive me. The wonderful thing for me was that I loved you at once as a person and wanted to stay on and talk for hours. Forgive me if I have written all this before.

Our garden beds were queer as anything this summer, thanks to a *very* late spring, a miserable, cold, wet summer, and the depre-

*KSW and EL finally met in April 1967 when Elizabeth visited her friend Ellen Flood in New York.

dations of deer in the vegetables. (Next year we're going to have to fence the vegetables.) Also Andy reactivated the farm and Henry Allen, our factotum, had to spend most of his time on a pig, sheep and lambs, geese, poultry etc. [. . .] and I myself could do less actual planting. It's time I *cut down* but I don't; everything just looks shabby and ill-kept. My skin—the curse of Job—has been worse than ever and I'm on the highest dose of the destructive prednisone (cortisone) to suppress it that I've ever taken outside a hospital. It takes up too much of my time but it could be something so much worse that I should be thankful. It injures my pride because it makes me moon-faced and bloated.

We're on our way to Florida and there I hope to subside and get less tense. However, *two* puppies are following us there this year. Same address as last year. If you have time, do write me your news. In fact, I guess this letter will be mailed from the South. We are going down by train from New York City—another sign of age.

Affectionately and gratefully,
Katharine

BEFORE THANKSGIVING [1967]

Dear Katharine,

I am so glad to have your letter, and to know where you are, as I had just been reading about the flower arrangers with great interest, and I wanted to tell you how much I enjoyed it. It is not a word too long, and you need not worry in the least about losing friends in the South, as I doubt very much whether any of the flower show arrangers ever see *The New Yorker.* And of course so far as *I* am concerned we are in perfect agreement.*

*KSW's 1967 columns, "The Flower Arrangers" and "More About the Arrangers," included her objections to the "overstudied" and "abstract" arrangements designed to meet flower-show guidelines. She noted, "Americans are most successful when they do not copy any style." Some garden club members wrote to defend their policies, and KSW replied good-naturedly to their letters.

Second Sunday in Advent

Each day I set out to do what I have to do, and one thing that I want to do. Today is yours. First to tell you how I loved being with you, and to explain why I did not write before to tell you so. I was in great distress when I was in New York (and so much so that I did not stay as long as I had planned but came on home right after I saw you) about Ann Bridgers who was dying of cancer in a hospital in Raleigh. You may remember that she was one of the authors of "Coquette."* Ann and her sister Emily [Bridgers] are the friends who have most encouraged me in writing, in fact who started me out in writing about gardens when I had never done anything but poetry. Now Emily is dying of cancer. As they are much older than I, I knew I would be likely to outlive them, but I don't yet see how I can do it.

When I got back from New York I found a letter from the director of the University [of North Carolina] Press saying that at last, after dickering all this time they had decided to get out a new edition of *A Southern Garden,* and wanted me to get it ready in a month, which I couldn't do. [. . .] At first he said he would allow me as much extra space as I needed, and then as I worked on it all summer he changed around and said none of what I had written would do, and that he would be away for his vacation for a month, at the end of which time the book would be reprinted with a few paragraphs from me. No notes, no list of dealers. I finally got hold of Billy Hunt, who was the one who goaded the Press into finally getting the book back into print. Billy got behind the assistant director, and [he] finally gave in. [. . .] Then they took the material I had written, and the list of nurseries, and got it all off to Raleigh, and I never even saw a galley. So all of that anguish and work, and it is still not what I wanted. [. . .]

*Coauthored with George Abbott in a 1927 production starring Helen Hayes. Bridgers died 5/3/67.

Well. Anyway I am sending you a copy, as I want you to have it from me. [. . .]

And now my only nephew, a Lieutenant in the Navy, is in charge of a group of Seabees building bunkers in the demilitarized zone.

I wish I were as young as you all. I cannot imagine taking on two puppies! Though I always said I couldn't live without a dog. The one in the Raleigh garden is Mr. Cayce, my beautiful springer. What I like about your writing is hearing about your family, and all of the things I love like Lafcadio Hearn,* and things I don't know about, but mean to look into. Hannah loves it too, and so do all the Mitchells. Laura† always comes to spend a day with me and make Christmas puddings. She was not in doubt of course as to the source of the Southern flower shows, but is very discreet.

Aff,
Elizabeth Lawrence

SARASOTA, FLORIDA
DECEMBER 21, 1967

Dear Elizabeth,

Your letter delighted but distressed me. To think you are in so much pain as to have to use Darvon constantly is unbearable. I don't quite know where or what the pain is. (I have Darvon on hand always and do use it when the muscles of my back go into spasm but it makes my head woozy, and a little of it is of small help.) Also I did not know you had been in all this sorrow over friends dying or dead or that you had the frightful weight of anxi-

---

*KSW had written about Lafcadio Hearn's *Glimpses of Unfamiliar Japan* (Houghton Mifflin, 1894; reprinted C. E. Tuttle, 1976), in her 11/4/67 piece, recalling that it had been a gift from Annie Shepley ("Aunt Poo"), who had married a Japanese man, Hyozo Omori.
†Laura Braswell, Joseph Mitchell's sister living in Charlotte.

ety about a nephew in Vietnam. You have had too much to bear in the past few years. On top of it, apparently, you had distress all year about the new edition of *A Southern Garden*. It is absolutely wonderful to have the book back in print and to have a copy of it from you, with your inscription, and so beautifully wrapped. It looked like a Christmas gift but I couldn't wait to open it. [. . .] I do feel that your unhappiness about this new edition is unwarranted. I have read right through the new part, which I found just as delightful as the old and of great importance, and it is beautifully written, just as the original book was. Now I am reading the whole book through in the hours before I go to sleep or at six or five when I wake, and I am finding it absolutely charming all over again. How I wish that just such a book could be written for every climate zone! I like the photographs; the picture of you in your Raleigh garden is *enchanting*, a real garden nymph.* [. . .] I have accomplished absolutely nothing in the nearly two months here and find my time was consumed with household help, that aren't helpful, puppies, Christmas for a huge family, and just getting started to live in a furnished house in which every possible appliance has broken down since our arrival—septic tank, washing machine, vacuum, refrigerator, portable dishwasher, and today the refrigerator, just as our little family of five from Maine† is due to arrive.

This can be all for now as I have endless errands to do and *no* transportation since I can no longer drive. I hate to drag Andy all over the place. May the New Year treat you more kindly. I love your book and thank you for your generosity in sending me a copy. I wish it had arrived in time for me to mention the new enlarged edition in that "Winter Reading" "Onward and Upward" bit I wrote in October and early November, which was

---

*EL, in her thirties, in a long summer dress, posed on the rock steps of her Raleigh garden with her dog, Mr. Cayce.

†Joel and Allene White and Steve, Martha, and John.

published in the December 16 issue. The selection of the few books covered was an arbitrary one, and the piece is not one with which I am pleased. Like you, I prefer the bits I write about the past, and if only I could get some domestic peace of mind I have chapters on this I want to write. My skin has been cutting up badly in the hot weather we've been having and this means weekly visits to a dermatologist. But my leg arteries are *better* than a year ago—a miracle. I look freakishly bloated by cortisone for the skin, but can do little about that except swallow my pride.

Good luck to the book and much love, and Happy New Year.
Katharine

[JANUARY 1968]

Dear Katharine,

As usual I started a letter to you long ago to tell you how much I enjoyed your "Winter Reading, Winter Dreams," and especially for my young friend Leonie Bell* to get recognition for her drawings and her firsthand material. I wish you would come to the Daffodil meeting sometime. It is a small group of delightful people, most of whom turn out to be someone I have some connection with already (like Mr. Krippendorf's daughter and granddaughter, and Polly Anderson, who always comes from California). At the first meeting I went to, Polly was sitting in the lobby of the motel when I came in, and she said, "Here is your West Coast correspondent."

[. . .]

You and I [. . .] seem to see eye to eye on everything but Mrs. Ewing.† I was brought up in such a swamp of Victorian senti-

---

*Coauthor with Helen Van Pelt Wilson of *The Fragrant Year* (Barrows, 1967).
†See the note on page 5. KSW had written about her youthful delight in reading Ewing's popular children's book, *Mary's Meadow,* which upon rereading she found "sentimental" and "moralizing."

ment that Mary's meadow, to me, is like being thrown into the briar patch. When we were children my grandmother used to read one of Dickens' novels to my little sister and me each summer, and at all of the touching passages she would weep, and we would weep, and my sister's little friend, Veronica—who would always lie on the sofa with her face in a pillow—would shake so that we were afraid she was hysterical. Long after we were grown, she told us she was shaking with laughter.

[. . .]

I admire you extravagantly for all you do. I often think of my mother's saying that she had always thought she could take life easier as she grew old and found it harder, instead. She had always said that when she was seventy she would have an "upstairs maid," and when the time came she didn't even have an upstairs.

Hannah and I are planning to go on the National Trust for Scotland's tour of Castles and Gardens. Everyone says we will freeze in May, and be seasick in the channel, and we are both decrepit. I was better for a while after an operation on my shoulder, but now the pain in my neck and joints has all come back. I can type only a short time at a stretch, and that makes it harder to get through with work and correspondence.

I never knew such a storm in this part of the country. We had almost a week of freezing rain and sleet. Now it is like spring, but freezes again at night, and the ice is still thick on the terrace. The storm did a lot of pruning, but I expect it was a good thing. A small garden gets overgrown so quickly.

I hope you are better, and getting some peace. If there is any.

Aff,
Elizabeth Lawrence

Dear Elizabeth,

Please forgive a dictated letter, which means that it's even less coherent than my scrawls I have copied. I'm delighted that you enjoyed "Winter Reading, Winter Dreams." Your young friend, Leonie Bell did not really like the review, I'm afraid, because I criticized the text to some degree, but we have had a correspondence and I think she understands better what I was driving at. She sounds like a delightful person and an amazing one and sent me a photograph of her wonderful children. She is really an artist.

I, too, was brought up on Dickens and wept over it, and I had an awful dose of Victorian novels read aloud because my five-year-older and eleven-year-older sisters were read aloud to and I listened. I loved Mrs. Ewing when I was young, and I liked *Mary's Meadow* again when I read it this year but I was surprised by the sentimentality. However, I felt that I had not done justice to the book in that mention of it, because those children did come alive for me.

[. . .]

Your trip to the castles and gardens of Scotland sounds wonderful and I admire you for going. The reason I am dictating is that I have joined you in the pain in the neck. It struck me suddenly about ten days ago, and it is really agony in the morning and now is stretching to be painful all day. I have been to the doctor, but he gave me a superficial examination and said it was roughening of the bones and told me not to bend my neck and not to work over a desk. Great! I simply have to. The bulk of the seed orders are out—and does this take neck bending!—but not the plant orders. And now income tax and I do a big correspondence on business matters for Andy as well as myself and have all these children and grandchildren and their problems and pleasures which require letters.

I'm in a down mood and feel that the peace I had hoped for is not going to arrive this winter, but perhaps all will suddenly change. [. . .]

Affectionately,
Katharine

[DECEMBER 1968]

Dear Elizabeth,

My health has gradually deteriorated since I last wrote you as you can tell by a garden piece in the Dec. 21 *New Yorker*. It's only a part of the article I planned and the better first half had to wait till my health was better. But I did squeeze in a few pre-Xmas garden book reviews, as promised, including one on your revised edition, probably chock full of errors. Writing is agony now and this is my feeblest effort yet. It should probably be my last but I hope not. [. . .]

How are *you*? I hope the trip to England was a good one and I do hope your health is better than it was. We're at the same address as last year—Sarasota, Fla. After the Xmas rush, write me a line about *yourself.*

Ever aff'y,
Katharine

[DECEMBER 1968]

Dear Katharine,

I was certainly glad to see your handwriting in the morning's mail. Joseph Mitchell told me when he was here in the late summer that you were not well. [. . .]

As for me I have been better lately, but still ache more or less all of the time. The worst of it is that I can type only a short time, and get less and less done. Hannah has a bad knee, so we were afraid we would never get to England and back without breaking down, but we managed very well by not trying to do too much. On the National Trust Cruise we were put to shame by staying aboard several times while Princess Alice (Queen Victoria's granddaughter) and Lady Violet Benson—both in their eighties—went tripping off on those steep Scotch hills.

New Year's Day

I have just found this under some notes on my desk. Evidently I took it out of my typewriter to answer or do something in haste, and thought (when it disappeared) that it had been mailed. I am distressed that you did not hear from me before Christmas—with love and New Year's wishes.

Aff,
Elizabeth

[DECEMBER 1968]

Dear Katharine,

I was amused by a letter I had this morning from Mr. Stanley Rowe, Chairman of the Board of the Cincinnati Nature Center. They bought Mr. Krippendorf's place, and I gave them the manuscript I have written, about bloom time throughout the year, based on Mr. K's letters. Mr. Rowe says that Marion Becker (*Joy of Cooking*) sent him *The New Yorker* with your article. He says, "The article caused me to raise my sights as to the possibilities of a wider sale of your new book than I had previously anticipated. I will suggest to Frank that he order some copies of *A Southern Garden* for the book shop at The Nature Center."

[. . .]

With more love and gratitude,
Aff,
Elizabeth Lawrence

[DECEMBER 23, 1968]
FRIDAY AFTERNOON

Dear Katharine,

The response to your "Onward and Upward" is a tribute to you. I am sure that you, like me, like it best when people who are not really gardeners read you for yourself; and so I was pleased when my rector, *New Yorker* in hand, waylaid me on Sunday as I was leaving church by a side door. I said, "How did *you* happen to read Mrs. White?" and he said, "I *always* read Mrs. White."

Yesterday I had a letter from one of your following in Denver, also a non-gardener, who said, "Louisa called me last night, and said 'If you haven't read your *New Yorker* look on page 81.'" In the same mail there was a letter from Marion Becker (*The Joy of Cooking*), who said, "I am sure Katharine White's wonderful review is the best Christmas present you could have." It certainly is.

Billy Hunt telephoned from Chapel Hill on Sunday to say that what pleased him most is that you have vindicated *him* for hounding the Press until they got *A Southern Garden* back in print. I said, "I hope you see that [the editor] sees," and he said, "I've already seen to that, and he is vastly impressed by Mrs. White though he wouldn't listen to me."

[. . .]

I was startled on Christmas Eve to find a magnificent wood duck in the pool. It jumped out as I walked down the path, and flew off to Elizabeth Clarkson's garden where it was born. Sometimes there are as many as twenty-two on her big pool.

I hope you are better, and that you had a good Christmas.
[. . .] it was wonderful to have my nephew, who was in Viet Nam
this time last year, and to have my niece and her husband.

With love and gratitude,
Aff,
Elizabeth Lawrence

Part Three

"LETTERS ONE BY ONE"

1969–1977

. . . you have drawn without knowing it a portrait of a dear and noble person.

ELIZABETH TO KATHARINE, JUNE 1977

This final section of letters is perhaps the most moving. Katharine was making many trips to the hospital during these years but, miraculously, she was able to write a final "Onward and Upward" piece. Then she directed her attention to helping Andy and to getting together her collection of gardening books and papers to send to the archives at Bryn Mawr College. Unable to be up for many hours, her memory sometimes fogged by drugs, her eyesight fading, she was determined "to rise like the phoenix." Although her letters are few during this period, she dictated long narratives—about an emergency trip to the hospital, about goings-on around town. Elizabeth, too, began to think of what she would do with her books and papers. Her greatest concern was the unfinished manuscript based on her letters with farm women who read the market bulletins. Katharine offered a good analysis of what she thought Elizabeth hoped to accomplish in her book. This was exactly what Elizabeth needed.

In March 1977, Katharine proposed to Elizabeth that they leave their letters in archives for future scholars. They agreed to do it, and as Katharine met with the librarian from Bryn Mawr, Elizabeth wrote to the archivist at Northwestern State University in Louisiana (chosen because it housed the letters of Caroline Dormon, one of her most beloved correspondents). In April 1977, Lawrence's registered package arrived safely in Natchitoches, Louisiana. Reading the letters between Katharine and Elizabeth, Carol Wells, assistant librarian, observed, "I got a feeling of moral interdependence on a creative level. Somehow, I had viewed the creativity of successful people as a strong force that perhaps needed channeling but not encouragement. Now, on this new-to-me plane, I see again that no man is an island."

SARASOTA, FLORIDA
JANUARY 2, 1969

Dear Elizabeth,

Thanks for your wonderful letter—I have read it over and over. Your rector is already one of my favorite readers.

[. . .]

I *have* no following in Florida if, indeed, I have one at all. My neighbors and friends, most of them gardeners, never read *The New Yorker* unless I press into their hands the copy with my yearly "Onward and Upward" and this is embarrassing to do and is seldom done by me.

[. . .] I long to hear how the trip to England went and I'm so glad your nephew came safe home from his year in Vietnam— the best Christmas gift of all.

Wonderful about the wood duck! Here the birds are scarce and the noise of building highways, new sewers, and new houses is bad. This is probably our last year in this house as the house is for sale and we won't buy it.

Andy called me on my wording of "literary prose."* He's been too poorly and too absorbed in the first version of his new book

*KSW in her review of a new edition of EL's *A Southern Garden* had admired her "simple, literary prose."

and could give me little advice before I hurried the miserable thing in to catch the last issue of the year. More on this later when I am in a better state. He says *all* prose is literary. I meant, of course, literary versus scientific or botanical prose, and *The New Yorker* editors didn't call me. *I* think it's O.K. There are all kinds of prose—yours is literary. Some is reportorial, some is scientific only. I'll stick by my guns.

I'm so thankful you are well enough to write. I have worried about you.

Much love and thanks for your lovely letter.

Affectionately and gratefully,
Katharine

[JANUARY 1969]
MONDAY AFTERNOON

Dear Katharine,
   [. . .]
I am on your side as to the forms of prose, but after consulting the *OED* I am not able to prove anything. Under 1. "The ordinary form of written or spoken language, without metrical structure: esp. as a species or division of literature."

1575 LANEHAM: The thing which heer I report in unpolisht proez . . .

1718 LADY M. W. MONTAGU: I . . . will . . . continue the rest of my account in plain prose.

If there is unpolisht prose, I should think there would also be polished prose, and if plain there must be fancy.

I am so glad you mentioned this, as otherwise I would have missed two other quotations: Chaucer: "Gladly quod I by goddes sweete pyne I wol yow telle a litel thyng in prose." And Coleridge: "The definition of good prose is—proper words in their proper places."

And so, if there is good prose there must be bad.

Did I tell you Warren said, "Is Katharine White, Mrs. E. B. White?" And I said, "How did *you* ever hear of E. B. White?" (as he is a reader of scientific rather than literary prose), and he said, "My dear Libba, have you forgotten that I read *Charlotte's Web* aloud *ten* times?"

I am still getting letters about "Onward and Upward," in every mail.

With love to both of you.
Aff,
Elizabeth Lawrence

P.S. Wednesday: letters continue to come.
    [. . .]

JANUARY 20, 1969

Dear Elizabeth,

Thanks for the cheering literary notes, definitions from the O.E.D., and the quotations. Coleridge's definition is one of the best, but Laneham's and Lady Mary Montagu's quotes are fascinating.

Poor Warren! He must *hate Charlotte's Web* by this time, just as when I came home from Miss Winsor's School all full of excitement about a new science course (Physiology and Biology) and my father raised his hand wearily and stopped me, saying "Do I have to go through that course a *third* time?" I was the youngest of his three children, all Miss Winsor's students.

I'm glad you're getting letters but what I hope to hear about is reviews of your last year's book in the *Charlotte Observer* and elsewhere.

What do you suppose my latest trouble is? Shingles—a bad case—on top of the dermatitis. I haven't worn clothes for two weeks, except to visit a doctor, and am more or less in torture. There go my hopes aglimmering again—so much writing to do for the book and so impossible.

Much love,
Katharine

[FEBRUARY 1969]

Dear Katharine,

I was distressed to hear about the shingles. My grandmother, who had many illnesses, said shingles was the most painful thing that ever happened to her. She was in bed for weeks, and I read all of Richard Harding Davis to her.

I am still getting letters about "Onward and Upward." [. . .] I am impressed that so many of my friends are *New Yorker* readers. I have heard from a number that I hadn't heard from for some time. Did you know about Mrs. Klaber's violet book.* She says it will have 108 sheets of color plates, 26 pen and ink drawings, and nine end pieces; and probably be from $25 to $50. Dr. Russell says it will be the definitive book on violets for the next fifty to a hundred years.

[. . .]

Aff,
Elizabeth Lawrence

SARASOTA, FLORIDA
FEBRUARY 14, 1969

Dear Elizabeth,

A tiny note because I am still so sick, having now got onto the intercostal neuritis part of shingles. Your mother was right about the pain.

*Doretta Klaber, *Violets* (Fairleigh Dickinson, 1976).

[. . .] Thanks for the tip on Mrs. Klaber's violet book and for the note on Japanese iris. On this last I think I am fixed. The author, Harold Bruce, of the Winterthur book is sending me a couple of roots that grow in a friend's garden. The real thing. Someone else from California seems to be sending me some roots but I don't think it is the real thing. It is that non-hardy thing they call iris in California that has to be lifted or heavily covered in cold climates. Have forgotten the name.

Love, haste,
Katharine

P.S. [. . .] I have to go to New York to the Columbia Presbyterian (probably Harkness) next week or whenever a room can be found for me—for tests and treatment of all kinds. Maddening now that the weather should be warming up. [. . .] I'm going to send Andy back South if I can as he's in the midst of a new book* if I can manage alone. I think the whole business is due to mismanagement by the over-busy Florida doctors who have little interest in any northern visitor as a person and act by routine on 15 min. office visits—not a second more. I'm fed up with Florida. I may have to wait here longer, tho'. New York hospitals haven't a bed empty.

MARCH 31, 1969

Dear Katharine,

All this time I have been wondering and worrying about you, and where and how you are [. . .] and decided to send a letter in care of *The New Yorker*, and at least let you know how concerned I am.

I do hope you won't be too miserable to laugh at the enclosed

---

The Trumpet of the Swan.

schedule of the Southeast Daffodil Show in Atlanta.* I suppose "arrangement" is a word not to be mentioned any more.

You will be amused to hear that the University Press is planning to reprint the new edition of *A Southern Garden*. It is entirely due to you, as they were completely apathetic. I don't know what the first printing was. Probably two thousand copies, which is what the first edition was. I am still getting letters from unknown readers of you and me.

I am off to the daffodil meeting tomorrow. It is in Nashville this year, which is nice for me as I shall see my only living Aunt,† and three generations of cousins; and friends from all over the country. I really don't care that much about daffodils. I'd rather see them in my own garden. It's the people I like.

With love, and I do hope you are better, and not in the hospital.

Aff,
Elizabeth Lawrence

NEW YORK
APRIL 4, 1969

Dear Elizabeth,

This is written flat on my back in a hospital but even so I could laugh at the schedule of the Southeast Daffodil Show in Atlanta—"Artistic Division." The "visions" are wonderfully full of pretentious wordings and vague aspirations and touching yearnings.

I have been here since late February and discovered, on arrival and x-rays, that I have a busted back again—a compression fracture of one of my dorsal vertebrae. Also a gigantic dermatitis outbreak again. [. . .] In any case to make a long story as short as

---

*Enclosure not preserved.
†Helen Lawrence Vander Horst.

possible things have gone from bad to worse since December 21 and finally we had to make a hasty retreat North the last week of February. I have been in Harkness Pavilion ever since in room 1116. The sad truth is that all the cortisone has given me osteoporosis and it could be that I have had other minor fractures in the pelvis or the spine. Nevertheless, there is nothing else to do but to let it heal itself. Meanwhile I am in bed or up on a walker. The pain has been very severe and it will be so, the doctors say, for two or three months more. Andy had to go back to Sarasota to pack up my possessions and his in our rented house and now, after a period of weeks in New York, he will be off to Maine tomorrow to make arrangements, if he can, to take care of me at home. I shall be confined to the second floor for quite a time and thus no gardening or garden pleasures. The difficulty will be to get the nurses or nurses aides that we need and a hospital bed and all sorts of things.

My goose is cooked as a writer and so is my hope for a book on which I was working and trying to write some background chapters because sitting is the most difficult position for me and I doubt I can do anything by dictation. This letter is dictated. At times of self-pity I think this is one of the worst ways to get old but one can't choose. However, I haven't given up yet and maybe I can do something with a tape recorder.

I am delighted that the University Press is planning to reprint the new edition of *A Southern Garden*. It is entirely due to your book, not to me. I hope you had a lovely time in Nashville with all your relatives and friends. Maine is still deep in slush and old stacks of snow and I have received the cheerful news that field mice have burrowed in under the snow in my spring bulb bed and have likely killed the Old Pillar rose and the Golden Wings rose and the pale lavender clematis that grew on a trellis behind the South bed that I planted with bulbs last fall. However, there might be a daffodil or two elsewhere but I expect great winter-kill and mouse damage. The mice probably have ringed my old-fashioned roses too.

I'll be here two or three weeks more but, with luck, will then be released to be taken home in an ambulance plane. It is dreadful for Andy and he was all through the first version of a new children's book except for the last two chapters when I became such a burden. It should be I who would be going to Maine to make the arrangements.

Much love and do write me from time to time if you have the time. For the next few weeks my best address would be in care of *The New Yorker.*

Affectionately yours,
Katharine

[JULY 8, 1969]

Dear Katharine,

I hope you won't be discouraged by this return post answer to your wonderful tape recording* (you are better than my niece and nephew) but I am off to New York on the early plane in the morning (if I can stand up, whatever I have hit in the small of the back the last two mornings, and I couldn't, but so far Darvon gets me going eventually) to a wedding, and I do want to tell you how relieved I was to get your letter and to know that you can at *least* enjoy the flowers. Also to tell you that you must not, under any circumstances, consider giving up the books. You are the only person, except me (and that is on such a small scale), who reads the books she reviews. It broke my heart when Dr. [Edgar T.] Wherry wrote me that mine was the best review he had of his

*Apparently not preserved.

Southeastern Fern Guide. I, of course, know nothing about ferns, but I know Dr. Wherry and the Rock Garden Society, and I studied the book very carefully to see what it would mean to dirt gardeners like me. So few reviewers of garden books get beyond the blurbs. I sometimes think that you really have no idea what "Onward and Upward" means to very many people.

I have so much to say, but am in the state where I took a potted plant to my sister to keep while I am gone, and left my reading glasses on her terrace. When I went to see if I had left them, after searching half an hour here, she said, no, they can't be here.

I am glad you are *some* better. Do get lots better.

Aff,
Elizabeth

P.S. I am so glad you liked the *N.C. Natives* [i.e., *Wild Flowers of North Carolina*].

[OCTOBER 1969]

Dear Katharine,
    [. . .]
    I wonder whether you know that a Sylvania sun lamp with fruit and flowers expresses peace and contentment in the home.* I am sure you have been sent that hideous book, translated from the French and put out by Morrow.† I reviewed it, as I feel sure most of the Flower Arrangers will love it.

With love to you both,
Elizabeth

---

*EL enclosed a clipping about a flower arrangement that used a Sylvania sunlamp to express "peace and contentment."
†Perhaps *Flower Decoration in European Homes,* by Laurence Buffet-Chaillie (Morrow, 1969).

OCTOBER 17, 1969

Dear Elizabeth,

Your funny little letter and Miss Dormon's two books [*Indian Boy* and *Bird Talk*] were a joy to receive and I thank you both. I don't know her address, so would you please seal and mail the enclosed inadequate letter to her. The address is of course in my files but I can't bend over to search for it. I was delighted with your clipping and want to know what paper it came out of just on the chance I might be able again to write and use it or have Andy use it as a newsbreak. I'll have to try a Sylvania sun lamp to see whether it brings peace and contentment to this unpeaceful and discontented home.

[. . .] I *am* stronger than when I left Harkness but it has been a horrible summer, and nurses, practical nurses, aides and kind neighbors still surround me and help me for eighteen hours of each day. Most of my time has gone into tending my disintegrating carcass. It has been terribly hard on Andy, who is now ailing himself. Nevertheless he has nearly finished a third children's book* that he has promised to send his publishers by Thanksgiving. I haven't been allowed to read it yet for he never lets me do so until he himself is reasonably satisfied with his manuscript. He is on the third revise now. I know all about it and its wild (I mean not human) chief character and all about his travels as they occupy Andy's thoughts continually. He says the book is doomed because it will be compared to its disadvantage with *Charlotte's Web*. He also says it will be said he is plagiarizing or repeating himself and he says perhaps he is but he does like some parts of it very much. He will turn it in anyway because he has spent so much time on it and we need the money. This has been an incredibly expensive year for us, despite Medicare. I'm betting that even if it's not Andy's best it will be better than most "juveniles."

The Trumpet of the Swan.

I won't go into the grim details of my health but it has been bad enough for me to spend most of my free time on my affairs, tidying up my chaotic files, assembling ancestral letters to go to Yale and Bowdoin, and my own personal literary correspondence to go to Bryn Mawr. My eyesight is somewhat on the blink, too. As for the garden, it's going to pot even though I get around when I have time, using a "walker." [. . .] The one thing I can't do is fall as I'd break every bone in my body. (This is one reason for the aides to follow me around and keep me on my feet but the chief reason is to give Andy an uninterrupted sleep at night and eight hours a day free to write and get some needed recreation.) To return to the garden, I can't now even take off deadheads or pick my own flowers, but when not in bed, I do get around and point. We are cutting down the size of the vegetable garden and I want to cut the end off one perennial bed but Henry says it will be more work than leaving it the way it is. He is overworked and helpers for him are hard to find. [. . .] Very late fall, and roses and annuals are still in bloom, plus lovely chrysanthemums. I could ramble on and on so no more. As you see [from the hand-written letter] secretarial help is also scarce and two of my helpers are pregnant.

Well, hope springs eternal. Today I at last went at the start of a new chapter for my mythical book. We shall stay right here this winter.

Much love from Katharine.

OCTOBER 27, 1969

Dear Elizabeth,

Help! Help! I'm trying to find how often the old-fashioned Night-blooming cereus opens its white flowers at midnight (or after), in order to recapture an event of my quite young childhood for the Northampton (Mass.) chapter of my improbable book. In this cold region of Northampton, of course, it was a houseplant and I remember being taken by my Aunt Helen to one of her friends' house to watch and wait from midnight on to see the magical happening. I was chiefly excited by being allowed to sit up so late and I got the impression, almost surely erroneous, that it happened on only one night in the year. My guess now would be that a tropical houseplant in a frigid New England house of that era had sparse bloom but a brief period of bloom when it opened about one flower a night and that probably this night was the first or second flowering of that year. Would this be nearly correct? My childish memory was that it opened a flower just once a year, for such a to-do was made about it by my Aunt Helen. [. . .]

Much love,
Katharine

[OCTOBER 1969]

Dear Katharine,

   Like you I remember great excitement about the rare and great occasion of the cereus that was to bloom at midnight. It was in the rectory greenhouse at St. Mary's. But my memory is hazy as to the actual performance. Some years ago some woman, whose name I have forgotten, called to tell me that her night-blooming cereus was in bloom, and Hannah and I went to see it. We did not have to wait for midnight. As I remember we went at nine o'clock and found some flowers open, and by ten all that were to open that night were out. I wrote a piece about it, but my files are not good enough for me to lay my hands on it. I do remember that it had a number of flowers in bloom at once, and that it bloomed more than one night. I think it was *Epiphyllum oxypetalum*. Ernesta Ballard says it blooms over a period of several weeks. […] Last summer, Novella, who used to nurse my mother, called to ask the name of "that flower that blooms at night." After several guesses she said it was in a pot. When I said night-blooming cereus she said that was it. She said she had had it for seven years, and these were the first flowers.

[…]

Aff,
Elizabeth

MARCH 25, 1970

Dear Elizabeth,

This miserly little check is what you would have received if your clipping about the Sylvania lamp had been used as an end of column filler, or, in *New Yorker* parlance, as a "Newsbreak." It *could* have been so used by Andy, who still writes the taglines or headings for newsbreaks and who, therefore, is still on the *New Yorker* staff as I am not anymore—I'm merely a contributor, although I must say that I put in a good many hours a month answering or writing letters that are called for just because of having been an editor of the magazine for over thirty-five years.

Much has happened since I last sent you a call for help. For one thing, I have become sicker and sicker and less able to function as a writer or even as a correspondent. A part of this is merely mechanical. The cold winter has stirred up an old nerve pinch in my cervical spine, which has given me occipital neuritis at times and now seems to involve two fingers in both hands [which] cramp up or go into muscle spasms when I write in longhand. This makes my handwriting almost totally illegible except to those who have known it for years—people like Andy and Harriet Walden at *The New Yorker*, who used to be my secretary. I lack a real secretary here. I can't type myself, both because of my spine and my fingers, and so my writing becomes long-winded and rambling. Poor typist as I am, my natural medium for composition is the typewriter and I am less prolix when I use it.

All this is leading up to the fact that I have turned in my final *New Yorker* reviews of garden books, for I resigned the post of critic in this field as of March 1st.

[...]

I never again can write for deadlines or under pressure (hence no more reviews) and very likely I am past writing anything publishable. As I now have some heart trouble my main job should be to help Andy and tidy up this house, which is still in chaos so far as my files and papers go. I do have at least three other pieces under way for my mythical book, but they are non-timely and it's the book I shall work at.

[...]

Andy is sick, too, and is just home from a morning of X-rays. This is great anxiety to me. In spite of all, he has a third children's book coming out in the late spring.

Much love,
Katharine

P.S. later—Results of the x-rays were happy from Andy's and my point of view—he has an active duodenal ulcer, probably his old ulcer reactivated. He has cured these up fairly easily before and hopes to again. [...]

I don't know whether this will be mailed or not. We've had nothing from NYC—can't send anything there or to many other points. The lull in the mail, especially the absence of *The New York Times,* is a momentary blessing but after that the deluge. I am still surrounded by nurses and aides and have to fight for time to write at all. A better letter later. The night-blooming cereus is in the next piece. I go back—about Northampton.

[MARCH 1970]
EASTER DAY

Dear Katharine,

Thank you for the nice Easter present.* But I can't bear for you not to be happy about your "Onward and Upward."† It is delightful, and I read it with great pleasure. I was particularly interested in what you said about *The Wild Flowers of North Carolina*, because I have found it to be so true.‡ Mittie Wellford and I were able to identify things in tidewater Virginia by taking it to the creeks with us on our rambles. But I didn't realize how good the pictures really are until you said so, and I took another look. Do you all know the book about the Botanical Garden at Chapel Hill, *From Laurel Hill to Siler's Bog*, by John Terres (Knopf, '69)? I had walked over the Mason Farm with Dr. Ritchie Bell, and Laurel Hill with Billy Hunt, looking for wildflowers, but I had no idea that there were red-tailed hawks, bobwhite quail, great horned owls, wild turkeys, gray foxes, golden mice, and muskrats about. (I *did* know about the buzzards!) I relished the bit about Mr. Whittle and the New York Botanic Garden.§ It does me good. They are so snippy about us. I do feel for him, though. I have to look it up every time I mention New York or Brooklyn. Linda Lamm (Joseph Mitchell's sister) asked me the other day what the difference is. I couldn't tell her, but I can now, I have looked it up in Fowler.

[. . .]

I hope to have a small paperback (or something) to send you before the summer is over. When I couldn't find a publisher for

*The $5 check.
†"Knots and Arbours—and Books" (*NY* 3/28/70).
‡*Wild Flowers of North Carolina* by William S. Justice and C. Ritchie Bell, "a model for any state field guide."
§In reviewing *Common or Garden*, KSW faulted Tyler Whittle for having placed the New York Botanic Garden in the Bronx.

my book on gardeners I have known, I took out the section about Mr. Krippendorf, taken from his letters, and gave it to the Cincinnati Nature Museum. I was disappointed, as Frank McCamey has taken beautiful photographs, and I hoped for something like the Winterthur book,* that it has a measly "spread," but I am glad to get into print the material that Mr. K. gathered from his more than fifty years of experience, and to know that it will be used at the Center.† [. . .]

We have had a happy Easter. Chip, my nephew who did two tours in Viet Nam, and was at Hue during the Tet offensive, is now out of the Navy, and with DuPont in Richmond, so he can come home often. He looks as gay and lighthearted as when he first came home with his commission, but when I asked him how he goes on living he said he didn't know. He said, "I choke it down, and go on for a while, and then it all comes back."

I stopped at this point to listen to College Bowl. Both sides missed the question about *Charlotte's Web,* but any member of this family could have answered for them! One boy said, *The Wind in the Willows.*

[. . .]

Hannah and I have reservations for the Castles and Gardens Cruise again this May. A very foolish thing, as Hannah is having trouble with her knee, and I am right where I was before they dug the calcium out of my shoulder. Only this time they say there isn't any calcium. Fortunately Darvon helps some. I do hope this will find both of you feeling better and spring in the air.

Aff,
Elizabeth

Winterthur in Bloom by Harold Bruce (Winterthur, 1968), which KSW had admired in "Winterthur and Winter Book Fare" (*NY* 12/21/68).
†*Lob's Wood* (Cincinnati Nature Center, 1971).

Elizabeth and her sister, Ann, in the Raleigh garden, the subject of Elizabeth's *A Southern Garden*, published in 1942.

Elizabeth and her mother in the young garden in Charlotte, North Carolina. Elizabeth's sister's house is in the background.

Elizabeth's pool and garden in Charlotte, looking toward the back of her house and terrace.

Elizabeth studying fragrance, a subject both gardeners wrote about in their columns. Elizabeth sent Katharine specimens of leaves and flowers from her garden "for your nose."

APRIL 7, 1970

Dear Elizabeth,

Your wonderful letter about the "O and U In The Garden" piece cheered me up in the hospital, from which I have just returned after a week's stay of complete bedrest. [. . .] I can only *guess* that I wrote you before being rushed to the hospital a week or more ago unable to breathe and in an attack of congestive heart failure due to the fluid deposited around my heart and lungs by the cortisone drug, Prednisone, which I have to take to suppress my rare form of dermatitis. Our well-trained and darling doctor, who comes from one of the Carolinas (Greensboro, N.C. His name is Murray and his father is a doctor still in practice. Maybe you know the Murrays), and the local volunteer ambulance corps saved my life by rushing oxygen here and giving it to me here and during the nine mile trip to the Blue Hill Hospital. I spent a day and a night under an oxygen tent. I am home again after a week and weak as a kitten, but I still have no oxygen in this house. We shall remedy that on Monday. Tomorrow I am supposed to resume my natural life.

I still think my article is lousy and it is full of awkward wordings and even of errors in fact that distress me, because I had to do last minute corrections on answers to queries by long distance phone so that I finally gave up and said, "Do what you like," which was a big mistake. I know the piece is just a bore for most people; [no one] except for you and the Editor-in-chief of *The New Yorker* and another faithful reader have said or written one word about it. Oh, yes, one other. Our southern doctor, who to my surprise read it without my telling him it was published at last, said, "I found it pretty technical—it is out of my field." Now I'm *supposed* to write pieces that can be enjoyable and readable by any one. Even my own children haven't spoken or written about it, or my friends on *The New Yorker* staff, and this to me is ominous.

It was a flop, but if you liked it, that's enough for me. You are one of my "shining exceptions."

I am distressed that your shoulder still gives you so much pain, even though the calcium is gone. I think you are courageous but sensible to take your trip with "Hannah." I have never known just who she is or her last name. Does she live with you or is she a friend and neighbor? My advice to everyone is to travel while they can still manage to walk a step. I am even more delighted to learn about your book but it makes me mad that it couldn't have had the Winterthur treatment—fully illustrated with beautiful photographs. I wish I had known about the book on gardeners you have known when you were offering it to publishers for I do have some influence with several publishing houses who have published *New Yorker* books. Good photographs of Mr. Krippendorf's garden and your section about him taken from your correspondence would have been just my meat. In any case I look forward to the "small paperback" you'll be sending me some time this summer. And what about the whole book on gardeners you have known? What publishers have you sent it to? I can't believe that any book by you would be turned down all around the line. Do you have an agent? I am now unfamiliar with the good ones, for only a few of the literary agencies I used to deal with are run by the same people or even exist. I could find out, though, through *The New Yorker*, which are the good ones today.

Spring is very late here and has been stormy and tempestuous. The frost is not yet out of the ground and we still have nights as low as 22. We haven't yet dared remove the evergreen boughs that cover the borders. I must stop as my typist who is also a mainstay on getting meals is about to leave.

How wonderful to have "Chip" back safe. What he said about his memories of the war haunts me.

Affectionately,
Katharine

P.S. Our mails are woefully out of joint and I since have had more letters from people who like the piece or are polite about it. Only a couple from total strangers, though, one of whom seems to expect me to design and plan a whole new garden for him. No soap.

[APRIL 1970]

Dear Katharine,

[. . .]

Hannah is Hannah Withers, a friend and neighbor and a dear one, and one of your ardent fans. She loves all of your pieces including the last one—we had fun over Mrs. Huffman's getting in *The New Yorker,** and your tact in not mentioning *The Observer*— not that Mrs. H. is likely to have read *The New Yorker.* Hannah collects garden books, so she is always interested in what you have to say about them, and like me she likes the way you write, and the things you write about. I did not know her until we came to Charlotte to live, but we found that we had been at St. Mary's together when I was twelve.

Mittie Wellford and I picked the perfect time for the visit to the tidewater, though it was by accident. It was the height of the daffodil season. We found Silver Bells in the Wellfords' garden at Sabine Hall. [. . .]

Mittie and Hill live on their farm on the Rappahannock River. Hill and I saw deer tracks when we went to hunt arrowheads in a ploughed field, and Hill showed me a beaver hut and a muskrat burrow in the marshes, and Mittie and I found coon tracks in the sand when we walked along the beach at low tide. They say the Rappahannock is the least contaminated river in Virginia. And they say there are bald eagles.

It is dear of you to be concerned about my book. I have taken another section to enlarge into a book in itself. It is about the

*Mrs. Huffman had designed the flower arrangement using the Sylvania lamp.

Southern Market Bulletins, and the old ladies who advertise in them, and the farmers and their dogs. I have been working on them for more than thirty years, since Eudora Welty introduced me. I send for the plants, and they write to tell me about them. The market bulletins are a social history of the rural South. It will all soon be gone, and it seems to me important to keep a record of it. The University has already turned the manuscript down, but I am still collecting material, and when I get some rewriting done I shall start out again. I have never had an agent, but perhaps I should. [...] Eudora Welty asked Mr. Russell to take me on long ago, but he didn't think he could do any better than I would.

The last of the daffodils are coming into bloom, and I am surrounded by a sea of dogwood. I hope you are having spring and feeling better.

Aff,
Elizabeth

APRIL 26, 1971

Dear Elizabeth,

Andy and I thank you for the charming little book, *Lob's Wood*. It is a wonderful memorial to the fabulous and mysterious Mr. Krippendorf of *The Little Bulbs* and also to his chosen correspondent. It is such a pretty little book with that beautiful photograph of the tall hardwood trees and the great swirls and glades of daffodils along their borders and the color page of flowers. I'm glad that the woods are now a great public reserve near Cincinnati. Did Mr. K. leave them to the Nature Center and money to keep up all these acres? Or must this be raised each year? I don't know how long ago you lost your friend and I do wish I knew more about him. Was he a man of great inherited wealth who never had to work to earn and so could spend all his life on the hard work outdoors he loved so much? Or did he make a fortune and retire to this life? Good Heavens how he labored! It makes me tired just to think of it. How many hands did he have to employ to provide these millions of flowers? (He speaks only once of "the boy" but I suspect that there must have been a good gardener and a phalanx of helpers despite Mr. Krippendorf's own prodigious energy.) I suppose everyone in Cincinnati knows the answers but not I and now all my Cincinnati friends are dead. [. . .]

I must say that after reading *Lob's Wood* I sometimes wish I were living in a milder climate. We've just survived a winter to top all others in the Weather Bureau statistics. Spring *is* here but I haven't a daffodil in bloom yet although others do near here. The ground is still frozen and unworkable except in a few south beds around the house. We expect and already see great winterkill. What happened (and it has never happened before since 1933 when we bought our farm) was that the ground remained unfrozen until just after Thanksgiving and then came a big snowstorm, catching us short before we had been able to cover the perennial beds with spruce boughs as we always do after the ground has frozen, nor could we bank the house with boughs or protect shrub and climbing roses and other tender things—not even my newly established clump of single white Japanese iris by the new pond. Then came snow storm after snow storm—an accumulation of 110 inches or more in all, and in drifts far more than that. This kept the ground from ever really freezing until about a month ago after the snow had melted. I am sure that if I could get into the woods I would find snow and ice in some sheltered places because only in the last week have the fields been bare.

. . . It is now April 29 and our cold nights still persist with temperatures in the upper 20s and hoar frost over everything in the morning. Nevertheless a few daffodils are now out and oddly enough, since they never came first before, a lot of the large dark blue hyacinths. [. . .]

I want to ask you about crocus. Most of my crocuses are planted in the grass and around the lawn trees. The purples and striped ones and the whites have come up but only a couple of yellows. [. . .] Could it be that these yellow ones are the ones that mice can eat with impunity?

[. . .]

I am miles behind on Andy's and my correspondence so this can't be a real letter. I guess I did tell you at Christmas the bad news of Andy's motor accident last July. The after-effects have never really left him. [. . .] He made a hurried trip to New York to see our old friend Dr. Frank Stinchfield, the orthopedist who has done so much for my spine, and as a result of that he now wears, when he can bear to, a soft sponge collar around his throat but he finds it so hampering that he doesn't wear it continuously. He also hangs himself twice a day when he can remember to.* Our newest dog, Susy, a white Highland terrier, jumps right up on his lap when he is hanging himself from a rafter and sits there, very pleased to be involved in the operation. At this time of year Susy is gray with mud.

We are having a frightful rabies scare here and the dogs can't be allowed to run loose although they have been inoculated. There are rabid animals all over the state of Maine. They have been holding clinics for cats and dogs to receive their anti-rabies shots but most of the people who keep cats don't bother to get shots for them. A rabid skunk was killed by a dog just over the Brooklin line so it's very near to home. They have even found a rabid deer and many foxes. Never a dull moment in the country,

---

*Years earlier, EBW had rigged up pulleys in the barn so that he could put himself in traction, which he described and drew in a very funny letter to his brother, Stanley Hart White (*Letters of E. B. White*, pp. 424–425).

it seems. This means that we can't let the dogs out at night except on a leash.

I am very anxious to hear about *your* health and I hope you are continuing your column, which I wish I could read regularly. Thank you again for the lovely *Lob's Wood*. When you have nothing else to do, which will be never, do tell me a little more about the fascinating mysterious Mr. Krippendorf.

Affectionately,
Katharine

P.S. I've managed to finish a labor of 5 years or more this winter and have sent off to Bryn Mawr the annotated list of *New Yorker* connected or *Sub-Treasury of American Humor* connected list of books I am leaving to my college (Bryn Mawr) libraries and each book is starred so my children will recognize them. The annotations are of things I remember that no one else may for future biographers or literary historians. I am sending now, since this house is a tinder box, a small collection of personal letters from writers of note. [. . .]

[MAY 1971]

Dear Katharine,

I am terribly distressed to learn about Andy's accident and I shall say a prayer for a good report from the tests.

I thought you would like to see the use made of your kind words.* They were the only thing that even made any impression on the Press.

I miss your "Onward and Upward," but I hope you will be able to go on with the book. All of your readers are looking forward to it—including me.

I am still working on *The Market Bulletin*, and it is such fun. I

*Apparently, UNC Press quoted White's praise for *A Southern Garden*.

cut out an ad today by a farm boy 21—almost 22—who is being married in December, and wants a job and is ready right now. He says he has had 18 years experience!

But I find it hard to do my garden column, and the garden, and my files and correspondence, and really get down to the sustained work of a book. So I sometimes feel as you do, but I keep working at it, and I am sure you will too.

With love to both of you.

Aff,
Elizabeth

DEC. 12, 1971

Dear Elizabeth,

This can't be a real letter as my eyes are recovering from a bad conjunctivitis and I can't see much at the moment. We've had a good year up till September and then both of us began to go down hill on health. I often wonder about yours and do hope you are well and writing another of your wonderful books. I hope to rise like the Phoenix and get to work on mine again but one never knows. I work every day a few hours, but this year it has been entirely work to free Andy to write, which is more important.

Ever so much love and a Happy Christmas and New Year.

Katharine

[DECEMBER 1971]

Dear Katharine,
    [. . .]
Mr. Krippendorf told me once when I was there that his father and uncle were German cobblers who came over to this country and set up a shop in Cincinnati. Soon after they started a small factory Mr. Krippendorf's father had a heart attack, and he had

to stop school at the age of 14 or 16 to take over the management. He said he walked between the machines to see where two movements could be combined in one, and by the time he was nineteen he knew all there was to know about making shoes. He said he was at that time an expert judge of leather, but that he had since lost the sensitivity of his fingertips. By the time he was twenty-one he had made enough money to buy the farm that was later called Lob's Wood, and when he was married (in 1902) he and Mary drove out there in a buggy (30 miles) to spend their honeymoon. At first they lived in town in winter, but when Rosan was eight they sent her to spend school nights with her aunt, and stayed in the country all of the year. Until they had a car, Mr. K. went back and forth on the train on week days. Mary took him to the station in the morning and met him in the evening in a pony cart. He got up at daylight and worked in the woods, and worked again until dark.

Krippendorf-Dittman shoes were good but not expensive. Mary and Rosan wouldn't have thought of wearing them, but when Mr. K. learned that I wore the sample size he used to pick them out for me when the salesmen came back to the factory. When he first wrote to me he was about sixty-eight, and was still driving himself into town five days a week. Later he went in only three days, but it was not until just before he stopped writing to me that he sold the business and was in the country all of the time.

[Aff, Elizabeth]

DECEMBER 27, 1971

Dear Katharine,

How good you are to write to me when your letter about *Lob's Wood* has never been answered. (April 26)

I sat down at once and wrote about Mr. Krippendorf, then I had to take it out of the typewriter, and I laid it aside until I could answer what you asked about the crocuses, and there it has stayed in a pile of unfiled and unfinished notes and manuscripts.

I don't know of any crocus that is poisonous to mice or any other rodent. I can't remember any reference to it, and I have just checked in Mr. Bowles's Handbook. Mr. Krippendorf told me they leave *Crocus Tomasinianus* alone, and I have found this to be true.

When I put out some corms of *Crocus aucyrensis* years ago, a chipmunk ate them as soon as they were planted. I thought he got them all, but later there was a flower, and during the years it had reseeded, and I always have a few, recently more and more. This is a lovely golden one—very early in the year. *Crocus speciosus* has seeded itself too, and I have lots of the tiny white *C. ochroleucus*. It was covered with 9″ of snow not long ago, and when the snow had gone it went on blooming.

I find that once the crocuses seed themselves, the chipmunks are apt to leave them alone. It is the new corms that they like. This must be true at Lob's Wood, too, for I found lots of them in bloom the last time I was there, in October. Mr. K. used to plant them in the gravel paths close to the stones that edge them.

The Sunday editor has dropped my column, which distresses me, as it gave me a chance to write about such a wide range of subjects, and kept me in touch with so many interesting people. But I was spending too much time on it, and now I am working hard on my *Market Bulletin* book. I have been reading the bulletins and writing to the old ladies for thirty years. I'm working on herbal teas at present. The old ladies are wonderful correspondents.

I love the delightful photograph of the geese, and we all loved reading about them in *The New Yorker*.*

---

*The Whites' 1971 Christmas card had a photograph of EBW with some of his geese. In his "Letter from the East" (*NY* 7/24/71), he wrote about the drama of watching his old

We are having weeks of spring after our 9″ of snow. Dr. Mayer says he has 35 varieties of camellia in bloom, and the autumn cherry in my garden is full of pink flowers. We have been able to have lunch under it several times.

Caroline Dormon died early in December.* She was not able to live alone, and had so many terrible falls, her niece had to put her in a nursing home. She died shortly afterward. Mr. Clinton is publishing one of her books,† and it is so sad that it did not come out in time for her to see it.

With love to both of you.

Aff,
Elizabeth

[JANUARY 1973]

Dear Katharine,

I rejoice to hear from you.‡ I have worried and worried, and asked Joseph Mitchell. Finally I saw him at his niece's wedding in Wilson [North Carolina]. It was a beautiful warm, bright day in November, and we sat in the woodsy garden, which I had helped Linda Lamm to plan, and talked for hours. He told me that, as I had feared, you were not well. Joseph hasn't been well either, but he was fine then, and in the best of spirits and fun.

[. . .]

Last January I fell and cracked my *other* knee. This time it wasn't so bad, as I had just gone to a new young specialist in ar-

---

gander become a foster father to three adopted goslings, turning it into a meditation on the sadness of a summer's day.

*Dormon died November 23, 1971.

†*Louisiana Trees* (LSU Cooperative Extension Service, 1971). A. S. McKean, who actually edited Dormon's work, was listed as author. Republished in 1984 under Dormon's name.

‡Perhaps a letter is missing. Both EL's and KSW's handwriting and dates become less reliable.

thritis, and he knew not to put my leg in a cast. I had a light brace I could take off at night, and a walker. Then I had summer flu and for weeks thought that was the end of me, but now I am fine— only older and more arthritic.

Don't give up on your book. I am working on three but concentrating on one—my *Market Garden* book that I have been writing on for thirty years, and every time I try to get it ready to publish (but still no publisher) I get a whole new vein of gold. It is your kind of a book because the Southern country people are just like the Maine people. And I feel it is so important to preserve their letters, and the culture that is revealed in their advertisements. The bulletins are put out by the states from Florida (have you ever seen it?) to Virginia and West Virginia, and along the Gulf Coast to Louisiana. Just this year the Louisiana Bulletin has been discontinued. South Carolina is threatened, and I feel they will all go before long, and all of that way of life will be lost. Most of the people who write to me are octogenarians. Most are barely literate—but they write beautiful and loving letters. They plant by the signs, and ask me to pray for them (it is the Bible Belt)—one of them (who is only fifty) says she is called the Herb Doctor. She deals out medicine (her family laughs at her), and is learning to make love potions from a woman who is half-Indian. (I can't put that in of course, as I use their real names.) She is one of the most religious, and begs me to pray for her son who has quit going to church, and drinks, and for her daughter who is ill, and all of her son's friends, and for God to give her guidance. I do my best, though personal prayers were (are?) not in my line, and it is hard to find one in the *Book of Common Prayer* that fits all of Mrs.— needs. I decided that the Collect asking for assistance "among all the changes and chances of this mortal life" would come nearest to covering them.

[. . .]

I hope I can get the manuscript in order and up to date, and if I can't find a publisher I'll leave it to the University.*

[...]

Aff,
Elizabeth

JANUARY 7, 1974

Dearest Elizabeth,

Your letter should have been answered long since but for a series of poor health happenings before and over the holidays. I was filled with delight to hear from you but desolated to learn of your two broken or cracked knees. Thank Heaven you are now without a cast but I don't know whether you still have to use a "walker." Since I have been using one for five years now I sympathize with you, but at the same time I love my "walker" and find myself secure on it so hobble about the garden on it in spring, summer, and fall; and when the streets aren't icy, I take walks on the highway with it. In winter with snow and ice I don't get out much and that is my state now. [...]

I have always been fascinated by your *Market Garden Book* but now you have told me more about it and I am even more anxious to have you finish it. It would be a real contribution to the history of the culture of the South, and I am sure that after you do finish it one of the university presses would see its merits and publish it even if a commercial publisher thought it too specialized. I have never seen any of these market garden bulletins from the southern states. Are they like *Joe's Bulletin,* which so far as I know ceased publication quite a few years back? I used to love the ads and ex-

---

*EL was working on a manuscript that was later edited by garden writer Allen Lacy and published posthumously: *Gardening for Love: The Market Bulletins* (Duke University Press, 1987).

changes in that and I have subscribed to it—but it dwindled and got less good after the first editor died.

[. . .]

As for finishing my book, I have now almost given up hope. First of all I can't write well any more because I am used to writing on the typewriter and correcting from that. When I write in longhand, I get long-winded and my writing is so illegible that nearly everything now has to be copied for me [. . .] Your correspondence with the octogenarians must be fascinating and rewarding. You are doing a sociological service by this book but I can see that it must take a lot out of you to comfort them by prayer and quotation. Everything you write is also a literary joy.

[. . .]

Affectionately,
Katharine

P.S. May 1974 be kinder to you than last year was.

MARCH 11, 1974

Dear Elizabeth,

I see to my horror that the postmark on your *Market Garden* reports from Georgia and South Carolina is January, and I am ashamed that I haven't thanked you for them and for your letter. I've been waiting for a chance to write you a good letter, but things in general have gone from bad to worse and the good day has never come. I am dictating this from bed where I have been lying flat with a heat pad for six days, thanks to a new compression fracture in my spine.

[. . .]

I had a good time reading the Bulletins and when I told Andy that I found an ad for a pony for $50 he immediately said that he'd like to get that pony—why, I don't know, because all horses give him horrible hay fever. He is allergic to horse dander. We did once have a horse that was used mainly for plowing, and my daughter-in-law and I drove it until once it ran away with her and upset the little carriage. The sales and notices of Horses and Mules, Poultry, and other farm things interested me just as much as the plants and flowers; also the employment ads. It all gives me a picture of a very different life from the life of a Maine farmer, and Maine farms are getting fewer and fewer. If we buy anything, it is mostly from a neighbor.

I haven't been able to detect from my hasty reading of these sheets the characters that stand out in the Plants and Flowers Exchange or Sales, but they all fascinate me. As for the price of Hay and Grain, they make us envious. We are now reduced in this region to one grain store, and we have to have grain for our laying hens, our geese in winter, and for the chickens and pullets come spring. We buy baby day-old chicks, and for the first time in history we had leucosis in the hen pen and lost five or six hens but apparently the epidemic is over, and I guess we're going to have enough fowls to freeze for the fall. [. . .]

One interesting thing has happened right in the next town of Blue Hill, which is that a young couple who moved here six years ago are getting ready to put out a publication on "New Gardening." It's called *The Farmstead Magazine, Maine Gardening and Small Farming.* They've been living in a house which, when they bought it, had no heat or electricity or plumbing. They have by now achieved a telephone and electricity for the house. I'll try to send you a copy of the first run of the magazine when it comes out in May. It's being distributed only in Maine. I am somewhat suspicious of these youthful organic farmers although we really do practically organic gardening ourselves—but once in a while I will use a pesticide, and of course Rotenone. The problem for me now is the expense of keeping up the garden. I'm broke all the time and while Andy isn't,* we just can't keep adding manpower and I'm no longer any use outdoors except on planning. I have suggested to Andy that I give up my long perennial borders and put in shrubs, which would be a distinctly labor-saving thing— but somehow I can't bring myself to do this, and I think I'll just leave the perennials and let them peter out. Our seed order and plant order was just as big as ever this year but maybe this will be the last year.

Most of my reading, I must admit, has been political this year. We get the *New York Times* and the *Bangor Daily News* and two local weeklies. One of these weeklies is *The Ellsworth American,* which is an absolutely fascinating newspaper, started and owned by Russell Wiggins, who was once Managing Editor of *The Washington Post.* He has managed to make a unique paper, almost all of which one wants to read.

The worst event, from the point of view of everybody living in this region, has been a thousand gallon oil spill in Blue Hill harbor. I didn't know a thing about it until the *Blue Hill Packet* arrived today. Blue Hill at last got the money to start its sewage system to cover the center of town, the hospital, George Stevens Academy, and a few houses and stores. The company which was to start the project came from Portland, and the first thing they did was to bring in a huge tank full of diesel oil which sprung a leak that ran in under the ice that was still in the harbor. I hope they have contained it, and so far we haven't seen it on our shores just a little way up Blue Hill Bay. It's a pretty difficult thing to mop up with floating ice floes, etc. It covered the shore of the town park for the children of Blue Hill, so they may have a bad summer.

We've had the oddest winter I've ever known, and March has been as warm as April. All my little bulbs, still under their cover

*KSW kept her own garden account; EBW's account was for the farm.

of boughs, are coming up, and I know that the cold (and the snow we haven't had) is likely to catch up with us later in the month or in April or even in May. On the whole, it's lucky it was warm because although our fuel supply never gave out, gasoline has been a scarce commodity hereabouts, especially the last week in each month.

[. . .]

This is a very scattered and deadly letter but it takes you much love.

Ever affectionately,
Katharine

[MARCH 18, 1974]

Dear Katharine,

What a wonderful letter. How can you dictate when you are flat on your back, or at all. I am sure I never could do it. I hope you will give me permission to quote what you said about the *Market Bulletins*. I was amazed at your point of view, and it gives me a new outlook. There are no market bulletins of this kind north of Virginia. I did get a sample of the Connecticut one, but it was mostly quoting market prices. An old lady in Alabama put in a want ad for red shanks, and when I wrote to her, she asked me to tell my friends about her prize pigs. She asked me to write again. She said letters help a lonely person. She also asked me to come to see her. Several do that, and if I could still drive on the highway I certainly would. My sister's niece, who lives in South Carolina, has bought a farm. Her husband said, "And Aunt (they call me Aunt too), guess where we found it—in *The Market Bulletin*." It has woods and a creek and wild flowers. The *Georgia Bulletin* played right into my hands by having an anniversary, and quoting from their first issue (1920). A young boy, 21, wanted a job on a farm, for room and board and two dollars a week. As to publishers, my cousin Alex Lawrence, after publishing a number of books on Georgia history (one, *A Present for Mr. Lincoln*) not best sellers, but at least one of them out of print, and he hasn't even a copy of his own (I told him his sister said she went to the library in Lancaster, Pennsylvania, and under L found *The Little Bulbs* by Elizabeth Lawrence, and *Storm over Savannah* by Alexander Atkinson Lawrence. Alex said, "I bet she donated both."), told me recently that he has given up. The Georgia University Press is worse, if possible, than Chapel Hill, which has already turned down the first manuscript of *The Market Bulletins*—not funny enough, they said. Some years ago Caroline Dormon told me not to send anything to Louisiana. And Mr. Claitor, who published her books, has had a reprint of *Gardens in Winter* on his *published* list (books in print I mean) for several years. He still has my original drawings that Caroline did for me, and I can't sleep at night. All I can do is to write. My nephew, Chip (who voluntarily went to Viet Nam twice, and who has never read a word I have written, or expects to), has volunteered to be my literary executor, and I am instructing him to give all unpublished manuscripts and files to the Botany Library at Chapel Hill. Maybe some student, or someone will be interested in a lifetime of research.*

[. . .] The *Observer* dropped my column several years ago. They wanted the space for a staff member to do a how-to column. He calls me to ask the answers to the questions. I was heartbroken at first, because I found to my amazement that a weekly column is the most delightful way to write. You don't have to hold yourself down to any lengthy subject (like eleven *Market Bulletins*, from 1920 on) but can go into whatever interests you at the moment. Then I learned so much, by being asked about so many things I

*Before her death in 1985, EL sent most of her papers to the Watson Library at Northwestern State University of Louisiana in Natchitoches, which houses the Carolina Dormon papers.

Caroline Dormon, gardener and garden writer, in front of her cabin at Briarwood in rural northwest Louisiana. Elizabeth visited Dormon at this cabin.

Carl Krippendorf's woodland estate near Cincinnati, Ohio. Elizabeth wrote about "Mr. K." in *The Little Bulbs: A Tale of Two Gardens* and in *Lob's Wood*.

Elizabeth Lawrence, under the *Clematis armandii*, in a photograph used with her column "Through the Garden Gate."

Elizabeth, in pixie haircut and hat, posed in the Charlotte garden in the 1970s.

didn't know, and having to find out. And the instant response is so stimulating; I would go to St. Peter's at eight, and someone would already have read the morning paper, and would comment or disagree, or have something to add. But it was really the best thing that ever happened to me, as I was putting too much time on it.

Your problems are mine. My small garden is all perennial borders, except for the gravel paths and scrap of pine woods in the back. Last year when I was out of commission for months, I had *no* one to do anything. Finally, Dr. Hechenbleikner* said, "Elizabeth, if I send you my best student, will you pay him two dollars and a half an hour?" I said I would pay *any*thing. Jamie [Stimple] can come only twice a month—if then, and if it doesn't rain on the day he saves for me—but he works hard for eight hours, and as I have been able to do some myself, lately, we are getting along better, at least.

This is the loveliest spring we have had in years, in spite of severe freezes at the end of summer days, and the magnolias being blackened when in full bloom. The daffodils have so much substance (as Mr. Krippendorf used to say), and some that are nearly always blind (like the tiny double Queen Anne's jonquil) have bloomed for the first time in some years. My autumn cherry has bloomed off and on since the leaves fell last fall, and has been in its glory for at least two weeks. The pool is now full of petals, but there seem to be as many as ever on the tree.

[. . .] Wednesday I am being driven to Annapolis, and what I don't answer now certainly won't get answered when I get back. Fuzz has turned out to be an ardent and insatiable gardener, and expects me to supply not only her, but all of Maryland. She called to ask me to bring her more strawberry begonias, and

*Dr. Herbert Hechenbleikner, who established the arboretum at the University of North Carolina in Charlotte.

said Christopher wants twin sisters, and Peggy Sue wants Lenten roses.

Much love and better times to both of you.

Aff,
Elizabeth

DECEMBER 11, 1974

Dear Elizabeth,

It's so long since I have written you that I am ashamed. I haven't heard how your health is and because I haven't heard from you for so long, I worry about it. How are you? If you are not able to write to tell me, I'll understand, but maybe you'll get some sort of word to me through Joe Mitchell or his family. I haven't seen Joe in years.

I am now eighty-two and Andy is seventy-five, and we are beginning to feel our years a great deal. [. . .] I am up and around and trying to do something about Christmas.

As for my garden, it's gradually degenerating for lack of help. I can't do any more than point and discuss what we will do; and dear Henry Allen, who has been with us more than twenty years, takes care of it. I still order the seeds for our vegetables, of which we try to grow more and more to help keep down the cost of living, and the flower seeds, but the flower gardens do get neglected. I am not buying anything new for the borders any more—I just divide and transplant. I do get a lot of bulbs each fall and grow some of them indoors, but most of them outdoors. I hope you are able to enjoy your own garden and your friends.

I should tell you that in order to make more room in our shelves, and because I no longer write garden pieces for *The New Yorker,* I this year (with the help of my secretary, who is typing this letter) made a complete list of all my horticultural, garden and allied subjects, books and sent it to Bryn Mawr. Out of the list they have chosen about 120 books, but a few of my most valuable books they already had; and I guess I ought to sell them to help pay for my Christmas presents. For instance, I have some of the original editions of Mrs. Loudon, the big ones with the color plates, which Bryn Mawr happened to have; and I have that elephant folio volume of famous botanical artists, of which Sitwell was one of the editors.* The librarian at Bryn Mawr said these were valuable books and advised me to sell them. Do you know of a good bookseller who wants garden books, to whom I could send the remainder of my list, in case they wanted to buy any for secondhand use? Don't bother if you don't know for I can try the Seven Gables Book Shop, when I have time to get around to it. Seven Gables deals mostly in non-garden books, but might take a few of the special and valuable ones on botanical illustration, etc. Your books, except for one copy of *A Southern Garden* that I am keeping, and those by Carolyn Dormon, are among those that Bryn Mawr wanted. They are to be a gift this year, and I can use Bryn Mawr's evaluation of them as a tax deduction.

[...] I have given my personal correspondence with *New Yorker* writers to Bryn Mawr and there is now a collection called the Katharine S. White Archive. Eventually, in my will, Bryn Mawr is to have all my *New Yorker*–connected books; so Bryn Mawr thus becomes a little center for research by biographers and historians on the magazine. Perhaps I have told you about this before, and if so, I apologize. I simply hate to part with these books, and I shall miss them terribly, but it seems to be essential to do this from the financial viewpoint. Luckily I have two copies of *A Southern Garden* and will give Bryn Mawr only one of those. I just thought you ought to know that your books will be there for many generations of students and researchers.

*Sacheverell Sitwell and Wilfrid Blunt, *Great Flower Books, 1700–1900* (Collins, 1956).

Lots of love to you, and the best of New Year's, from both Andy and myself.

Affectionately,
Katharine

APRIL 1975

Dear Katharine,

[. . .] I was miserable last summer, but I am better than I have been for some time, and I try to work in the garden a little each day. I have a college student who is a splendid worker, but he also has a job at the college, and can seldom give me more than two Saturdays a month.

I am very much interested in what you are doing with your books, and I am pleased that Bryn Mawr wanted mine, [. . .] I have told the children that I want them to have any of my garden books that they want, and the rest, unless they want to sell them, in which case they are to send the list to Mrs. Woodburn, are to go to the University of North Carolina in Charlotte.* I found, when I began to look into it, that giving books away is not as easy as I thought. Hannah says if you sell them you *know* they go to someone who wants them. I asked Mr. Harkness, when he was president of the Rock Garden Society, whether they would like my complete file of the *Rock Garden Bulletins*. He said they have no place to keep things, and would just sell them separately to members who wanted to complete their files. So the children might as well do that. I also have a complete file of Mr. Houdyshel's catalogues. I would be most interested in hearing what you are offered for the Sitwell and Blunt elephant *Great Flower Books*. I have it too. As I go over the book lists, I make notes of current

*After EL's death, her niece and nephew sold the collection to the Cherokee Garden Library housed in the Atlanta History Center.

prices, so Chip and Walton will have an idea of the value of what I have.

I thought you knew Mrs. Woodburn, but anyway, she knows you, and is, of course, as interested in buying books as in selling them.

[. . .] With dearest love to you and Andy (I wonder what he is up to now).

Aff,
Elizabeth

FEBRUARY 4, 1976

Dear Elizabeth,

I am ashamed that I did not communicate with you before Christmas. I think of you often and I have been worrying about your arthritis, and I am very sorry to hear it is so much worse. As for your mind, I am sure it hasn't failed. Possibly, like Andy and me, you find yourself forgetting names and even words, and this is hampering but I am sure you are right on the ball from everything you write, and I hope that you will persist in the *Market Bulletin* book.

You did guess right in thinking that you didn't hear from me at Christmas because I was ill. On the fourth of November I had had my breakfast in bed as usual, and Andy was out around the farm doing chores, and I had called Shirley Cousins to come up and talk about the menu. She came up, and suddenly I couldn't breathe. I had just time to get out the words "Call Mr. White," and then I lost consciousness. I didn't come to until several hours later, but have been told what happened in the meantime. Andy and Henry Allen—our man-of-all-work and a pillar of strength in this household—had begun trying to get oxygen to me from a small oxygen tank we had in my room, because this breathing problem had happened, in a minor way, five years ago. That time I didn't lose consciousness. The machine was inadequate, it turned out, so they weren't very successful. Andy had also phoned the volunteer ambulance in Blue Hill and the Blue Hill Hospital and our doctor—all of them nine miles away from us. Shirley had the bright idea of calling the local fire department in Brooklin, which is also a volunteer affair. However, they have a resuscitation team and a huge tank of oxygen, and in no time flat one of the volunteer firemen and his R.N. wife arrived, and I really think they saved my life—or at least my brain—until the ambulance arrived twenty minutes later with more oxygen. I spent thirty-six hours in the Intensive Care Unit of the hospital and hardly remember a thing about it. [. . .] They called it congestive heart failure, which was caused by excess fluid around the heart and lungs. Now we have a huge oxygen tank ready to use here but I still think I'd rather have the Fire Department come than have Andy struggle to administer the oxygen if an attack ever happened again. [. . .] Anyway, I was well enough to have my son Roger and his wife and their little boy, age five, here for Thanksgiving. It was quite a scrabble to get together Christmas gifts for all my nurses that come and go, and their children, and the household help, to say nothing of our now huge family. (3 children, 9 grandchildren, 5 great-grands and a 6th expected any minute.) We just gave up Christmas cards this year, and also my annual letters to many people at Christmas.

Your book sounds to me fascinating and I'm sure that it will be published when you get through with it. I wish I knew all these mountain women who sell wildflowers. The wildflowers of North Carolina are very varied, if I remember right, and there are a great many of them. I gave to Bryn Mawr a great many of my garden and horticulture books. They chose the books they didn't have and wanted, from my list, and among those they wanted were the local guides to the wildflowers of the various states. I can't now remember whether it was North Carolina or South

Carolina that had such a particularly good wildflower manual. Whenever I give away books I immediately regret it and find that I need to look up something in one of them. A few years back I sold some of my collection of children's books* and have wished ever since that I hadn't—but there just isn't shelf space here to keep everything.

It is now February 5. I started to write this letter in pencil way back the first of the month, and much has happened since then. We are all still shaking from the terrible windstorm of February 2. It caused a flash flood in Bangor that inundated over one hundred cars in a parking lot in the center of the city but miraculously no lives were lost, thanks in part to the heroism of a man in rescuing a woman shut in her car who had only one inch of air left to breathe. He had arrived at the scene of the flood in his four wheel drive truck, hoping to be of use. The truck wasn't needed but he plunged in and swam to the car and pulled the woman out by her legs and held her above water until a boat rescued them. There was terrible devastation around the coast, particularly east of here in Eastport and Machias, where buildings were knocked right down by the waves and the wind. A huge Japanese tanker went ashore to the west of us. We probably had it less hard than most places but our son [Joel] had a wild time with his crew of men rescuing the small boats from the small boat storage house which stood on a dock over a sheltered harbor. They didn't lose any boats, I am thankful to say. The big yachts are in aluminum storage houses, less near the water. The wind was just right to pour into our sheltered harbor, and the wind and the waves were higher than any in the memory of anyone now alive. Bridges were put out of commission on highways all along the shore, and we had gusts of wind between 80 and 100 knots at times. This old

*KSW had reviewed children's literature for *The New Yorker* (1935 to 1950) and had donated many of the books to the Brooklin public library.

house roared and shook but nothing happened except that one window blind was blown off onto a tall lilac bush by our entrance door, and our television antenna was bent double.

I keep hoping to see something by Joe Mitchell in *The New Yorker*. I suppose he is writing but it comes slower and slower. If you know anything about him and any news of his health, I would be very glad to hear it. One by one my generation of writers fall by the wayside. The latest is Frank Sullivan, who is apparently dying slowly in a hospital in Saratoga Springs. We had known he was sick and I did get a note off to him at Christmas, and apparently he had asked his doctor to write of his condition. The doctor said he would probably never leave the hospital again, which, if true, is sad news indeed. Frank and I are almost the same age as our birthdays fall within a few days of each other's.* I am sure this is the worst thing about growing old, and I am sure you feel the same way; the sad news and the disappearance of one's old friends.

Speaking of *The New Yorker*, I hope you didn't miss a story by Peter Taylor, who, after a long silence, came back with one of his best stories. I can't tell you the exact issue it was in but I think it was in January, and it was all about the south as usual. It always cheers me to see a piece of work by someone who hasn't been published for quite a long while.

We have had a horrid winter, taken all in all, the coldest Andy and I can remember here, and I have been pretty much house-bound because my right leg has very bad circulation and just turns to ice if I go out in very cold weather. The worst is that we have not had a very good snow cover and so I expect that we shall have a lot of winterkill—of trees, of blueberry bushes and the blueberry crop, which is very important to Maine in general, of

*KSW was born September 17, 1892; Frank Sullivan, September 22, 1892.

fruit trees, and of course of perennials. It's a guessing game to know what to order.

Andy had a brainstorm earlier, at the time of our forty-sixth wedding anniversary, and he decided that I would most like, instead of a piece of jewelry, a small greenhouse. We always have a terrible time raising our seedlings because our little plant room off the kitchen is too small, and so we have to farm out some of the flower seeds to various greenhouses. That is expensive and unsatisfactory for they charge just as much if I provide the seed as if they provided it. Andy also thought it would get me out-of-doors if he put the greenhouse near enough to the house. Unfortunately our anniversary date was November 13 and it was already too late to dig the foundation because the soil was beginning to freeze, so we won't have the greenhouse for this year's seeds. Henry Allen, our gardener and general caretaker, is as happy at the prospect of a greenhouse as I am, but I don't know whether I'll know how to manage a greenhouse. There was no place to put it against the house so it has to be free-standing with a small potting shed built to hold a heating unit and supplies etc. I think it's far too extravagant to be going into this expense this year when our income is less, but Andy is determined to put it through, and I guess it will be a going concern by July, at the latest. I'm very ignorant of greenhouse procedures, and if you know the title of a good short greenhouse book for amateurs, I hope you'll tell me. We have one but it's far too big and ambitious for us to use.

No more now but my love. I think of you often.

Katharine

[FEBRUARY 1976]

Dear Katharine,

After our unusually severe weather in January and early February, the "Bermuda High" has taken over. We have had a record high of over 80, but now it is cooler. We have been almost a month without frost—very rare at this time of the year. We almost always have a freeze when the Oriental magnolias bloom with the flowering quinces, but this time they all came through, and now the flowering cherries are out. Two years ago I ordered "weeping March flowers" from an old lady in South Carolina, and late in February they bloomed for the first time. They are the little white swan's neck daffodil that is still found in a few old gardens. I have also gotten it from the *Southern Carolina Bulletin* as *Narcissus moscha-tus* and as horse neck (the name used in 1779 by Martha Logan, whose "garden was her delight") and from Mississippi as "pure white goose neck jonquils." In the South people still think all daffodils are jonquils. Now I am working on the identity of the "foxtail lily" that I got from a South Carolina advertiser. They are bulbs, and I thought from Miss Elizabeth Seabright's description they would be *Camassia Leichtlinii,* but the foliage came up in the fall instead of the spring, and it is much wider. It might be *C. Cusickii,* which has leaves an inch wide, but it doesn't seem likely as that species is rare. Unlike my other old ladies who are eager to help, Miss Seabright resents questioning. She says why don't I write to Clemson College. I tried to mollify her by telling her that the professors can't tell me the things I want to know, but without success.

Aff,
Elizabeth Lawrence

[APRIL 5, 1976]

Dear Katharine,

I started to write to you so long ago, and never got back to it, because I have so much I want to say. One is, did you know that I owe all of the pleasure I have had all these years of collecting *The Market Bulletin* material, to you? When Mary Ellen was Mr.

Shawn's secretary, I sent a piece about the Mississippi [Bulletin] to *The New Yorker*. She returned it with a note. She said it was too sketchy, and that I should do it in detail. I am sure that advice came from you, and you see I took it.

The other thing I want to say is that your writing me about your giving your books to Bryn Mawr, made me give thought to mine, and also to my records. Dr. Meyer,* who is botanist in charge of the National Arboretum, is making a survey of plant material in Southern gardens. He spent a day with me last summer collecting material, and before he left I got up courage to ask whether the Herbarium would have any use for my files. I was mortified to let him see them. They are so sloppy, dirty, and illegible, having never been intended for anyone but me. He pulled out several cards at random, said he had no difficulty in reading them, and that the Herbarium is the place for them to go as I cannot let him have them as long as I am using them. He told me to write a letter to him for his files, and put a statement in my file for my nephews, who are my executors.† He also wanted copies of *A Southern Garden* and *The Little Bulbs*, as the Herbarium has only *Gardens in Winter*. I was amazed to find out how poor their files are in garden literature—such as [not having] a complete collection of such things as Mr. Houdyshel's little brochures, and both American and English magazines. I want to ask about unpublished manuscripts.

[. . .]

This is the most beautiful spring I have ever known. No frost for weeks on end. The Oriental magnolias did get caught at the height of their bloom, but the quinces, the pear, the crabapple, and the cherries were never touched, and now the dogwoods are

---

*Dr. Frederick Gustav Meyer was the research scientist in charge of the herbarium from the late 1950s until his retirement in 1991.
†EL's literary executor is her nephew Warren Way; power of attorney was held by Walton Rogers, her niece's husband.

in perfection. Bernard Harkness (who retired some years ago as head of the Rochester [N.Y.] Park System) and his wife, and her Aunt and three other delightful old ladies from the Methodist Home, came to see me yesterday. Bernard and Mabel were on their way home from a trip of the Delta Queen. The Aunt is ninety-one. She fell and hurt her head seriously last winter, but is sprightly as ever. She had made so many engagements that they hadn't time to stay to tea. The cherries were gone, but Lady Banks' rose was showing down from the top of a tall pine.

[. . .]

Aff,
Elizabeth

P.S. Did I ask you if you were reading *Children of Pride*—the letters of the Jones family of Liberty County, Georgia, before, during, and after the Civil War? Especially interesting to me as all of my father's family were right there in the path of General Sherman's March to the Sea. A woman called here the other day to ask the name of a plant with long, narrow leaves, and pink flowers, that the Confederate soldiers used to poison the stupid Yankees by telling them the leaves made excellent tea. Then she said, "Oh dear, I hope *you* are not a stupid Yankee!" I told her no, it was probably my family who did the poisoning. The plant is oleander.

APRIL 18, 1976

Dear Elizabeth,

Your old February and later April 5 letters were a joy to get. First, I'm afraid that you don't owe the idea of the *Market Bulletins* book to me, for unless my memory has totally forsaken me, I don't think I ever read your piece about Mississippi, rejected by *The New Yorker* so long ago. I have no memory at all of it and the usual procedure at that time was that factual articles, unless they were humorous or reminiscent pieces, were not read in my Department, which covered fiction, humor, memoirs, and poetry or verse. The advice to make the article less sketchy and more detailed must have come from one of the Fact Dept. editors unless Mary Ellen made an exception because it dealt with horticulture and therefore sent it to me. If it was very long ago perhaps I had not even begun writing "Onward and Upward in the Garden." The first piece in that series dated March 1, 1958, and was run under the Book Dept. heading, for I had had the sudden idea of *reviewing* catalogues and Shawn ran it under *Books*. Then I decided on a title and began writing the series you used to read. If your review was before 1958, I am pretty sure that your piece on Mississippi never came my way.

I am delighted to hear that your files and notes are to go to the Herbarium of the National Arboretum. They should be valuable to any arboretum. I have to confess that I don't know where the National Arboretum is situated—probably in or near Washington?* I am a member of the New York Botanic Garden so as to get their publications, and also of the Arnold Arboretum of Harvard, which I used to visit as a child. It was an easy carriage ride from our house. Also the then director was Charles Sprague Sargent, whose big estate and beautiful plantings were near where we lived. My friends and I were given permission to ride our bicycles through Mr. Sargent's many driveways provided we picked nothing on his land. I am certain that Dr. Meyer will also want any unpublished manuscripts you have as well as your books that he lacks. How wonderful that you have a complete set of Mr. Houdyshel's little brochures. I started to keep them after you put me on to Houdyshel but he died soon after that.

[. . .] I am slowly reading *The Book of Abigail and John,* letters of the Adams family—Harvard Press—and it's wonderful. The

*In Washington, D.C., on Bladensburg Road near New York Avenue.

Revolution comes alive. I had no idea of the horrible smallpox and dysentery epidemics that carried off so many New Englanders (and probably others around the country) until I read the book. It shouldn't be confused with *The Adams Chronicles*, which is a totally different book.

[. . .]

Henry, our gardener, has just come in with news that he had moved a lot of flats of seedlings out into the cold frame, and that the cold plus the heat killed them off over the weekend. A lot of labor had gone into his raising them and we needed that greenhouse, but it couldn't be got ready last fall as the ground had frozen when Andy thought of it. It means that I shall just have to buy some plants and they won't be the colors I want of petunias. Life is like that. No more for now, but do keep on with your *Market Bulletin* book.

Ever affectionately,
Katharine

JANUARY 13, 1977

Dear Elizabeth,

Your letter to Andy* was wonderful, but unfortunately he couldn't make out your handwriting and he put it aside to answer later. [. . .]

Andy is very pleased that you found passages in his book that interested you. I myself have been reading the book [*The Letters*] through slowly, although of course I had read it many times in proof. [. . .]

I talked to Joe Mitchell not long ago because the widow of his

---

*In December, EL had written a ten-page letter to EBW telling him how much she was learning from his *Letters* and *Elements of Style* and how her own research was going. KSW had a secretary type EL's letter for the files, and then in her own shaky hand she filled in more than a dozen words the secretary hadn't been able to read.

dear friend, who is one of my best friends, has had a stroke and is in the therapy wing of the New York–Cornell Medical Center. You will recognize her as the contributor of many fine stories to *The New Yorker* over her own name of Jean Stafford. Andy's sister is in just the same state but she won't consider speech therapy so we have not much hope that she will get well as soon as Jean. However, the horrible thing is that Jean probably won't write again. This all happened to her right after she wrote a review of the *Letters of E. B. White* for *The Saturday Review* (her piece made perfect sense) so I feel almost as though her doing this chore may have brought on her stroke.

We are having a bitter winter here and I wish I were where you are. Monday night we had the worst storm of the year and lost our power and heat. This is now a special anxiety to us because last year Andy gave me a small greenhouse as an anniversary present. We have been having flowers from it and every day now we have a camellia blossom or two to bring into the house, because with the help of a southerner who lives here in summer— Dr. Joseph Wearn—nine camellia plants came all the way from California by Greyhound bus and arrived at our county seat, Ellsworth, in perfect condition. Do you have camellias? I imagine you must have a lot of them. So far we have had blossoms from Ville de Hants and from a deep red one whose name I now forget, and now from a lovely pale pink. They're not all blossoming at the same time and this will prolong the pleasure. They are called something like "Magnoliafolia"—I don't know it really.

Katharine

[MARCH 1977]

Dear Katharine,

You did not answer my question when I asked what you would like me to do with your letters. I doubt whether you realize how

many and how interesting they are, and on such varied subjects—not gardening alone. In the meantime I had a letter from
Carol Wells, Assistant Librarian at Northwestern State University, Natchitoches, Louisiana, asking me to give her any letters I
might have of Caroline's for the Dormon Collection in the University's archives. [. . .] I then asked whether she would like your
letters, if you would allow me to give them to her. The minute she
got my letter the Librarian, John Price, called me in great excitement to tell me what a treasure that would be. I told him I had no
idea how you felt about it—perhaps you would like them yourself, but I would ask you.

Please tell Andy that Dr. [W. B.] Mayer lent me a bound volume of *St. Nicholas* for Summer 1914. It fell open at The St. Nicholas League and there was a silver badge won by Elwyn B. White,
and a story about his father and a dog. I was writing poetry for it
at that time, but I never got it done until after the deadline.

After a miserable winter, everything has suddenly come into
bloom.

I hope you are both better—
Aff,
Elizabeth

MARCH 21, 1977

Dear Elizabeth,

I'm sorry I failed to answer your question. By law, the actual
letter or letters belong to you and the contents of the letters belong to the writer. I can't believe that any of my letters are worth
preserving in any library or in anyone's files; but you may do anything you want with them, of course. I'm surprised that you did
not tear them up after reading them, and I just can't imagine that
they are interesting today. But that is your decision. If the Northwestern University has the practice of making xerox copies of the

letters it receives, I might be glad to have such copies—but *not* if anyone has to pay for the xeroxes. As a matter of fact, I am now so old and have such bad eyesight that I can't think what I would do with them. I *need* to write and earn because I have become such an expensive creature for poor Andy to maintain, what with my eight-hour day nurses and my ten-hour night nurses, that if I could manage to write and earn something I'd be happy, but I'm almost sure it is beyond me to create even just one more "Onward and Upward in the Garden." My longhand writing wanders, and my dictated letters are even worse. The faint hope that copies of my letters to you might enable me to scratch out just one more *New Yorker* piece is the only reason I ask about the xeroxes.

[. . .]

The rewarding thing this year has been the nine camellia plants that Andy got for our new miniscule greenhouse. They have bloomed and bloomed. [. . .] I think I just picked the last blossom for this year. It was a Guilo Nucio, named, I believe, for the man who runs the nursery from which Andy purchased them. [. . .]

You spoke about the St. Nicholas League and this rings a bell in my mind. When I was quite young I got a silver badge for writing something on the subject given, which that month was "a surprise." My surprise was the long nest of the Trap Door Spider, that some relative gave me when I was a little girl. The door part fascinated me with its perfect hinge and just enough space for the spider to stick her foot into a tiny hole on the hinge of the door and close the door behind her. Andy, by the way, once wrote me a so-called love poem in which he made the spider a male who spun a web. Only females make the big orb webs. He was yet to write *Charlotte's Web* and yet to study up on spiders. He, however, is the owner of a gold badge from the League. My five-year-older sister Rosamond got a gold badge for a photograph of wild ducks, but I always thought it was a cheat because they were actually very tame ducks and were swimming in a park in Worcester, Mass., where our artist aunt* lived for a few years. I think I was discouraged by Rosamond's gold badge—I never submitted anything else. Andy wrote an essay for *The New Yorker* on the St. Nicholas League and he is going to use it in his next book, which will be a book of essays selected from his various earlier volumes. I rather dread the publication of this book as I am sure Harper will now think that they will be able to let all his books go out of print. So far, only two of his books are no longer available in Harper editions, but those two are available at least in University Microfilm editions.

This is the first day of spring but you wouldn't know it here as we had snow—although only an inch or two—yesterday. At least it's less slippery now and I can get out to walk as the highways are clear. Did I ever tell you about the time I was walking on our highway, with my nurse, facing the traffic as one is counseled to do, when a ruffian-looking fellow in a huge truck swung right over in front of us on the wrong side of the road, where there was a curve just ahead. He leaned out and said to me, "Are you prepared to meet your Maker?" I replied, "If you stay on this side of the road I expect to meet him any moment." I refused the literature he held out because I knew that he was probably one of the Holy Roller sect of which we have quite a number in this region. My nurse was more sensible and accepted the literature and thanked him and said, "I have my own church but I will read about yours."

I hope your book is nearing completion and I look forward to it for I know nothing really about *Market Bulletins* published in your region. One of the sorrows of this year for me has been that Jean Stafford [. . .] has had a stroke. She is better and at last is at home after a long stay in a New York hospital. Her third husband

*Annie Shepley ("Aunt Poo").

(and the only one with whom she had a happy marriage) died several years ago, and she is all alone in the world and I worry about her. She has been reviewing children's books of late years for *The New Yorker* but this year the stroke came just after she had written the lead for the review but before she had listed any of the books she wanted to recommend. [. . .]

I'm afraid I've rambled on and on, but at least I have finally answered your question.

Affectionately,
Katharine

MAY 31, 1977

Dear Elizabeth,

When you wrote asking about my letters to you, I should have written at once to ask whether you do not want your letters to me, which would be of far more importance to any library than mine to you. I did not write and only because disaster has hit me. I am losing my eyesight thanks to "macular degeneration" of the rods and cones that began years ago far at the back of my retina. Why nothing was told me of what this meant, I cannot guess. If I had been warned, I could have learned touch typing and other things to aid the blind. It may be that this will leave me with enough peripheral vision to get about, and I am far from the stage of having to be led around. What I can't do is to read, or write legibly. I am writing now in pencil hoping my secretary can make out the words. I can't *see* what I write. I still can read a little by adding a magnifying glass in one hand, but in writing I can't use a pen or pencil and also hold a magnifying glass.

I have been collecting your letters, but it took much longer than I thought because in the files labeled "Elizabeth Lawrence" there were only two letters. I, therefore, am gradually going through all my horticultural files and have found many others.

They are wonderful and I realize that I never could have written "Onward and Upward in the Garden" series without you.

I think you should take these and offer them to the same place that holds my letters because it will give you a big deduction on your income tax. You are a known and important garden writer on horticulturist matters. If by any chance you don't want to give them, I would love to add them to my *New Yorker* connected archive at Bryn Mawr College. But I think that *you* should have them. Your letters at Bryn Mawr would be available to scholars but not to anybody without my permission; and after me, without Andy's; and after him, without William Maxwell's.* Even Maxwell is so old that I may have to add another name as my archive is so full of personal letters from *New Yorker* writers.

[. . .]

Much love, and admiration,
Katharine

[JUNE 1977]

Dear Katharine,

I am terribly distressed to hear that you are having trouble with your eyes, and I do hope you will be like my sister and that it will not be as bad as you fear. After two successful operations for cataracts, her glaucoma was much worse, and then an infection, which was eventually cleared up by heavy doses of cortisone (and its side effects), but they told her that the damage would be permanent. They were wrong. Her sight has slowly improved, so that she can now read large print, see television well enough to enjoy it, and can see to write. Your writing is perfectly clear. My sister, like you, has great courage.

I would be proud to have any writing of mine in your *New Yorker*

---

*Maxwell was for four decades a fiction editor at *The New Yorker* and was himself a distinguished writer of fiction.

collection, but I agree that my letters to you would be more useful in the Louisiana archives along with yours to me than at Bryn Mawr. The horticultural material is more valuable with both sides of the correspondence and the Libraries files of *The New Yorker* available in one place. Do keep the copies of your replies to my letters, and I hope you will add them to your collection. Mrs. Wells would be glad to make xerox copies of the ones that you like, and there is no charge.

After sending the first folder of your letters to Mrs. Wells, I found another and larger folder, and sent that to her too, but before I sent them I reread all of them, and relived all of those years. I loved your letters as they came one by one, but reading them all at one time I felt deeply all that you have meant to me, your generosity, your concern, and your loving kindness. I feel about you as I did about Mr. Krippendorf that you have drawn without knowing it a portrait of a dear and noble person.

[. . .]

With love to both of you,
Elizabeth Lawrence

JUNE 11, 1977

Dear Elizabeth,

Thank you for your lovely letter. There is no chance that my eyesight can improve, as your sister's did, because although I have cataracts, the basic trouble is that the rods and cones in the eye that make us see, just are not there any more. (It is called "macular deterioration.") I shall always have peripheral vision and won't have to be led around, but now I can only read a little by holding a very strong magnifying glass just above the print. My glasses have as much magnification in them as is possible, but I need the extra glass, held in the hand also.

I am touched that you felt on rereading my letters that I had encouraged you and given you affection and support. In return I must say as I'm sure I have before that you have done the same and far more for me. First, you set me a model of good writing on gardening and horticulture. Second, you have taught me almost everything I know about horticulture; and third, you were encouraging about my attempts to write "Onward and Upward in the Garden." Your affection has been very acceptable and I value it.

Today the man who is in charge of the archives at Louisiana (not Mrs. Wells) called me this afternoon while I was having a nap. I did not catch his name because I was dead asleep, recovering from guests. He said he was delighted to have your letters and called you "fabulous," which indeed you are. We agreed that I should keep your original letters to me for my Bryn Mawr [archive] and he would send me copies and that you should keep my letters for your archive at Northwestern State University of Louisiana (or whatever it is) but copies of all should be sent to me. This is the usual procedure. Only a few of my letters, written when I was still at *The New Yorker*, have carbon copies. Therefore, he will send me copies of the other. Mr. [Leo] Dolensky, the young Bryn Mawr librarian, will make copies of your letters and send them either to you or direct to the University of Northwestern Louisiana. The point is that legally the originals belong to the recipient. And my archive needs your letters even more than your collection needs mine. Mr. Dolensky, as it happens, is coming here for lunch on Wednesday. I'll explain all of this to him. This will be a fair and even exchange, don't you think?? However, I have packed three cartons of horticultural correspondence for Mr. Dolensky—some of your early letters are in that—I haven't time or strength to unpack this and must rush to empty the rest of my files.

Excuse a bad letter—I'm dead tired. We have seen the sun only one day in the last two weeks or so.

John White, my youngest grandson, graduates from George Stevens Academy tomorrow. He is going to a special technical school in Eastern Maine to learn all about Diesel engines so he can be the Diesel engine specialist at his father's boatyard after he is through the course.

No more now, but my best love and EBW's.

Much love,
Katharine

P.S. Your letters will be the mainstay in my horticultural BMC archive. Mine will be a feeble part of your collection.

Epilogue
"SIGNS OF DURABILITY"
LETTERS OF E. B. WHITE AND ELIZABETH LAWRENCE, 1977–1980

On July 20, 1977, Katharine White died at the hospital in Blue Hill, Maine. A few days later, Elizabeth Lawrence received a personal letter from a secretary who had been asked by Andy to let her know that Katharine's "ordeal was mercifully short" and that she had died after only a day's stay in the hospital. There was to be a simple graveside memorial service on July 23 at the Brooklin cemetery. Later, Andy sent a poem he had written to friends as an expression of appreciation for their letters of condolence.

> To all who loved my lovely wife.
> To all who spoke their sorrow,
> I send this printed card of thanks
> So I can face tomorrow.
>
> I'd hoped to write a full reply
> To each, to say "I love you."
> But I'll reveal the sticky truth:
> There's just too many of you.
>
> Andy

Over the next several years, Elizabeth and Andy continued to write to one another on occasion, especially proud that Katharine's New Yorker *columns had been published in 1979 in a book,* Onward and Upward in the Garden, *for which Andy had written an introduction.*

[JULY 27, 1977]

Dear Andy,

I am touched by your thinking of me. I had not seen the notice in the *Charlotte Observer*, but Elizabeth Clarkson called me. She said your Letters and your essays in *Harper's* make her feel you are a dear and well-known friend.

My only consolation is that Katharine did not have to be blind. I don't see how you will manage without her. I always think of you as one.

With love,
Elizabeth

[JULY 1979]

Dear Andy,

Thank you for having the publisher send me *Onward and Upward* (it really is). I have been re-reading and re-reading ever since, with great pleasure and great sorrow. I can't bear not to be able to tell Katharine again what a wonderful book it is. I think of her and of you continuously, and want to write to you, but Katharine told me that you can't read my handwriting, and also I think of Eudora Welty who feels she *has* to answer every personal letter personally, and said she carried around a suitcase of more than two hundred, and meant to catch up in time.

Dannye Romine, book editor of the *Charlotte Observer*, also sent me a copy for review. This is to ask for permission to quote a paragraph from a letter you wrote to me,* "Katharine just spent three days in bed, in pain, caused by a back injury brought on by leaning far out over a flower bed to pick one spring bloom—the daffodil Supreme. It seems a heavy price to pay for one small flower. But when she is in her garden, she is always out of control. I do not look for any change, despite her promises."

I am not sure about your *s*, whether it is the daffodil supreme, or the daffodil Supreme, Rijnveld, 1947, 3a. But I don't think it likely that any *Observer* reader will know the difference.

I thought the paragraph fits in with your loving introduction [to *Onward and Upward in the Garden*].

[. . .] I am having a miserable time trying to say something worthy of the book in the space allotted to me.

Aff,
Elizabeth

JULY 26, 1979

Dear Elizabeth,

I was delighted to get your letter in this morning's mail and to learn that you are enjoying those garden pieces again and plan to review them for the *Observer.* You surely do have my permission to quote from the letter I wrote you. I suspect that my "daffodil Supreme" was just my figure of speech. For one thing, I am quite ignorant of garden matters and doubt that I had heard of the flower you mention. Perhaps it would make it easier for your readers if you didn't capitalize the "S" and let it go as "daffodil supreme."

K's gardens are still lovely, but something has gone out of them that is irreplaceable—something she breathed into them

---

*EL and EBW had exchanged letters from time to time when KSW was living. This was a letter he had written May 8, 1974, thanking her for news of their friend Joseph Mitchell.

because of her love and her care. I try to keep her *tokonomas** going around the house by throwing bouquets together in my manly way, but it is a pitiful comedown. My spirit of dedication is all there, but my technique leaves much to be desired. The book has been getting some quite good reviews on the whole. If yours gets into the paper, I hope you'll let me know.

Eudora Welty has my sympathy if she has a couple of hundred letters waiting to be answered. That's my situation right now, as a result of having just had my 80th birthday. My head is spinning, and most of my well-wishers are still waiting for an acknowledgement.

Yrs.,
Andy

[AUGUST 1979]

Dear Andy,

[The editor] didn't leave anything out, and changed only a few phrases—mostly for the better. But they always have to do *something*. Katharine White's "Garden" is not the same thing as "Mrs. White on Gardening," which is what I wrote, and it is misleading.†

I am sure you have seen the review in the *Charlotte News*,‡ but I thought you would like to know it was there.

I went next door to have sherry with my sister the other morning, and found her listening to a Book for the Blind—*E. B. White's*

---

*KSW had written about *tokonoma* in Japanese homes, "where arrangements are placed in a spirit of dedication, to be viewed for their spiritual value by members of the family and their visitors," in her 11/4/67 garden piece on "The Flower Arrangers."
†EL praised "the spirited pieces," EBW's "tender and amusing" introduction, and alluded to the friendship they had carried on through KSW's and EBW's letters to her.
‡"A Book for the Gardener in Us All" (8/18/79).

Letters. I keep thinking of things I want to say to Katharine—I always will.

Aff,
Elizabeth Lawrence

AUGUST 30, 1979

Dear Elizabeth,

Your review in the *Observer* was a pure delight to me. You are right—they always have to do *something.* But whenever I see the name Katharine spelled correctly in print, my heart leaps up. So I'll forgive the *Observer* this time.

I was much interested in your statement "I know of no other book that covers so many phases of gardening. . . ." This is something I suspected might be true, but because I am not a reader of garden books I was not in a position to make any such remark. And I thought your detailed listing of the subjects was fine to have in a review.

The *New York Times Book Review* section will be out on Sunday (September 2) with a report on *Onward and Upward* by Eden Ross Lipson. It is headed "Autobiography With Flowers" and is a long, sensible, and enthusiastic review. I was able to read it in advance of the publication date because I subscribe to the *Review,* and subscribers receive it several days ahead of Sunday.

My editor at Farrar Straus tells me that White Flower Farm bought a hundred copies of the book (to resell at the Farm) but then asked if they might please return them. They said the book was too full of praise for the Farm, and they had a policy against blowing their own horn. I got a chuckle out of that one, never having noticed any fierce streak of modesty in their literature. My guess is that they didn't like Katharine's comical remark that she had never found anything "unreliable" in the common pussy willow. Or perhaps they didn't care for her reference to Amos

Pettingill as "the sage of White Flower Farm." Anyway, Farrar Straus obligingly took the books back.

Thank you, Elizabeth, for writing such a good piece and also for sending me the one from the *News*.

Sincerely,
Andy

[DECEMBER 1979]

Dear Andy,

I had a letter from my English friend, Pamela Harper,* who said, "I am reading, with much pleasure, *Onward and Upward in the Garden*, by Katharine S. White. She is new to me, though I am sure not to you, and it is delightful to read an American writer with a real feeling for words. Particularly so for me, because there are differences in style, choice of words and—sometimes—meaning of words, from English writers, thus I can stretch my own vocabulary and construction. And she has OPINIONS; such a change, though I very much doubt that she would have been permitted to voice them so openly in print had she not had both feet firmly planted in the world of publishing."

I will think of you and Katharine at Christmas and always.

Aff,
Elizabeth

[MARCH 16, 1980]

Dear Andy,

I do not want you to miss this purple effusion, and "our golden astonishments," the "poet's narcissus." Every March this ques-

---

*Author of *Time-Tested Plants; Perennials; Designing with Perennials;* and other garden books. She has lived in the United States since 1968.

tion comes up about narcissus, buttercups, jonquils, and daffodils.* The question is seldom answered correctly, but this beats
all. It was sent to me by Joseph Mitchell's sister, Linda Lamm.

I think of you and Katharine always, and will never cease to
miss her letters.

Affectionately,
Elizabeth

MARCH 24, 1980

Dear Elizabeth,

I look forward to the time when jonquils will carry sidearms
and capture Eastern Carolina through superior firepower. In any
event, one of my golden astonishments is finding a letter from you
in the mail.

At this season, we don't know the meaning of the word jonquil. Spring comes to Maine not with the arrival of a crocus or
a snowdrop, it comes with the stoppage of the cellar drain. This
happened five nights ago, in a very heavy rain, and I had to call
the Fire Company to pump me out. Every region to its own rites.

Tired snow still lies about, here and there, in the brown fields,
and my house will never look the same again since the death of
the big elm that overhung it. Nevertheless, I manfully planted (as
a replacement) a *young* elm. It is all of five-and-a-half feet high. By
Katharine's grave I planted an oak. This is its second winter in
the cemetery, her third.

Yrs,
Andy

*The "purple effusion" from the *News and Observer* (Raleigh, N.C.) began, "Once again the
exquisite jonquil has captured Eastern Carolina without firing a shot." The "question"
was whether the flower should be called buttercup, jonquil, or daffodil.

[JUNE 12, 1980]

Dear Andy,

I hope Katharine's garden came through the winter better than mine. We have had lower temperatures—to 2 degrees below, but this came after a very mild false spring when things were beginning. Shrubs on the borderline were badly cut back, and even things like sweet olive, that have never been touched were defoliated.

Your interview was carried in the *Charlotte Observer*, and it was like having a letter from you. I think about you. And I think about Katharine. I will never have another correspondent like her. Though, like you, I have many.

Affectionately,
Elizabeth

P.S. I hope the clipping from the Georgia Bulletin amuses you. The letters to the editor are not the least of its charms; and in the same issue there is a receipt for a Scripture cake:

> one cup Judges 5.25 (butter)
> one cup Jeremiah 6.20 (sugar)
> 1 tablespoon Samuel 14.25 (honey)
> etc.

There are eleven in all: flour, baking powder, salt, milk, raisins, almonds, and figs. All from the Old Testament—the King James Version. It is suggested that you make it a family project to look up the ingredients. I wonder why the eggs referred to are partridge eggs. If the cock crowed thrice, there must have been hens—but then that is in the New Testament, so perhaps they didn't have them in the desert.

JUNE 17, 1980

Dear Elizabeth,

This flower show program* was sent to me by Pat Strachan, of Farrar Straus, publishers of Katharine's book. She said the first prize went to an arrangement of black spray-painted calla lilies entitled "Dracula." How I wish K could have attended.

We had a fairly open winter for Maine, and the gardens came through quite well. There was little snow—not enough, really. I closed down the greenhouse for the cold months because of not wanting to use the oil furnace. Henry had some pansy plants out in the vegetable garden that he hoped to winter over, but we lost all of them, not surprisingly. We had a couple of days of false spring early on, and then settled back into a cold May and an even colder June. It is just beginning to feel summery. On the whole, the borders look fine, and the bulb garden was a riot. The clematis on the terrace survived better than it usually does. I'm sorry your things took such a beating. It must have been a really queer winter in the south, from all reports.

Letters and reviews still come drifting in from *Onward and Upward,* and the book has already shown early signs of durability. It has certainly enjoyed a good press and a good life so far. I'm sure you are not the only one who misses its author as a correspondent. K's letter-writing ranged all over the place. I recently had to examine the KSW–John Updike file in Bryn Mawr, to decide whether a scholar should have access to it, and I was amazed at the size of it, as well as the quality of the letters. It's comforting to know that so much of her total output will be preserved.

Thanks for your letter and the comical clipping from the *Geor-*

*From the "Whodunit?" Gramercy Park Flower Show in NYC, scheduling flower-arranging classes in categories named for detective novels, such as "The Witch's House," "Dracula," and "Death on the Nile."

gia Bulletin. I think I will forgo the Scripture Cake. (Let me eat bread!)

Yrs,
Andy

In 1984 Elizabeth Lawrence found she could no longer live alone in her house in Charlotte and moved to Annapolis, Maryland, to be with her niece Elizabeth. She died June 11, 1985, and is buried in the St. James's Episcopal Churchyard in Lothian, Maryland. E. B. White died at his home in North Brooklin, Maine, on October 1, 1985, and was buried next to Katharine in the Brooklin cemetery.

Acknowledgments

This book would not have been possible without the permission of Allene White as executor for the Katharine White estate and Elizabeth Way Rogers and Warren Way, executors for Elizabeth Lawrence. Above and beyond the call for permission, however, they (along with Warren's wife, Fran) have encouraged me by generously sharing their knowledge and perceptions. I also enjoyed corresponding with Allene's daughter Martha White, who has published a lovely essay about her grandmother and shared her scrapbook of photographs. Lunch at the shore in Blue Hill Falls, Maine, with the Whites and Carol and Roger Angell, Katharine's son by her first marriage to Ernest Angell, was memorable. Katharine's granddaughter, Kitty Stableford, gave me a good phone interview. Visits to the homes of Elizabeth Rogers (Annapolis, Maryland) and Fran and Warren Way (Fayetteville, North Carolina) have been far more than research opportunities: Their memories of "Aunt" have been the next best thing to having known her. Meeting their children also added another dimension to the history. This book is a testament to the enduring legacies of families.

I would not have been able to see the places where Katharine White and Elizabeth Lawrence lived and gardened without the hospitality of their new owners. Mary and Robert Gallant invited me to the saltwater farm the Whites had owned for many years in North Brooklin, Maine; in Charlotte, North Carolina, Lindie Wilson showed me through the house and garden where Elizabeth Lawrence lived and worked. As gardeners themselves, they were especially well-informed guides.

I am indebted to Katharine White's biographer, Linda H. Davis, who began her research soon after Katharine's death in 1977, and whose interviews with E. B. White provided an extraordinary opportunity to see her through his eyes. I began my own study of Katharine White by reading Davis's biography, *Onward and Upward*.

The people who assist in research and move manuscripts into print have also been essential, and I thank each of them for generous and professional support: librarians in Special Collections of the Library at Bryn Mawr College, which houses the White papers (especially Kathy Whalen, Miriam Spectre, and Eric Pumroy); Christina DiGiusto and Lorna Knight in the Kroch Library, Cornell University, responsible for the E. B. White manuscripts; Mary Linn Wernet, Watson Library of Northwestern State University in Louisiana, which houses the Lawrence papers; and Blanche Farley and Staci Catron-Sullivan at the Cherokee Garden Library in Atlanta, repository for the Lawrence garden library.

Elaine Maisner at University of North Carolina Press continues to encourage my scholarship long after we worked together on an earlier book; at Beacon Press, Deanne Urmy first "put a bee in my bonnet" by asking if I would be interested in editing the letters of Katharine White and Elizabeth Lawrence; and her successor at Beacon, Joanne Wyckoff, has carried the project to completion with skill and enthusiasm. Linda Lear helped me shape my book proposal and continues to be an incomparable ally and friend. Thanks to Molly Lineberger, who helped date the letters, and to Martha Rokahr, who typed them into the computer. Once more Betty Leighton and Ed Wilson have been careful readers of my work, and my familial support system includes librarians at Wake Forest University, especially Isabel Zuber and Elen Knott. LeAnne Howe, whom I met in residency at the MacDowell Colony, always brings me back to my own true instincts about my subjects.

Among gardening friends, I count upon the knowledge and intuitions of Curry and John Jamison and Pamela Harper, who generously have shared recollections of Elizabeth Lawrence and plants from their gardens. A memorable weekend with them included another friend of Elizabeth Lawrence, Dannye Romine Powell, a writer who knew just what I was trying to undertake. Bobby J. Ward (without seeming to notice my ignorance) has expertly answered many questions about the horticultural world. I remember with great affection and appreciation the late Hannah Withers, a friend who appears often in Elizabeth's letters. Linda Lamm Lawson had the added advantage of having known Elizabeth Lawrence and a friend who appears in Katharine White's letters—Linda's Uncle Joe Mitchell. Archival letters to Katharine White and Elizabeth Lawrence from countless readers gave me a wonderful appreciation of what their work meant to so many.

I acknowledge with appreciation the good ways that I have benefited from accessing information via the Internet and "reply" with special thanks to book dealers and horticulturists who maintain reliable Web sites. Cathy Craig, International Bulb Society, and Alan T. Whittemore, U.S. National Arboretum, were helpful respondents.

Finally, my debt to Katharine White and Elizabeth Lawrence in leaving us their letters is obvious, though deserves my saying so.

Index

Photograph Credits

59: Photograph by Nickolas Muray, courtesy of Div. of Rare & Manuscript Collection, Cornell University Library. From the E. B. White Collection, #4619, Box 220B, and the Estate of E. B. White, *60, top:* Photograph by William Mangold, 1954, courtesy of the E. B. White Estate; *bottom:* Courtesy of the E. B. White Estate; *87, 88, 139, 140, top:* Courtesy of the E. B. White Estate; *bottom:* Courtesy of Nora Mitchell Sanborn; *161, 162, top:* By permission of Warren Way and Elizabeth Rogers; *bottom:* North Carolina Collection: University of North Carolina Library at Chapel Hill; *201, 202:* By permission of Warren Way and Elizabeth Rogers; *221, top:* Courtesy of the Eugene P. Watson Memorial Library, Northwestern State University of Louisiana, and the Caroline Dormon Nature Preserve. Photograph by John C. Guillet, Guillet Photography of Nacitoches, LA; *bottom:* Courtesy of Mary Stambaugh and the Cincinnati Nature Preserve; *222, top:* Courtesy of *The Charlotte Observer; bottom:* By permission of Warren Way and Elizabeth Rogers.